The Visibility of Imported Wine and its Associated Accoutrements in Later Iron Age Britain

Emma Carver

BAR British Series 325
2001

Published in 2016 by
BAR Publishing, Oxford

BAR British Series 325

The Visibility of Imported Wine and its Associated Accoutrements in Later Iron Age Britain

ISBN 978 1 84171 276 5

BAR Publishing is the trading name of British Archaeological Reports (Oxford) Ltd.
British Archaeological Reports was first incorporated in 1974 to publish the BAR
Series, International and British. In 1992 Hadrian Books Ltd became part of the BAR
group. This volume was originally published by Archaeopress in conjunction with
British Archaeological Reports (Oxford) Ltd / Hadrian Books Ltd, the Series principal
publisher, in 2001. This present volume is published by BAR Publishing, 2016.

Printed in England

BAR
PUBLISHING

BAR titles are available from:

BAR Publishing
122 Banbury Rd, Oxford, OX2 7BP, UK
EMAIL   info@barpublishing.com
PHONE   +44 (0)1865 310431
FAX   +44 (0)1865 316916
www.barpublishing.com

Contents

Abstract   iii

Acknowledgements   v

List of Figures and Tables   vi

1.0 **Introduction**

Material Evidence   1

    1.1   Amphorae   1
    1.2   Drinking Equipment   2
    The Study of Imported Wine in Britain to Date   3

PART I

Setting the Scene

2.0 **Wine in the Classical World**

The Texts   6
    2.1   Wine Production   6
       2.1.1   Fine Wines
       2.1.2   The Quantity of Wine in Production
       2.1.3   Vintage Wine
       2.1.4   Wine Storage and Transport
    2.2   Wine Drinking Accoutrements   8
    2.3   The Use of Wine in Society   10
       2.3.1   Attitudes towards Drinking
       2.3.2   Wine Festivals
    2.4   The Ritual Use of Wine   11
       2.4.1   Dionysios
       2.4.2   Bacchus
       2.4.3   The Bacchanalia
       2.4.4   The Iconography of the Bacchic Mysteries
       2.4.5   Roman Funerals
           2.4.5.1   Wine in the Funerary Ceremony
           2.4.5.2   The Use of Masks

3.0 **Wine in Temperate Europe**

    3.1   References in the Ancient Sources   15
       3.1.1   Wine Drinking Accoutrements
       3.1.2   Attitudes towards Drinking
       3.1.3   The Ritual Use of Wine
       3.1.4   Funerals
    3.2   The Archaeological Evidence for Wine in Gaul   17
       3.2.1   The Distribution of Dressel 1 Amphorae
       3.2.2   Wine Amphorae in Mining Regions
       3.2.3   Burials
       3.2.4   Ritual or Ceremonial Sites

PART II
Wine in Britain in the Late Iron Age: a consideration of the evidence and its contexts

4.0	**The Evidence for Wine on Settlement Sites**		
	4.1	Presence of Wine Amphorae	24
		4.1.1 Hengistbury Head, Hampshire	
		4.1.2 Isle of Wight	
		4.1.3 Heybridge, Essex	
		4.1.4 Braughing, Hertfordshire	
	4.2	Presence of Bronze Vessels	27
5.0	**The Presence of Amphorae on Salt Production Sites**		
	5.1	Dorset, Hampshire and Sussex Salt Marshes	28
	5.2	Essex Salt Marshes	28
6.0	**The Treatment of Wine and Bronze Vessels in Burials**		
	6.1	Presence of Wine Amphorae in Burials	31
		6.1.1 Elms Farm, Heybridge	
		6.1.2 Folly Lane, St. Albans	
	6.2	Bronze Drinking Vessels as Imported Bronze Vessels in Burials	32
		6.2.1 The Function of Imported Bronze Vessels in Burials	
7.0	**The Appearance of Wine on Ritual or Ceremonial Sites**		
	7.1	Sacred Enclosures	35
	7.2	Shafts	36
	7.3	Temples	36
		7.3.1 Hayling Island, Hampshire	
		7.3.2 Heybridge, Essex	
	7.4	The Appearance of Imported Bronze Vessels in Hoards	36

8.0	**Conclusions**	38
	Further Work	40
	Figures	41
	Tables	75
	Appendices	78
	Appendix 1	
	Dressel 1 and 2-4 findspots	
	Appendix 2	
	The adoption of wine in post- Conquest Britain	
	Gazetteers	82
	Gazetteer 1	
	Dressel 1 and other wine amphorae findspots (where no bronze vessels are present)	
	Gazetteer 2	
	Finds of bronze vessels (without amphorae)	
	Gazetteer 3	
	Dressel 1 and other wine amphorae findspots (with bronze vessels present)	
	Bibliography	104

Abstract

The Visibility of Imported Wine and its Associated Accoutrements in later Iron Age Britain

This book deals with the appearance of an imported commodity and its associated accoutrements in later Iron Age Britain. Wine begins to appear in the archaeological record in southern Britain in the early 1st century BC and slightly later in the south-east of the country as evidenced by Dressel 1 amphorae. This particular commodity comes with unusually rich social and ritual baggage. Before examining the evidence in southern Britain the writer has, therefore, drawn upon the ancient sources in an attempt to place wine in its context within Roman society. The same sources are also gleaned for any information on how wine may have been perceived by those living outwith the Republic and early Empire.

During the later Iron Age in Britain wine appears on settlement sites, in burials, on sites associated with salt production and may also be associated with temple or sanctuary sites. The evidence for each context is assessed with regard to both wine amphorae (predominantly Dressel 1A, 1B and 2-4) and bronze vessels, some of which can be identified with examples from the continent. Close attention is paid to the **visibility** of both these groups of objects in each context.

Having examined the evidence, the writer believes that commerce is not the primary force behind the arrival of wine in Britain. The most important starting point to illustrate this contention is the fact that wine appears in burials. This fact represents a hitherto unexplored aspect of wine's appearance in Britain at this period, that is one of ritual. The writer analyses the use of wine in the funerary rites as they are understood and attempts to separate out the customs which may have come with the wine from those which may indicate an entirely indigenous use of the drink. The use of wine in late Iron Age burials is placed in its local context where evidence for a new religion is very convincing; the writer also looks to continental Europe for comparative material.

Wine does not appear exclusively in burials, it is also found on settlement sites. The writer examines the record and puts forward suggestions as to the mechanism of distribution, which correlates strongly with that of the salt trade.

Acknowledgements

The contents of this volume consist in essence of the postgraduate thesis I submitted to the University of Edinburgh in 2000. Thank you to the scholars and publishers who have allowed me to reproduce their illustrations. The sources are acknowledged accordingly. Thank you also to Rosalind Niblett, Matthieu Poux, Steve Preston and Mark Atkinson, Philip Crummy, J.D. Hill, Andrew Fitzpatrick, Pam Craven and Kevin Trott for providing information and papers prior to publication and to Rob Sands for producing maps from my data. Warmest thanks also to Professor I.B.M. Ralston, Mr Simon Collins, Mrs C.R. Austin and the Trustees of the Abercromby Trust, without whom I never would have been encouraged, started, finished or gone to Mont Beuvray respectively. Thank you also to Iain Shaw for putting up with the lost weekends.

"Eat, drink and be merry,
For tomorrow the sky may fall on our heads."

Later Iron Age Saying
(unprovenanced)

Figures

Fig. 1   Dressel 1A; Dressel 1B; Dressel 2-4 (Peacock, 1986)

Fig. 2   Vineyards at the end of the Republic (Tchernia, 1986)

Fig. 3   The distribution of Dressel 1 (1A and 1B where identified) amphorae in southern Britain

Fig. 4   The distribution of Dressel 2-4 amphorae in southern Britain

Fig. 5   Distribution map of amphorae of Dressel Form 1 (Callender, 1965)

Fig. 6   Distribution map of Dressel 1 amphorae in Gaul and Britain (Peacock, 1971)

Fig. 7   The distribution of Graeco-Italic and Dressel 1 amphorae in western Europe (Fitzpatrick, 1985)

Fig. 8   The distribution of Dressel 1A, 1B and 1sp. in Britain (Fitzpatrick, 1985)

Fig. 9   Distribution of Etruscan amphorae along the south coast of Gaul (after Bouloumié, 1982 in Laubenheimer, 1990: 17)

Fig. 10   Map of the east of France showing the sites of Hallstatt date where fragments of Marseillan amphorae have been found (Flouest, 1993)

Fig. 11   Distribution of Dressel 1 amphorae in western France: small dots represent single finds, medium-sized dots 2-10 amphorae, large dots over 10 amphorae (Galliou, 1984: 27, fig. 1).

Fig. 12   Findspots of Dressel 1 wine amphorae in Belgic Gaul (Haselgrove, 1990)

Fig. 13   Map showing distribution of Dressel 1 amphorae in north-east Gaul (Baudoux, 1996)

Fig. 14   Principal concentrations of Republican wine amphorae in northern Gaul (Poux & Selles, 1998).

Fig. 15   Map showing the mining regions of the Iberian peninsula at the end of the Roman Republican period (Domergue, 1990)

Fig. 16   Dressel 1 and Lamboglia 2 sherds and an anvil at the mine of Sortijón del Cuzna (Cordoba) (Domergue, 1990)

Fig. 17   Scene depicting workers extracting ore or clay in a mine, with amphora. Painted plaque from Penteskouphia, Corinth.

Fig. 18   Map showing groups of rich graves comparable with the Fléré-la-Rivière group (Ferdière & Villard, 1993)

Fig. 19   Plan of the tomb and enclosure at Clemency (Metzler et al. 1991)

Fig. 20   Map showing the distribution of Dressel 1 and 2-4 amphorae in settlement and burial sites in southern Britain.

Fig. 21   Maps showing distribution of Dressel 1 and Dressel 2-4 amphorae on the Isle of Wight (Trott, forthcoming)

Fig. 22   Map showing location of Heybridge (Atkinson & Preston, 1998)

Fig. 23   Elms Farm, Heybridge: schematic plan showing location of excavation areas (Atkinson & Preston, 1998)

Fig. 24   Location of Ermine Street site and other areas of excavation at Braughing (Potter & Trow, 1988)

Fig. 25   Map showing the distribution of strainers (Guillaumet, 1991)

Fig. 26   Reconstruction drawing of strainer (Guillaumet, 1991)

Fig. 27   Excavator with copper-alloy ewer from Elms Farm, Heybridge (1998)

Fig. 28   Prehistoric and Roman saltworks in Purbeck and Poole, Dorset (Farrar, 1975)

Fig. 29   The Salt Industry and its Hinterland (Bradley, 1975)

Fig. 30   Map showing the distribution of the Red Hills of Essex as known in 1975 (de Brisay, 1975)

Fig. 31   Map showing location of some late Iron Age burials and settlements in south-east England (Hüssen, 1983)

Fig. 32   The ceremonial enclosure showing the main features and the excavated areas (Niblett, 1999: 15)

Fig. 33   Diagrammatic section of the funerary shaft, burial pit and turf stack (Niblett, 1999: 44)

Fig. 34   Distribution of amphora burials in Britain (Callender, 1965)

Fig. 35   Graves marked by amphorae at the Isola Sacra necropolis north of Ostia (Toynbee, 1971)

Fig. 36   Map showing the distribution of burials with wine amphorae, those with bronze vessels and those with both.

Fig. 37   The bronze vessel from Kjaerumgaard after which this series is named (Boube, 1991)

Fig. 38   The distribution of Kjaerumgaard type jugs (Boube, 1991)

Fig. 39   Aylesford type patera from the cemetery at Ornavasso, S. Bernardo, tomb 161 (Feugère & de Marinis, 1991)

Fig. 40   Map showing distribution of Aylesford type paterae (Feugère & de Marinis, 1991)

Fig. 41   Patera No.2, with details, from Antran (Eggers 155) (Pautreau, 1999)

Fig. 42   Handle of Patera No. 56 with details, from Fléré-la-Rivière (Ferdière & Villard, 1993)

Fig. 43   Bronze oenochoe No. 1, with details, from Antran (Eggers 124) (Pautreau, 1999)

Fig. 44   Bronze oenochoe No. 53 from Fléré-la-Rivière (Ferdière & Villard, 1993)

Fig. 45   Plan of the grave goods laid out in the Warrior's Grave, Stanway (CAT Web Site)

Fig. 46   Plan of the deposition of objects in the grave at Antran (Pautreau, 1999: 27)

Fig. 47   Pre-Roman Iron Age features at Oram's Arbour, Winchester in 1975 (Biddle, 1975)

Fig. 48   Site plan of the main area investigated at Gun Hill (Drury & Rodwell, 1973)

Fig. 49   Plans of the Iron Age (left) and Romano-British temples at Hayling Island (King & Soffe, 1994)

Fig. 50   Plan of the temple precinct remains at Heybridge (Atkinson & Preston, 1998)

Fig. 51   Reconstruction of the fish-head spout from Felmersham (Kennett, 1970)

Fig. 52 Wooden pale decorated with metal sheet (No. 10) from Antran (Pautreau, 1999)

Fig. 53 Distribution of late Iron Age cremation burials and selected shrines and settlements in southern England (Fitzpatrick, 1997)

Tables

Table 1 Chronology of Dressel 1A, Dressel 1B and Dressel 2.4 (after Tchernia, 1986; Py, 1993; Tyers, 1996)

Table 2 List of chief Dionysiac subjects found in art from Roman Britain (after Hutchinson, 1986)

Table 3 Amphorae and bronze drinking equipment found in the graves of the Fléré-la-Rivière Group (after Ferdière & Villard, 1993)

Table 4 The condition of wine amphorae in graves

Table 5 Buckets in late Iron Age burials and hoards

Introduction

It is not easy to ascertain what meaning, if any, wine had to the native population in Britain in the later Iron Age[1] but it is this question which is the driving force behind this piece of work. Wine is a very emotive product - prior to the emergence of Christianity it held a place in many of the ancient religions, not least the cults associated with Bacchus and his Greek predecessor Dionysos. It has physical medicinal qualities but it can also have a psychological effect. Drink wine and it will make you happy, even ecstatic, drink wine and it may bring melancholy and madness. Such is the power of wine, it can bring out the best or the worst in the drinker. None of this escapes those writing on the subject in antiquity and all these qualities or otherwise are expounded upon at length (see Chapter 2).

It is this potential added dimension, one of emotion and spirituality which makes the appearance of wine in Britain all the more fascinating. Hitherto, the appearance of wine amphorae has been incorporated into models on economy and trade and through these devices has been used to signify prestige, wealth, status and influence in the politics and society of Iron Age Britain. These have been firmly planted within semi-historical models derived from fragmentary references to life in the Iron Age hinted at by writers such as Strabo and Tacitus. But wine appears as part of the grave goods assembled to accompany the dead in the rich burials of south-east Britain. Could it have held a special importance to the deceased or to the composers of the grave? In addition, there may be further evidence to indicate that wine was being deposited ritually in other circumstances, in temples, or even more intriguingly, in the ditches of enclosures.

Wine has a long and illustrious history before the period in question and is well attested archaeologically and in the ancient sources. An early example of a wine drinking set comes from Tell es-Sai'diyeh in Jordan and dates to 1200 BC (Edgeworth Reade, 1995). It illustrates the basic components of a drinking set; a *ewer* or *jug* from which to pour the wine, through a *strainer* into a shallow *bowl* ready for drinking. There are even earlier examples from the Royal Tombs of Ur dating to the mid-3rd millennium BC (in the Early Dynastic period of the Sumerian civilisation in southern Mesopotamia) where sieve-like objects made from gold and silver have been found associated with spouted jars and beakers.

The Egyptians also drank wine and by the Achaemenid period sets of vessels and strainers had become standard components of some tombs, predominantly those of the elite. Herodotus (III.6) tells us that the Egyptians actually recycled amphorae sending them to Memphis where they were washed and sent on for refilling. This kind of observation has implications for the visibility of wine, particularly for attempting to calculate the amount of wine in circulation.

In temperate Europe, wine was also possibly in use in the late Bronze Age together with its associated accoutrements which certainly were. The nature of the exchange of such a commodity between Etruscans and Greeks and the Celtic and neighbouring communities in the early Iron Age is the subject of many books and papers (see for example, Wells, 1980; Brun, 1987; Dietler, 1990, 1995; Gomez de Soto, 1993). Some of this evidence is described briefly in Chapter 3.

Material Evidence for Wine in later Iron Age Britain

The appearance of wine in the archaeological record is evidenced primarily by the empty containers, in which it was transported. This study deals principally with the amphorae types Dressel 1A, 1B and 2-4 which are found in Britain in varying quantities in the later Iron Age (**Fig. 1**). In addition, the writer has examined the bronze vessels sometimes found with wine amphorae and thought by many scholars to be the vestiges of wine drinking services. This is a matter of some controversy and the evidence is considered in some detail in Chapter 4 and 6. This group of objects consisting of imported amphorae and bronze vessels, has been selected for analysis because they represent the **visible** evidence of an **invisible** commodity in the archaeological record.

It should be noted that this study deals with imported wine and does not attempt to cover the beginnings of viticulture in Britain evidenced by the 'experimental' production of amphorae, for example, at Brockley Hill (Castle, 1978) and the increasing archaeological evidence for Roman viticulture in southern Britain (Williams, 1977). There is, as yet, no evidence to suggest that viticulture had been introduced prior to the Roman Conquest.

1.1 Amphorae

With some degree of confidence we can be sure that when Dressel 1 and Dressel 2-4 amphorae appear in the archaeological record they contained wine (Tyers, 1996; Peacock, 1986; Laubenheimer, 1990; Tchernia, 1986). Although there are examples when both types have been found to be carrying other products, these are few and far between[2].

---

[1] The author has used the term 'later' Iron Age in order to acknowledge the difference in the regional chronologies with regard to the Roman horizon. The period under discussion is the 2nd century BC to the 2nd century AD.

---

[2] Although the inside of the single Dressel 2-4 amphora found at

Dressel 1 amphorae from the shipwreck of Madrague de Giens, and Lamboglia 2 and Dressel 2-4 vessels dredged from Port-la-Nautique, have been tested for wine. If empty, the amphorae contained a red residue on their interior bottoms, if still sealed by corks, they contained a relatively transparent liquid. Phenolic acid derivatives and tartrate acid and its salts were observed in the remaining liquid and residues. These compounds are found in grapes in large quantities (Formenti & Duthel, 1996).

In addition to chemical testing, extensive catalogues and studies of amphorae stamps (for example, Callender, 1965 and Py, 1993) have enhanced our understanding of the production of amphorae and their provenance.

Recent work on the chronology of these amphorae has pushed the date of circulation back in time. The current thinking on this matter is summarised in the table below which indicates the outside limits of production.

Type	Date	Capacity
Dressel 1A	-135/-50	17-24 l
Dressel 1B	-100/-1	26-27 l
Dressel 2-4	-30/150	26-34 l

Table 1 Chronology of Dressel 1A, Dressel 1B and Dressel 2.4 (after Tchernia, 1986; Py, 1993; Tyers, 1996)

All three types of amphorae were produced in workshops associated with the vineyards of Campania, Latium and Etruria, on the Tyrrhenian coast of Italy. André Tchernia produced a map showing the location of known amphorae production workshops and vineyards in this area producing wines of high repute at the end of the Republic (**Fig. 2**).

The writer has produced a database as part of this study consisting of finds of Dressel 1A, Dressel 1B, Dressel 1sp.[3] and Dressel 2-4. It does not claim to be comprehensive but does serve to illustrate that there are many new finds. Fitzpatrick's survey published in 1985 listed 75 Dr.1 findspots (including Dressel 1sp.); the attached appendix (**Appendix 1**) contains no fewer than 105, an increase of nearly 30% in 14 years. As was noticeable in the earlier survey, many of the new find spots contain only fragments of Dr.1 amphorae, in some cases literally only one sherd. The finds have been plotted and are shown in **Fig. 3**. The history of the study of imported wine is discussed below but it can be seen that essentially the distribution is still concentrated in two areas - Dressel 1B in the south-east of Britain and Dressel 1A on the south coast, with a particular concentration now noticeable on the Isle of Wight.

The finds of Dressel 2-4 in southern Britain have also been plotted and the results of this are shown below. Although the area covered has much in common with that of Dressel 1, there are fewer find spots and a more even distribution may be indicated (see **Fig. 4** and **Appendix 1**)[4].

There are three other types of amphorae which appear in Britain in the 1st century AD associated with wine:

1. **Rhodian (or Camulodunum 184)** This type was in circulation from the Republican period until the 2nd century AD; examples have been found at Sheepen (Sealey, 1985), Hod Hill (Richmond, 1968) and Lexden C (Foster, 1986);

2. **Pascual 1** This type is mostly found in Britain in Augustan-Tiberian contexts but production may continue into the later 1st century AD. These were made in Catalonia and on a smaller scale in southern Gaul; they contained wine from Layetania. Findspots in Britain include Hengistbury Head (Cunliffe, 1987).

3. **Pèlichet 47** This type was in production from the later 1st century AD and continued in circulation into the 2nd and 3rd centuries (Tyers, 1996). Findspots include Braughing (Potter & Trow, 1988) and Sheepen (*ibid.*).

This study is primarily concerned with context rather than the distribution or quantity of particular types of amphorae. The archaeological context in which examples of these amphorae have been found has not overtly contributed to the discussion, thus, they are acknowledged as carriers of wine in the period under review, but they have not been treated separately.

1.2 Drinking Equipment

Vessels associated with drinking are made of copper-alloy, pottery, glass and wood during the period under review. The writer is concerned primarily with vessels of copper-alloy because a) these make up elaborate drinking sets associated with wine in the rich graves of late Iron Age Gaul (Feugère & Rolley, 1991; Ferdière & Villard, 1993) and b) some of these vessels have been found in Britain, as is the wine, which implies a relationship worth exploring.

This relationship, however, is not clear cut. The first point to establish therefore is, what constituted a drinking set? If that is possible, is there any evidence in Britain for such a service?

The literary evidence for drinking sets is discussed in Chapters 2.2 and 3.1.1 and the comparative archaeological material is explored in Chapter 3.2.3.

In answer to the second question, most of the bronze vessels found in Britain, and relevant to this study, are

---

King Harry Lane, Burial 272 (Stead & Rigby, 1989) was analysed and found to contain olive oil.

[3] In cases where the identification of Dressel 1 has not been conclusive (ie. either 1A or 1B) the finds are referred to as Dressel 1sp., after Cunliffe (1987).

---

[4] Prior to press. Sherds of Dressel 2-4 have also been retrieved from the excavations at Cadbury Castle; see Barrett, J.C., Freeman, P.W.M. & Woodward, A. *Cadbury Castle, Somerset The later prehistoric and early historic archaeology* (2000) English Heritage. These are not included in Fig. 4.

found in burials and are therefore described in Chapter 6.2, where their typology, distribution and function are also addressed.

Although bronze vessels do appear on settlement sites they are very rare; those that have been found are discussed in Chapter 4.2.

The Study of Imported Wine in Britain to Date

The first significant study on this subject was that of M.H. Callender's *Roman Amphorae (and index of stamps)* published in 1965. Callender produced the first map illustrating the distribution of imported wine showing the find spots of Dressel 1; it essentially highlights the south east of Britain with one outsider, at this time, on the south coast (**Fig. 5**).

Six years later, Peacock, in his study published in 1971, made two observations which have underpinned the study of imported wine in Iron Age Britain ever since. Firstly, the two areas where wine arrives in Britain became more distinct as shown in his distribution map (**Fig. 6**).

Since that time the two areas have often been treated separately, either in discussions of archaeology on the south coast, or of the south-east. The earlier Dressel 1A finds have been associated with the area bordering the south coast based on the discoveries at Hengistbury Head, amongst other sites. Peacock suggested that this related to the southern tribes' relations with the Veneti who controlled the wine trade across the channel. After their uprising in 56 BC the trade was diverted to the east coast where an alliance between Rome and the Trinovantes existed (as recorded by Caesar[5]). Peacock's later revision (1984) recognised that as Dressel 1A were produced over a long time span, relating the fall in that trade with the Venetic uprising 'now seems decidedly hazardous'.

The second distinction of the distribution, noted by Peacock in 1971, is that amphorae on the south coast appeared on settlement sites and were mostly Dressel 1A and **fragmentary**. On the other hand amphorae in the south-east were, almost without exception, Dressel 1B and were notable for their appearance in burials and their **completeness**.

Two other scholars who presented overviews of the evidence in the 1970s were Rodwell (1976) and Dannell (1979). Rodwell considered the appearance of Dressel 1

amphorae in the light of a discussion on the 'Belgic' problem. He observed two distinct and different forms of burial practice: burials **with** amphorae and those **within** amphorae, the former a pre-Conquest phenomena, the latter, he argued were, for the most part, representative of a post-Conquest Roman custom.

Dannell argued for a political explanation for the appearance of wine and the trade in samian ware in Britain. He made two points: firstly, that "the use of amphorae as ritual grave goods may have a greater political significance in representing the boundaries of the protected area, than in a profound change in social habit." Secondly, he noted that despite industrial scale production contemporary with the production of Dressel 1, other Italian products, such as Campanian black-ware, were not imported into Britain until the end of the 1st century BC. He examined the trade routes in an attempt to explain this phenomenon arguing that the arrival of Dressel 1 amphorae was due to a direct link with the Mediterranean rather than northern Gaul. At this point the record for northern Gaul was still sparse with regard to Dressel 1.

In 1982 Colin Haselgrove described the archaeological evidence from south-east England in terms of a prestige goods system, thus identifying imported goods in particularly valuable terms, within this system. The prestige goods system was used as a model to identify hierarchy within the archaeological record and the importation of wine was included in the analogy.

Where Peacock's map really was inadequate was in its representation of the distribution across the Channel. The British framework established however, Fitzpatrick approached the material in 1985 and quickly discovered that the hitherto blank areas on the opposite side of the Channel were wholly inaccurate (as Peacock himself acknowledged in 1984) (**Fig. 7**).

From Fitzpatrick's map it was also clear that the distribution of imported wine in Britain was now wider than previously realised, with finds recognised from the south-western tip of Cornwall as far north as Worcester (**Fig. 8**). Dressel 1B finds were still dominating the distribution in the south-east. The picture along the south-coast however, begins to become more complex with a larger number of Dressel 1B finds indicating a continuity not apparent in previous accounts[6].
The picture on the continent is much more vivid than previous maps had reflected, the distribution becoming much more dense and concentrated especially along the river systems. Recent work by Baudoux (1996) and Poux & Selles (1998) has revealed even greater concentrations.

Despite a growing realisation that the evidence demands a greater degree of analysis it has continued to be 'shoehorned' into an existing idea of trade networks

---

[5] "In the meantime the Trinobantes, the strongest state, perhaps, in those parts ..... sent deputies to Caesar, promising to surrender to him and to do his commands, and beseeching him to protect Mandubracius from outrage at the hands of Cassivellaunus, and to send him to their state as ruler and sovereign lord." (Caesar, *Gallic War*, V.20)

---

[6] The statistical problems associated with the preparation of this distribution map are described in Fitzpatrick, 1987.

involving imports. Professor Barry Cunliffe, in his classic text book, *Iron Age Communities in Britain* (1991) summarises this view. A simple historical model is presented dividing the late Iron Age in Britain into three phases:

> *Contact Period* c. 120-60 BC
> *Caesarian episode* c.60-50 BC
> *Impact Period* c.50BC to AD 43

The Contact Period on the south coast is characterised by a Roman demand for raw materials (metals, hides, corn and slaves) which created a new market in Britain due to an inherent increase in their value. The excess created by this enhanced value was used to procure exotic items such as Italian wine which was, in turn, used by the local aristocracy to display their status. The south-east of Britain was likewise dominated by an elite, seduced by a prestige goods economy during the Impact Period, who used wine, amongst other luxury goods, including imported bronze vessels in which to serve it, to reflect their wealth and position as is evident in their rich burials.

This model implies a simple demand and supply between the Roman need for raw materials and the native desire for imported luxury goods, a relationship which the author believes can no longer be substantiated. The evidence has previously been set firmly into an economic framework where wine is seen as simply imported as a status symbol which is then used by a tribal elite to endorse their advantage.

The author believes a review of the evidence provides an opportunity to create a new, more complex model, by posing the following questions:

a) does the appearance of imported wine into later Iron Age Britain constitute a trade?

b) is it possible that wine held a ritual significance to the people of later Iron Age Britain?

c) were wine sets consisting of elaborate bronze vessels, such as flagons, paterae and ladles such as those found at Fléré-la-Rivière or Antran in France also imported during this period?

d) with regard to wine, how similar are the circumstances of its discovery to those identified in Gaul?

PART I

Setting the Scene

Wine is so much part of the culture of the classical world that its appearance in Britain cannot be seen in isolation. In Chapter 2 the ancient sources are examined for references to wine and practices associated with this commodity. Practical advice has survived from writers such as Pliny and Cato with regard to the production and transport of wine and there are many references, not least in Athenaeus, to the use of wine in society. Much of the chapter, however, is given over to a discussion of the god of wine, Dionysios, and his Roman counterpart, Bacchus.

Chapter 3 describes briefly the literary and archaeological evidence for wine in temperate Europe, concentrating mainly on the evidence from late Iron Age France, as a source of comparison for the assemblage from southern Britain.

Wine in the Classical World

The ancient sources provide a valuable insight into the practical matters of producing wine and how to drink it, together with Roman and others' attitude towards it both socially and ritually. There are passages describing at length the manners and etiquette of wine drinking in the Roman world and the equipment used. There are also, in less abundance, descriptions of how wine was or was not adopted by people in other parts of the Empire. This chapter endeavours to summarise and assess the information contained in contemporary or near contemporary texts to the period under review. Particular attention is paid to the observations of writers with regard to i) practical observations of wine production and transport, ii) wine drinking accoutrements, iii) the use of wine in a domestic or social environment, and finally iv) the ritual use of wine in Roman society. The intention is to gain an impression of how wine was used in Italy and elsewhere on the continent before attempting to assess how it was used in Britain.

In addition, it is considered worthwhile in view of the appearance of wine in burials (see Chapter 6) to discuss briefly literary references to the burial rites of the Romans themselves.

The Texts[1]

Information on attitudes towards wine in the classical world and also the practical aspects of producing it have been collected predominantly from Pliny *Natural History*, Strabo *Geography* and Athenaeus *The Deipnosophists*.[2]

The three main authors who provide Celtic ethnographic observations are Julius Caesar *De Bello Gallico*, Tacitus *Agricola* and *Germania* and Diodorus Siculus.[3] Unfortunately, potentially the most useful ethnography on the Celts has been lost, that of the 23rd Book of Poseidonius' *History*. This was written in about 80 BC and was concerned mostly with the Roman wars in southern Gaul in the late 2nd century BC. However, some of what he wrote was repeated by other, later authors for whom the text was available, sometimes *verbatim* (for example, a passage by Athenaeus describing Celtic food and drink[4]). Tierney (1964) analysed Poseidonius' contribution and concluded that all the later authors owed much of their ethnographical input to the earlier writer. He suggested that Athenaeus, Diodorus Siculus, Strabo and Caesar are

the most important sources for the lost text. This view was modified by Nash (1974) who argued successfully that much of what the later writers included in their accounts would have been common knowledge at the time. She also pointed out that Caesar had spent eight years in Gaul himself and that it was therefore inappropriate to suggest that all observations on the Celts originally stemmed from Poseidonius. In addition it should be noted that Athenaeus in particular, but also Strabo, were always careful to quote the source from where information had been derived.

T.C. Champion (1985) made the following comment on using ancient texts:

"The explicit assertions of Caesar and Tacitus are credible unless they are self-evidently erroneous (which they rarely are) or unless there is archaeological or other evidence (and there rarely is) with which they cannot reasonably be reconciled."

The present writer is of a similar opinion. There are no observations in these texts which deserve to go uninvestigated. It is likely that the truth of an observation may be askew, especially when writers have borrowed from other authors or have never visited the place they describe. Also inevitably, especially in the cases of Caesar and Tacitus who were describing either their own military prowess or that of a close relation, successes may have been over-played and losses toned down. In addition, one would expect a certain amount of "rubbishing" of the enemy. However, that having been said much of the information of relevance to this study requires only to have been cited, the type of equipment used for wine drinking for example, is unlikely to have been fabricated. When reading either of the above mentioned texts, the tone, particularly in Caesar's work, is surprisingly straight forward and factual although Tacitus does appear to show more poetic licence in interpreting his father-in-law's career.

The comments and observations cited below are not conclusive but are chosen to illustrate certain points relevant to this study. Although some of the passages cited (through Athenaeus) are of Greek origin, the intention is to concentrate on the literature relevant to the use of wine in Rome.

2.1 Wine Production

"Among these topics, however, it occurs to me that while there are in the whole world about eighty notable kinds of liquor that can properly be understood as coming under the term "wine"; two thirds of this number belong to Italy which stands far in front of all the countries in the world on that account; and further investigation going into this

[1] The writer has used translations from the Loeb Classical Library where available; for full references see bibliography.
[2] Pliny and Strabo were writing in the 1st century AD; Athenaeus wrote *The Deipnosophists* at the end of the 2nd century/beginning of the 3rd century AD.
[3] Julius Caesar and Diodorus Siculus were both writing in the 1st century BC; Tacitus wrote *Agricola* and *Germania* at the end of the 1st century AD.
[4] Athenaeus *Deipnosophistae* IV.151

subject more deeply indicates that this popularity does not date back from the earliest times, but that the importance of the Italian wines began from the city's six hundredth year [154BC]." (Pliny, *Natural History* XIV.13.87)

The use of wine and its production already had a long history in Italy by the mid-2nd century BC as illustrated in Etruria and also via the Greek city states in southern Italy[5], but the Italian wine industry in the Roman world really came into its own during this period. The earliest surviving prose in latin on wine is the 2nd century BC work *de Agri Cultura* by Marcus Porcius Cato. Viticulture was established much earlier in Greece, the first literary evidence being provided by Hesiod's *Works and Days* in the 8th century BC. It is from Greece that many of the customs associated with drinking wine, for example, the *symposia* and the ritual association with Dionysos, are derived.

2.1.1 Fine Wines

Athenaeus and Pliny wrote extensively of the types of wine available, their history and their qualities. Just as now, some areas were renowned for producing the finest wines because of the soil and the amount of sunshine and other geographical factors. At this point in time, before Spanish[6] and French wines had really started to get a foothold in the market, Italian and some Greek wines were considered the finest. Of particular note were wines from Latium and Campania. Strabo mentions Falernian, Statanian and Calenian wines as of the highest quality (*Geography*, V.iv.3) and 50 years later Pliny still ranks the three varieties of Falernian wine from Campania as the best available (*Natural History* XIV.viii.59-72).

In illustrating this point further Pliny discusses the history of important and prestigious wines:

> "And besides, did not Caesar also, when dictator, at the banquet in celebration of his triumph apportion to each table a flagon of Falernian and a jar of Chian?[46 BC] Caesar also gave Chian and Falernian at his triumph over Spain [60 BC], but at a banquet during this third consulship he provided Falernian, Chian, Lesbian and Mamertine: this is known to be the first occasion on which four kinds of wine were served." (Pliny *Natural History* XIV.14.17)

A considerable pride was shown in Italian wines and their history.

---

[5] See general introduction and bibliographies in Torelli, M. (ed.) *The Etruscans* (2000) and Unwin, T. (1991: 94-133)

[6] Emperor Domitian issued an edict (c. 90-2 AD, Suetonius *De Vita Caesarum*, VIII.Domitianus.7), the objective of which was to increase grain production by reducing the amount of land under the vine. It has been argued (Levick, B. 'Domitian and the Provinces' *Latomus* 41, 50-73) that a secondary intention was to reduce the amount of competition threatening the Italian wine industry from the provinces.

"But where can we better make a beginning than with the vine? Supremacy in respect of the vine is to such a degree the special distinction of Italy that even with this one possession she can be thought to have vanquished all the good things of the world." (Pliny, *Natural History* 14.1.7)

The fact that wines from Campania were so highly regarded is notable. It is known that the contents of Dressel 1A and later Dressel 1B were from this area (Tchernia, 1986 amongst others).

2.1.2 The Quantity of Wine in Production

Wine was produced in vast quantities in the ancient world. To serve as a simple illustration to this point, the following remarks from Pliny:

> "Marcus Varro records in the following words the wines that ranked highest in his own younger days: 'When Lucius Lucullus was a boy he never saw a full-dress banquet in his father's house at which Greek wine was given more than once, but when he himself came back from Asia [80 BC] he distributed more than 100,000 jars in largess; also Gaius Sentius, who was praetor in our time, used to say that the first time Chian wine entered his house was when the doctor had prescribed it for him for heartburn; but Hortensius left over ten thousand jars to his next of kin." (*Natural History* XIV.14.17)

Cato, an earlier author (234-149 BC), wrote an extensive treatise on farming (*de Agri Cultura*) and included much information on viticulture and the successful running of a vineyard as a business. He indicates the amount of wine allowed per year to be allocated to each slave:

> "the total of wine for the year for each man, seven amphorae. For the slaves working in chains add more in proportion to the work they are doing. It is not too much if they drink ten amphorae of wine apiece in a year" (in Unwin, 1991:103)

As Unwin points out, using Tchernia's estimates for the capacity of Dressel 1A and 1B wine amphorae which is between 17 and 27 litres, this works out as a mean average allocation of 220 litres or 293 0.75 litre bottles a year (1991: 103). Tchernia also estimates that Italian wine being imported into Gaul in the 1st century BC probably reached the extraordinary quantity of 40 million amphorae over the century (100,000 hectolitres) (1983:92). The excavator of the villa at Settefinestre estimated that this Italian estate would have produced 4,260 amphorae for export each year (Carandini, 1980: 6-7).

2.1.3 Vintage Wine

The literature provides evidence of the high value placed upon vintage wines and also serves to emphasise the sophistication of Roman viticulture. Of particular interest are Pliny's comments:

> "So large are the sums of money that are kept stored in our wine-cellars! Indeed there is nothing else which experiences a greater increase of value up to the twentieth year - or a greater fall in value afterwards."(*Natural History* XIV.6.55)

To this we can add the following observations:

> "As a matter of fact old wine is better not only in taste but also for the health." (Athenaeus *Deipnosophistae* 1.26).

Athenenaeus also gives the optimum age for different wines, as between five and twenty five years (Athenaeus *Deipnosophistae* 1.26-27).

> "Carefully sealed wine bottles were immediately brought, their necks labelled: ALERNIAN, CONSUL OPIMIUS. ONE HUNDRED YEARS OLD. While we were examining the labels, Trimalchio clapped his hands and said with a sigh: 'Wine has a longer life than poor little man. So let's wet our whistles. Wine is life. I'm giving you real Opimian. I didn't put out such good stuff yesterday, though the company was much better class.' Naturally we drank and missed no opportunity of admiring his elegant hospitality." (Petronius *Satyricon* XV.34)

Keeping and laying down wine was therefore common practice (perhaps not for 100 years!).

2.1.4 Wine Storage and Transport

The use of amphorae for the transportation of wine is attested in Roman texts many times (see Pliny, Strabo etc.) and archaeologically, for example, Ostia (see Dressel, 1879; Tchernia, 1986: 236).

The following comment from Strabo has often been cited to illustrate the possibility that barrels were used to transport wine in Gaul:

> "Aquileia[7], which is nearest of all to the recess of the Gulf, was founded by the Romans as a fortress against the barbarians who were situated above it; and there is an inland voyage thither for merchant-vessels, by the river Natiso [Natisona] for a distance of more than sixty stadia. Aquileia has been given over as an emporium for those tribes of Illyrians that live near the Ister; the latter load on wagons and carry inland the products of the sea, and wine stored in wooden

jars, and also olive oil, whereas the former get in exchange slaves, cattle and hides." (Strabo, *Geography* V.1.8)[8]

Iconographic evidence adds weight to the possibility that wine was transported by barrel in northern Europe, for example, the famous "wine-ship" from Neumagen[9].

In addition, Pliny notes the use of barrels in the Alps for storing wine:

> "Even in regard to wine already vintaged there is a great difference in point of climate. In the neighbourhood of the Alps they put it in wooden casks and close these round with tiles (with hoops?) and in a cold winter also light fires to protect it from the effect of the cold." (Pliny, *Natural History* XIV.27.132)

He also makes this observation which may have implications for the 'lone amphora' deposits (see Chapter 6.1).

> "Districts with a milder climate store their wine in jars (dolia) and bury them in the ground entirely, or else up to a part of their position, so protecting them against the atmosphere; but in other places people keep off the weather by building roofs over them." (Pliny, *Natural History* XIV.27.133)

These accounts illustrate four important points with regard to wine exports. Firstly, that the wine imported in Dressel 1A and 1B was of the highest quality. Secondly, that the quantity of wine in circulation around the Mediterranean and throughout the Empire was vast. Thirdly, that Roman viticulturalists and their clientele were well aware of the advantages of laying down wine and the implications for chronologies based on wine amphorae that this may have. Finally, amphorae were not the only method of transport for wine but they are the most visible[10].

2.2 Wine Drinking Accoutrements

This section identifies the type of equipment used in the Roman world for wine drinking. The equipment was specialised and through textual and iconographic sources it is clear that a "wine set" can be identified. The components in their simplest form are a jug or ewer

---

[7] Situated along the Adriatic coast, west of Venice.

[8] Of interest with regard to relations between wine and industry, in particular mining (see Chapter 3.2.2) Polybius (*Histories*, XXXIV 10) writes "Near Aquileia, in the territory of the Noric Taurisci, in my own time a gold mine was discovered, so easy to work, that by scraping away the surface soil for two feet, gold could be found immediately. ... Accordingly, on the Italians joining the barbarians in working this mine, in two months the price of gold went down a third throughout Italy".

[9] See illustration in C. Wells (1995: 612)

[10] The earliest evidence for barrels in Britain known to the writer are those found at Roman forts and summarised by G.C. Boon (1975) and thus out of the scope of this study.

(oenochoe), a bowl, a strainer and sometimes a ladle. In addition, cauldrons and hot water heaters are described or depicted as part of the same ensemble. The set varies in richness and detail according to the occasion for which the accoutrements are produced. The objects can, of course, have other uses individually; a ewer and bowl appearing together may have been used for washing which also had a ceremonial aspect.

Athenaeus (*Deipnosophistae* II) describes the equipment which may be used at dinner. He mentions wooden, silver and gold cups together with cups which have lettering. He also talks of wine coolers and ladles. In one of his long tales, he includes a description of a wine set: "On the tripod lay a bronze cooler, a wine jar, a silver bowl holding a pint, and a ladle; the pitcher was of bronze." (*Deipnosophistae* IV.142) It is not clear exactly what a "pint" is. Whilst describing strainers he mentions that "Hellanicus in his *History of Egypt* writes as follows: 'In the houses of Egyptians are kept a bronze phialê (type of bowl), a bronze ladle and a bronze strainer.'" (*Deipnosophistae* XI.470) We are not told of the significance of this, merely that it is mentioned.

Also in *Deipnosophistae*, Athenaeus quotes from Homer[1] :

"Before every feaster in Homer a cup is set. In the case of Demodocus, at least, there are furnished a basket, a table, and a cup 'for drinking whensoe'er his heart bade him.' And 'the mixing-bowls are crowned with the beverage,' that is, they are filled to the brim, so as to be 'crowned' with the wine. This they did because they regarded it as a good omen." (Athenaeus, *Deipnosophistae* I.13)

More revealing, particularly about the problem of identifying objects associated with wine as opposed to water, is the following extract:

"For in ancient times there were two sorts of tripods, both of which came to be termed cauldrons. The one called "bath-pourer" was also made to stand over a fire. Thus Aeschylus: "This was contained in the household cauldron, tripod-mounted, which ever keeps it station above the fire." The other is the so-called krater ('mixing bowl') ...Wherefore the tripod is proper to Apollo because of its prophetic truth, while to Dionysus it is proper because of the truth of wine. Now Semus of Delos says: "Bronze tripod; not the Pythian, but rather what is now termed cauldron. Of these some were not intended for fire, and in them they mixed wine; others were pitchers for the bath, in which they heated water, and they were made to stand over a fire." (*Deipnosophistae* II.37)

There are, unfortunately, no further statements indicating any special feature of cauldrons by which we can distinguish their use. This applies to all the objects associated with wine drinking. Bowls, strainers, ewers and ladles were used for serving wine but they also had other uses. However, in some cases the ewers may be distinguished in the archaeological record by iconographic evidence in the form of references to Bacchus and in some cases a vine leaf is used as decoration on bronzeware.

A frieze from a villa at Marbella,[12] in Spain dated to the late 2nd century AD begins with images of bathing equipment including strigils and oil flasks (Dunbabin, 1995: 257). A bath was often a prelude to a meal (*ibid*: 258). The frieze goes on to depict a wide-mouthed crater with a ladle or strainer resting on it followed by a display of food. Amphorae, oenochoe, a crater and a table with a wine jug and beakers and a hot water heater are interspersed with the main images.

A further point and one which may have implication for the archaeological record is this comment from Pliny:

"Nay what is more, to enable us to take more, we reduce its strength by means of a linen strainer." (*Natural History* XIV.28.137)

A linen strainer would be unlikely to survive materially unless in very special circumstances. The lack of a bronze strainer in some assemblages where other elements of a wine set are present may not therefore prevent an association with wine.

There are many examples of drinking scenes represented pictorially. The drinking set as a whole is illustrated in an early Imperial representation of a banquet on the Tomb of Vestorius Priscus at Pompeii: table silver, three craters accompanying drinking cups of various shapes, wine jugs, a ladle and other implements are displayed. A frieze from Neumagen illustrates a servant with a pedestal table on which sit a two-handled cup, a patera, a jug and a mirror[13]. The lion (panther?) at the foot of the table may have Dionysiac connotations (see Chapter 2.4.4).

Katherine Dunbabin (1995:258) points out that one of the distinguishing features of the Roman *convivium* is the presence of the hot-water heater. This was used to heat water which would be added to wine for serving. She argues that a heater represents a fundamental difference in the handling of wine between the Romans and the Greeks. The wine was served individually in the Roman world and this opposes the communal idea of the Greek crater. In addition she notes that she has not found any passages in the Roman literature which mention the proportions of mixing wine and water in a crater. This was very important

---

[1] [1]Homer, *Illiad* i.470.

[12] A. Garcia y Bellido, 'El mosaico de tema culinario de Marbella' *Hommages à Marcel Renard* 3 (Brussels, 1969: 241-6); J.M. Blazquez, *Mosaicos romanos de Córdoba, Jaén y Málaga (Corpus de Mosaicos de España* 3) (Madrid, 1981: 81-3, no.55, figs. 22-3 pls.62-6); A. Balil, 'Un bodegon en mosaico hallada en Marbella (Malaga)', *Baetica. Estudios de arte, geografia e historia* 6 (1983: 159-70)

[13] See Veyne, P. 'The Roman Empire' in Veyne, P. (ed.) (1992: 192)

to the Greeks. It would seem also that drinking during a meal was more prevalent than in Greek practice where the emphasis on drinking was after the meal.

The hot water heater therefore was also part of the equipment used at banquets by the 1st century AD. An elaborate bronze escutcheon with a frontal mask of Pan with ram's and goat's horns was found at the Praetentura of the Roman fort at Iklely (Yorkshire). It is roughly dated to pre-2nd/3rd century AD and may have decorated a hot-water heater (Hutchinson, 1986:331 No.Me-124). This is the only example of such an object in Britain known to the author but is not discussed further because it is rather later than the period of this study.

Lids from Roman sarcophagi dating from between the 2nd century and the early 4th century AD frequently include scenes of heating a cauldron on a fire. Wine is sometimes shown being poured from an amphora into a bowl on the ground and sometimes directly from the amphora into a cauldron on a fire.

A further possible accoutrement is the tripod as indicated in this passage:

> "Hence also the tripod as prize of victory in the festival of Dionysus. For of those who speak the truth we say that they "speak from the tripod", and it must be understood that the mixing-bowl is Dionysus's tripod." (Athenaeus *Deipnosophistae* II.37)

2.3 **The Use of Wine in Society**

Many of the customs and rituals associated with wine prevalent in Rome were derived from earlier Greek culture; in this respect it is important to include a brief account of the Greek roots. The following section is divided into two parts i) social drinking and ii) the use of wine in ritual. There is considerable overlap as ritual was involved on what could be called social occasions and *vice versa*.

2.3.1 **Attitudes towards Drinking**

The Greek *symposium* and its antecedent the Roman *convivium* were drinking forums with much tradition and custom attached. They did have their differences, not only with the kind of equipment used (for example, the Roman introduction of a hot water heater) but also in etiquette. Wine was, in both cultures though, part of everyday life, and drunk by everybody, although the glimpses to be gained through the ancient writers tend to relate to their own experience, that is of the aristocracy or at least the educated people of the day.

Wine is praised for its ability to lead to truth and to intoxicate (Rösler, 1995). This was seen as a good thing but writers were also fully aware of the pitfalls of too much wine and there are many references to moderation and in a way, the art of drinking. Being able to "use" wine effectively was of great importance and is one of the

reasons that not being able to drink and remain in control was so chastised in accounts of the way Gauls and other peoples behaved with wine.

Athenaeus cites many examples, some from much older, mainly Greek texts and stories, of wise words with regard to wine drinking:

> "After this long and continuous catalogue given by Democritus, Pontianus remarked that wine is the source of all these dread evils; from it comes intoxication, acts of madness, and drunken violence" (Athenaeus *Deipnosophistae* 10.443)

> "Eubulus makes Dionysus say: 'Three bowls only do I mix for the temperate - one to health, which they empty first, the second to love and pleasure, the third to sleep. When this is drunk up wise guests go home. The fourth bowl is ours no longer, but belongs to violence; the fifth to uproar, the sixth to drunken revel, the seventh to black eyes. The eighth is the policeman's, the ninth belongs to biliousness, and the tenth to madness and hurling the furniture. Too much wine, poured into one little vessel, easily knocks the legs from under the drinkers." (Athenaeus *Deipnosophistae* 2.36)

He includes a familiar sounding drinking story about a house which became known as the "trireme":

> "A party of young fellows were drinking in it [the house], and became so wild when overheated by the liquor that they imagined they were sailing in a trireme, and that they were in a bad storm on the ocean. Finally they completely lost their senses, and tossed all the furniture and bedding out of the house as though upon the waters, convinced that the pilot directed them to lighten the ship because of the raging storm. Well, a great crowd gathered and began to carry off the jetsam, but even then the youngsters did not cease from their mad actions." (Athenaeus *Deipnosophistae* 2.37)

Heavy drinking was generally frowned upon. Cicero disapproves at length of overindulgence when it comes to eating and drinking (in *de Officiis* I 93-106) but as John d'Arms (1995:308) points out what was acceptable with regard to drinking could depend to some extent which emperor was in power at the time.

The following two epitaphs serve to illustrate the ubiquitousness of wine and also highlight the importance of bathing in Roman society.

> "In this tomb I lie, the famous Primus. I fared on oysters, and often I drank Falernum. Baths, wine and Venus, year after year, accompanied me to my old age. If I could do as much, let the earth be light on my bones. But in the world of the Manes a phoenix awaits me and makes ready to renew itself together

with me." (Inscription from Tomb of *C. Domitius Primus* at Ostia (CLE No.1318))

"Baths, wine and sex corrupt our bodies; but baths, wine and sex also make up our lives." (Epitaph of *Ti. Claudius Secundus* (CLE No.1499), Rome)

2.3.2 Wine Festivals

Most of the following information is taken from Professor Scullard's book on *Festivals and Ceremonies in Republican Rome* (1981) where he has actually pieced together the Roman festival calendar using primarily, Ovid's *Fasti*. Holidays in Rome consisted of *feriae* (holidays) and *ludi* (public games). Scullard described *feriae* as days on which religious rites were performed, civil lawsuits and quarrels avoided and all men including slaves had a period of rest. They were divided into two groups - public festivals (*feriae publicae*) and private festivals (*feriae privatae*) which were celebrated by families or individuals (eg. birthdays). Public holidays were of three types: annual holidays (*stativae*) which had a fixed date every year and were recorded in the official calendar; *conceptivae*, holidays which were held annually on a date fixed each year by the magistrates and priests and *imperativae* which were irregular holidays proclaimed by consuls, praetors or dictators and which met an emergency or celebrated a victory.

There were two large public, primarily agricultural, festivals held in Rome during the year which were specifically associated with wine.[14] The first was held on 23 April, the *Vinalia Priora* where wine from the previous year was drawn from a jar or skin and offered in libation to Jupiter. Liber was linked on occasion with Jupiter and was known as Jupiter Liber. A similar festival was held in Athens called Pithoigia, the Opening of the Jars, in honour of Dionysos when new wine was offered and tasted. A Spring festival held in Athens in honour of Dionysos had been an institution since at least the 5th century BC.

The second was the *Vinalia Rustica* held on 19 August. This festival was intended to gain protection of the growing vines and the *flamen Dialis* officially announced the vintage.

The *Liberalia* was held on 17 March and consisted of a procession of the *Argei*. On this day also older women would act as priestesses of Liber Pater, crowned with ivy they would sit in places dotted around the city where they displayed cakes made from oil and honey, with small altars on which they offered sacrifices on behalf of passers by. Liber was often linked with Dionysos and he was, in his own right, particularly associated with the vine.

Two other festivals linked with wine were the *Meditrinalia* held on 11 October where an offering of new and old wine would be poured and tasted in order to be healed. This was an important agricultural ceremony in early Rome. Columella (*de Rustica*) also mentions that sacrifices must be offered to Liber and Libera and to the vessels of the wine press after the wine cellars had been cleaned and fumigated. This also took place in October.

On the 19 April the *Cerialia* was held. These were games in honour of Ceres where offerings of milk, honey and wine were made.

The use of wine for festivals is documented in the Roman records from Vindolanda (Birley, 1999). These show that wine was used to celebrate other festivals not specifically to do with the production of wine. In the accounts of the Commanding Officer's Residence, for example, listed for the 25th June is '8½ litres for the festival of the Goddess' together with a further 6½ litres of wine. June 24th is the date of the festival of *Fors Fortuna*; during this week at least 46 litres of vintage wine and 68 litres of Celtic beer were consumed (*ibid*: 62-64). This evidence is relevant to the study of wine consumed in Roman forts after the Conquest. It may be of interest particularly in relation to northern Britain in explaining the nature of the use of wine during the Antonine period on the Scottish forts.

2.4 The Ritual Use of Wine

The growth of the vine and the production of wine itself were governed by ritual and ceremony. The Romans in particular, were a deeply superstitious people but the ritual attached to wine production and its uses, whether for social or ceremonial purposes, serves as a reminder of how important wine was on so many different levels.

Wine was used for libations in the Classical world by which time it already had a long history of associations and meaning. Wine and blood were both used in sacrificial ritual - there is a reference in *Aeneid* (Virgil, v.77-9; Griffin, 1995: 293-294) to wine and blood being poured out together as an offering to the dead. According to Pliny the Romans had not always used wine for libations but rather milk.

> "Romulus used milk and not wine for libations, as is proved by the religious rites established by him which preserve the custom at the present day. The Posturnian Law of King Numa runs: Thou shalt not sprinkle the funeral pyre with wine - a law to which he gave his sanction on account of the commodity in question, as nobody can doubt." (Pliny, *Natural History* XIV.14.88)

As already noted wine did not become popular in Rome until the 2nd century BC and the passage above relates to the early history of Rome. It was also during this time that women in Rome were forbidden to drink wine (Pliny,

---

[14] Wine festivals are still held throughout the wine growing regions of Europe, for example, the Fête des Vignerons, Vevey, Switzerland which is held roughly every generation, about every 25 years.

Natural History 14.14.88) although this was not the case by the period in question.

Wine was used for libations by the 1st century AD (and earlier) as Pliny records restrictions on the type of wine used in such ritual.

> "And since life is upheld by religion it is considered sinful to pour libations to the gods, not only with wines made from a vine that has not been pruned, but from one that has been struck by lightening .....; and likewise Greek wines must not be used for libations, because they contain water." (Pliny, *Natural History* XIV.23.119)

Ritual was not just associated with the finished product but all through its production from the vine's planting and pruning through to the fermenting and "bottling".

> "Moreover (these instructions proceed) the shape of the jars is important: pot-bellied and broad ones are not so good. Immediately after the rising of the Dog-Star they should be coated in pitch, and afterwards washed with sea-water or water with salt in it, and then sprinkled with ashes of brushwood or else with potter's earth, and then rubbed clean and fumigated with myrrh, as should frequently be done with the wine cellars also." (Pliny, *Natural History* XIV.27.133)

The Dog Star is mentioned in other earlier literature as significant as far as the timing of viticultural events are concerned (for example, Hesiod *Works and Days* 609-17).

2.4.1 Dionysos

One of the most important and well-known aspects of wine in the Classical World was the god of wine - Dionysos (the Greek god) who later became known as Bacchus in the Roman world.

Dionysos was already known in the 12th century BC as his name is recorded on the Pylos tablets and wine was familiar with the characters in Homer (Griffin, 1995; 289). Dionysiac religion is thought to have first become notable in Greece in the 5th century BC although the first appearance of Dionysos in Greek art is about 580 BC. This representation shows simply "a humble, barefoot figure who holds a branch of a grape-vine and walks by himself in a procession of deities" (Carpenter, 1986 in Unwin, 1991: 86-87).

The key elements in the mythology associated with Dionysos' are summarised by Unwin (1991: 86-87). Briefly, he was the son of Zeus and Semele, the daughter of Cadmus, the King of Thebes. He grew up on the slopes of Nysa where he was taught by the Muses and other gods. He is associated as the result of his education with one of his tutors, Silenus ("a drunk and obese old man", *ibid*: 88), Satyrs, Pan, Centaurs, Nymphs and Priapus (the god of garden and field).

Although having an origin as the god of wine, Dionysos eventually became part of the Olympian pantheon with a much wider significance. His influence spread to represent a more elusive quality, one described as incorporating the essence of nature (see Dodds, 1960: xii; Unwin, 1991: 89). He also thereafter became associated with the afterlife. His followers sought communion with him through drinking wine and through dancing.

If the cult of Dionysos was rejected madness struck; this is illustrated in the fate of Pentheus, King of Thebes in Euripides' play *Bacchae*. Professor Dodds in his introduction to the play states that it was about the emergence of a new religion in Hellas and that Euripides presents the Dionysiac cult as a sort of "world religion" carried from one land to another by missionaries (Dodds, 1960). This was a new phenomena as no native Greek cult had become popular in other regions before. Dodds emphasises the fact that at this time Dionysos was not specifically the god of wine, as he was later to be perceived in Rome, but that he represented a religious experience of a communion with God which transformed a human being. The Greeks believed wine to be one of the aids to that transformation although only at certain times, for example, in the Spring when the new wine was ready to be opened at the Feast of Cups in 5th century Athens. Writing much later the Greek Athenaeus notes:

> "To drink to the point of intoxication is not proper to any other occasion except the festivals in honour of the god who gave the wine, and it is not safe". (*Deipnosophistae* 10.432)

The second method of communing was wild mountain dancing which was practised by women's societies at Delphi. This tradition continued and Diodorus (4.3) describes the following: "they dance in imitation of the maenads who are said to have been associated with the god in the old days".

The rite gradually came under State jurisdiction and was practised every two years thus "canalizing mass hysteria" and keeping the cult within organised bounds (Dodds, 1960: xvi). Further evidence comes in the form of a document from 276/5 BC concerning the sale of the priesthood of Dionysos and thus civic regulation of the older ritual. In addition, the raw meal of an animal torn to shreads had been replaced with a portion of raw flesh laid down as an offering (Nilsson, 1957: 6-7).

2.4.2 Bacchus

By the 2nd century BC Bacchic rites were well established in Rome although it is not clear when they became popular. Early on in the rite's history however, Dionysos was associated with the Roman gods of Ceres, Liber and Libera. Some scholars (Scullard, 1981: 21) suggest that Dionysos or Bacchus were actually accepted in Rome as

Liber (a god of the fertility of the fields). Nilsson suggested that Dionysiac elements were introduced to Rome as early as the early 5th century BC (Nilsson, 1957: 12).

2.4.3 The Bacchanalia

Plautus made references to Bacchants and Bacchanalia in his comedies written in the 2nd century BC; he died in 186 BC the same year of its repression. In *Miles Gloriosus* (line 1016) he records the existence of secret organisations attended by men and women associated with the Bacchanalia. There are two main sources for this affair, firstly Livy's account (*History of Rome* 34.8) "embellished by romantic and exaggerated details" (Nilsson, 1957: 15) and secondly, the *Senatus Consultum de Bacchanlibus* of 186 BC. Livy writes of the cult:

> "To the religious content were added the pleasures of wine and feasting, to attract a greater number." (Livy, *History of Rome*, XXXIX, viii)

The historian goes on to describe the dark deeds carried out by those affiliated with the rite "When they were heated with wine, and all sense of modesty had been extinguished by the darkness of night ...." and more sinister "Nor was the vice confined to the promiscuous intercourse of free men and women, but false witnesses and evidence, forged seals and wills, all issued from this same workshop; also poisonings and murders of kin....."

An inscription was set up in 186 BC. It laid out the details of the suppression of the cult (Dowden, 1992: 37).

In the late years of the Republic, Bacchic rites again became popular. New Bacchic mysteries free from the fanaticism of the Bacchanalia were favoured by the aristocracy. Nilsson draws attention to a line in *Servius ad Verg. Ecl.* v.29 'Caesarem constat primum sacra Liberi patris Roman transtulisse' ie. Caesar introduced the Bacchic mysteries into Rome (Nilsson: 1957: 20). This may or may not be so, but it serves to illustrate that imagery associated with the cult of Bacchus may once again have become popular in the 1st century BC.

2.4.4 The Iconography of the Bacchic Mysteries

Valerie Hutchinson, in an extensive study on the evidence for the later cult of Bacchus in Roman Britain, has made a serious attempt to understand, not only the extent of the cult of Bacchus, but also to single out objects which can be assigned religious meaning. She has subjected evidence from archaeological contexts (temples, shrines, hoards and graves) to vigorous iconographic analysis. Hutchinson's position is as follows:

> "however complex its origins and however varied its content, [Bacchic religion] had by early Imperial times achieved a fundamental unity. This is evident both from literary sources and from ancient

monuments, which time and again display a crowded - yet basically consistent - tapestry of Bacchic subjects."

From all those objects which Hutchinson describes as 'Dionysiaca', 37% of the total in Britain come from military sites thereby implying that the Roman army was one of the major conduits through which the cult entered the country. The second major source of objects was towns; four in particular, London, Colchester, Wroxeter and Cirencester were rich in Bacchic material. Only 9% of the objects have been retrieved from villa sites although a larger percentage came from other rural sites intimating that the cult was not exclusively urban.

Hutchinson lists the objects which, for the purposes of this study, may help in identifying Bacchic associations (see **Table 2**). These images, or combinations of these images, may alert the researcher to an association with the Bacchic rite. However, particularly in the case of the animals listed in the table, their appearance is not exclusively Bacchic in origin. Lions, tigers and griffons, for example, can be seen in the elaborate bronze wine services of the Hallstatt period[15]. The assemblage of objects in pre-Conquest Britain under review have been assessed for any possible links with this cult (see Chapter 6.2).

2.4.5 Roman Funerals

The most illuminating and scholarly description of a Roman funeral is still that provided by Professor J.M.C. Toynbee (1971: 43-72). Drawing together many sources, mainly from the late-Republic/early Empire, she pieces together the procedures of the ceremony. The funerary rite was either inhumation or cremation but there were many stages and rituals attached to either rite both before and after the ceremony itself. In addition, there are many variations in the type of tomb. It is not proposed to describe in great detail after Toynbee, Roman funerary rites, but rather to flag up some aspects which will be discussed in Chapter 6 and which may or may not be represented in the British late Iron Age archaeological record.

There are two points upon which Toynbee is quite clear. Romans used cinerary urns; there is no mention in her account of unenclosed cremation. Secondly, Roman burials were placed outside settlement sites.

2.4.5.1 The Use of Wine in the Funeral Ceremony

Wine was used as part of the Roman funerary ceremony; it was poured onto the remains of the pyre as this passage illustrates:

---

[15] For example, the griffons on the tripod from the tomb at La Garenne, Sainte-Colombe (Rolley, 1988: 98) and the lions on the bronze cauldron from the tomb at Eberdingen-Hochdorf near Hohenasperg (Rolley, 1998: 99; Biel, 1988: 158).

"No servile flames were thine: fragrant harvests of Saba and Cilicia [incense and saffron] did the fire consume, and cinnamon stolen from the Pharian bird [the Phoenix], and the juices that drip from Assyrian herbs - and thy master's tears: these only did the ashes drink, those the pyre ceased not to consume; nor was the Setian wine that quenched the hoary ash, nor the smooth onyx that guarded his bones more grateful to the hapless shade than those tears." (Statius, *Silvae* II.VI.90)[16]

Statius intimates that wine was actually used to put the pyre out - "quenched the hoary ash". It is also apparent that exotic spices and herbs were burnt symbolically on the pyre. This practice is described again in an epitaph written by Ausonius, again referring to the practice of pouring wine on the ashes:

"Sprinkle my ashes with pure wine and fragrant oil of spikenard: Bring balsam, too, stranger with crimson roses.
Tearless my urn enjoys unending spring.
I have not died, but changed my state."
(Ausonius *Epit.* XXXI)

Whether these practices can be detected in the rich burials of the 1st century AD in Britain is addressed in Chapter 6.

2.4.5.2 **The Use of Masks**

For a Roman funeral, masks and images of the deceased would be made and put on show during the ceremony as Polybius[17] explains during the description of the funeral of an 'illustrious man':

"After the burial and all the usual ceremonies have been performed, they place the likeness of the deceased in the most conspicuous spot in his house, surmounted by a wooden canopy or shrine. This likeness consists of a mask made to represent the deceased with extraordinary fidelity both in shape and colour. These likenesses they display at public sacrifices adorned with much care." (Polybius, *Histories* VI 53)

As Toynbee (*ibid.* p.48) points out images or masks must still have been in use under the Empire from this account of Vespasian's funeral recorded by Suetonius:

"Even at his [Vespasian] funeral, Favor, the principal mime, wearing a mask of the emperor and mimicking, as the custom is, his deeds and words during his lifetime" (Suetonius, *Vespasian* 19)

Tacitus writes of the Germans:

"Apart from this they deem it incompatible with the majesty of the heavenly host to confine the gods within walls, or to mould them into any likeness of the human face." (Tacitus, *Germania* 9)

This is in direct contrast to the Roman practice of making images of their gods through statues, figurines and also representations on bronze, ceramic and glass. In addition, they create masks and images of their dead. However, masks do appear in the grave assemblage of Welwyn A, possibly at Folly Lane and in France at Neuvy-Pailloux (Indre).

---

[16] Statius, a poet, was born in Naples in about AD 40.
[17] Polybius was born in about 203 BC and died in 121 BC according to the best judgment of Shuckburgh (1889).

Wine in Temperate Europe

Wine in the late Republic was a major export from Italy to the surrounding areas and into temperate Europe, before the practice of commercial viticulture was adopted in southern France, and later in Spain. The non-Roman world's experience of wine during this period is touched upon in contemporary literature but it is the archaeological evidence which provides a more vivid picture of the scale of the venture.

3.1 References in the Ancient Sources

This subject has been well covered previously and most thoroughly in Tchernia (1986: Appendices II-V). However, the passages highlighted below draw attention to certain aspects of the literature which are relevant to this study.

3.1.1 Wine Drinking Accoutrements

There are very few references to the equipment used in the non-Roman world for drinking wine especially in the period under review. The most well known passage is from Poseidonius' *History of the Celts* recorded by Athenaeus; it describes a Celtic meal:

"The Celts place hay on the ground when they serve their meals, which they take on wooden tables raised only slightly from the ground. ... Those who dwell beside rivers or by the inner and outer sea [the Mediterranean and the Atlantic] also eat fish baked with salt, vinegar and cumin. The last they also drop into their wine. ...When several dine together, they sit in a circle .....The attendants serve the drink in vessels resembling our spouted cups, either of clay or silver, similar also are the platters which they have for serving food; but others use bronze platters, others still, baskets of wood or plaited wicker. The liquor drunk in the houses of the rich is wine brought from Italy and the country round Marseilles, and is unmixed; though sometimes a little water is added. (Athenaeus *Deipnosophistae* IV.151)

Several points are raised in this description. Firstly, it is evident that spices, in this case cumin, were added to wine in a dining situation, so this custom is not exclusive to funerals (Chapter 2.4.5). It may also imply indirectly that the wine was heated. Secondly, the type of drinking vessels that were in circulation are described; note the reference to silver cups. Finally, literary evidence that wine was imported from Italy and 'the country around Marseilles' as confirmed by the archaeological record.

Tacitus describes the German tribes' reaction to gifts of silver:

"One may see among them silver vases, given as gifts to their envoys and chieftains, but treated as of no more value than earthenware. However, the tribes nearer to us for purposes of traffic treat gold and silver and precious metals, and recognise and prefer certain coins of our money; the tribes of the interior practice barter in the simpler and older fashion." (Tacitus, *Germania* 5)

He states here that fine metalware was presented to leaders as gifts by the Romans, a system of 'potlatch' as noted by Tchernia with regard to southern France. This scenario is illustrated by Lotte Hedeager's work on the distribution of Roman imports, including wine and bronze vessels, along the German limes (Hedeager, 1978; 1992). Using Eggers' maps she showed how high status goods were found further from the border well into tribal territory and that more commonplace objects were found near or on the border.

Polybius, writing in the 2nd century BC, describes the wealth of the Iberian kings:

"One of the Iberian kings had such a magnificent and richly furnished palace, that he rivalled the luxury of the Phaeacians, except that the vessels standing in the interior of the house, though made of gold and silver, were full of barley-wine ..." (Polybius, *Histories* XXXIV 9)

This is the only passage known to the author which cites the use of fine metal vessels to contain a drink other than wine made from grapes[1]. Barley wine was actually brewed at Vindolanda in the early 2nd century AD and was obviously still being drunk when the Roman Emperor Julian wrote this verse about it in the 4th century:

On wine made from Barley

Who made you and from what?
By the true Bacchus I know you not
He smells of nectar,
But you smell of goat.
(in Birley, 1999:75)

3.1.2 Attitudes towards Drinking Wine in the non-Roman World

Roman writers record attitudes to wine in the non-Roman world in two ways - they either drink so much of it that they go mad or they drink none at all. It would appear that attitudes to wine varied from tribe to tribe.

---

[1] Other than the use of drinking horns; see Caesar *The Gallic War* VI.28 on use by German tribes and Athenaeus *Deipnosophistae* IV.150 for use by the Thracians.

The following two passages illustrate the excessive response to wine as described or imagined by, firstly Athenaeus, and secondly, Pliny:

> "And in the first book of the Laws he says: "(I am speaking) of intoxication itself, as practised by Lydians, Persians, Carthaginians, Celts, Iberians, Thracians and such tribes; while you, Lacedaemonians utterly abstain from it. Now the Scythians and Thracians drink nothing but unmixed wine, their wives as well as all the men; they pour it over their clothes and think that they practice a noble and happy custom." (Athenaeus *Deipnosophistae* 10.432)

> "It is stated that the Gauls, imprisoned as they were by the Alps as by a then insuperable bulwark, first found a motive for overflowing into Italy from the circumstance that a Gallic citizen from Switzerland named Helico, who had sojourned at Rome on account of his skill as an artificer, had brought with him when he came back some dried figs and grapes and some samples of oil and wine; and consequently we may pardon them for having sought to obtain these things even by means of war." (Pliny, *Natural History* XII.2.5)

Diodorus Siculus is also not of a moderate opinion in this famous passage:

> "The Gauls are exceedingly addicted to the use of wine and fill themselves with the wine which is brought into their country by merchants, drinking it unmixed, and since they partake of this drink without moderation by reason of their craving for it, when they are drunken they fall into a stupor or a state of madness. Consequently many of the Italian traders, induced by the love of money which characterises them, believe that the love of wine of these Gauls is their own godsend. For these transport the wine on the navigable rivers by means of boats and through the level plain on wagons, and receive for it an incredible price; for in exchange for a jar of wine they receive a slave, getting a servant in return for the drink." (Diodorus Siculus, V.26)

The mixing of wine with water was considered the correct way to drink in the Roman world; this was partly due to a wariness of its powers. The passage above emphasises the opinion that many may have had of the Gauls; the "barbaric" way in which they supposedly drunk wine reflecting their incivility and un-Roman attributes. It is interesting also to note the price which the Gauls were prepared to pay for wine. If there is any truth in the statement it is difficult to discern whether wine was indeed an exceptionally valuable commodity or rather that people were an exceptionally invaluable commodity.

Attitudes appear to be quite different in the north of Gaul where there are several passages referring to a conscious decision by some tribes not to buy and drink wine. Caesar mentions the refusal to buy wine by northern tribes on at least three separate occasions. The Nervii and Suebi are cited as not drinking wine and in general terms the Belgae also.

In this passage, which is part of his introduction to the book, the *Gallic Wars*, Caesar makes reference to the quotations he uses later of the Nervii and Suebi. The extracts are quoted in sequence.

> "Of all these peoples the Belgae are the most courageous, because they are farthest removed from the culture and the civilisation of the Province [Gallia Narbonensis], and least often visited by merchants introducing the commodities that make for effeminacy; and also because they are nearest to the Germans dwelling beyond the Rhine, with whom they are continually at war." (Caesar, *The Gallic War* I.1)

> "Their [the Ambiani] next neighbours were the Nervii and when Caesar inquired as touching the nature and character of these, he discovered as follows. Traders had no means of access unto them, for they allowed no wine nor any of the other appurtenances of luxury to be imported, because they supposed that their spirit was like to be enfeebled and their courage relaxed thereby." (Caesar, *The Gallic War* II.15)

> "They suffer no importation of wine whatever, believing that men are thereby rendered soft and womanish for the endurance of hardship." (Caesar, writing of the Suebi in *The Gallic War* IV.2)

Andrew Fitzpatrick addressed the archaeological evidence for this abstinence in a survey published in 1985. He concluded that wine amphorae were absent from Germanic areas but that contemporary bronze vessels did appear in the record (Fitzpatrick, 1985: 311-12).

3.1.3 **The Ritual Use of Wine**

The only literary account known to the author which intimates, by association only, a possible ritual use of wine by the Gallic or northern tribes at this time is the following:

> "In the ocean, he says [Poseidonius], there is a small island, not very far out to sea, situated off the outlet of the Liger River [River Loire]; and the island is inhabited by the women of the Samnitae, and they are possessed by Dionysus and make this god propitious by appeasing him with mystic initiations as well as other sacred performances; and no man sets foot on the island, although the women themselves, sailing from it, have intercourse with the men and then return again." (Strabo, *Geography* 4.4.6)

This account suggests that Dionysiac cults were active beyond Italy in the 1st century AD.

3.1.4 Funerals

The references made to funerals in the ancient sources are very well documented in Brunaux (1996) and it is not proposed to list the same here. However, attention is drawn to three passages describing funerary ceremonies in Gaul and Germany which are enlightening with regard to the differences between indigenous funerary rites and potential Roman influence.

This extract describes a funeral in Gaul:

> "Their funerals, considering the civilisation of Gaul, are magnificent and expensive. They cast into the fire everything, even living creatures, which they believe to have been dear to the departed during life..." (Caesar, *The Gallic War* VI 19)

In the same volume, a German funeral ceremony is described:

> "In burial there is no ostentation:[2] the single observance is to burn the bodies of their notables with special kinds of wood. They build a pyre, but do not load it with palls or spices [a Roman practice]: to each man his armour; to the fire of some his horse also is added. The tomb is a mound of turf: the difficult and tedious tribute of a monument they reject as too heavy on the dead." (Tacitus, *Germania* 27)

These two passages illustrate the difference in approach to what is essentially the same rite, that of cremation.

Tacitus makes an interesting comment with regard to the religion of the German tribes, in particular, of the Suebi:

> "Of the gods, they give a special worship to Mercury, to whom on certain days they count even the sacrifice of human life lawful. Hercules and Mars they appease with such animal life as is permissible. A section of the Suebi sacrifices also to Isis: the cause and origin of this foreign worship I have not succeeded in discovering, except that the emblem itself, which takes the shape of a Liburnian galley, shows that the ritual is imported." (Tacitus, *Germania* 9)

Tacitus' commentary infers that it was accepted that elements of ritual would be imported from one culture to another.

This study does not extend to the role of druids in British and Gallic society at this time on the grounds that the author does not know of any references which link the use of wine and druidic practice.[3]

3.2 The Archaeological Evidence for Wine in Gaul

In the second half of the 7th century BC elaborate objects associated with wine drinking in the Mediterranean world begin to appear in the tombs of the Celtic aristocracy of central Europe. Whether wine itself appears at the same time is still a matter of some debate[4].

Marseilles (or *Massalia*) was founded by Ionian Greeks from the city of Phocaea (Asia Minor) in 600 BC[5] and was one of several colonies founded throughout the Mediterranean during this period reflecting an intense period of commercial contact. Ionia exported wine, olive oil, pottery and silver and may have imported grain, metal and luxury goods in return. This signifies the first major phase of wine drinking accoutrements and wine itself into southern Gaul during the late Hallstatt/early Iron Age period. Marseilles was ideally situated to exploit the mouth of the Rhône which connected the new city with central Europe; its principal purpose was as a city of commerce and as such it also served as a conduit for Etruscan goods, including wine (**Fig. 9**).

The Massiolite type of amphora, containing Greek imported wine, first appeared in about 540 BC and was made until the end of the 3rd century/beginning of 2nd century when they begin to disappear from the record. One of the key problems associated with this type of amphora has been identifying when it ceased to be manufactured in Greece and began to be made in Marseilles; this is because of the consistency in the way that they were made (Bats, 1993). Reille and Abbas' (1992) recent work on mineral inclusions in the amphorae found at the kiln site of rue Négrel in Marseilles concludes that the amphorae from this site were being made locally, although Archaic in appearance.

Wells (1980) proposed a model explaining the relations between the Mediterranean world and central Europe as recognised by foreign imports. He simplified the record by defining three spheres of interaction and interdependence: the greater Mediterranean, the coastal and inland regions of southern France and west-central Europe.

Wells observed that amongst the products brought into Massalia and thereafter sent inland were wine amphorae and vessels for mixing and drinking wine (kraters, jugs and bowls). The evidence for wine itself being imported into west central Europe in the late Hallstatt period is insubstantial but vessels associated in Greece and Etruria with the preparation and drinking of wine are found, particularly in graves. For example, the famous Vix crater and the tripod and cauldron from La Garenne. Wells examined the cultural changes which he believed came

---

[2] Compared perhaps with Roman burials or Gallic burials as described by Caesar in the passage above.

[3] For example, on Britain, Pliny *Natural History*, XXX.III.13; on Gaul, Strabo *Geography* 4.4.4.

[4] See Bouloumié in Mohen, Duval & Eluère (1988) for a discussion on the adoption of the Greek symposion by the Celtic aristocracy.

[5] The foundation of Marseilles may be later than previously thought, c. 540 BC - see Postscript in Nash, 1985:61-63.

about as a result of the contact and interaction between the two societies.

Michael Dietler re-examined the evidence in a very influential paper published in 1990. He has long advocated the importance of alcohol in early societies using anthropological examples to illustrate how feasting could have played a major political role in early Iron Age France. He too examined the role of wine in Hallstatt society where a number of rich burials contain Mediterranean drinking equipment but there is a notable paucity of wine amphorae. In his case study centred on the area around Hallstatt, it appeared that Mediterranean goods were not redistributed but concentrated in a few of the wealthiest burials and in a small number of central fortified settlements. On the basis of this, he therefore argues against a burgeoning trade between the Hallstatt chieftains and the Mediterranean and dismisses the concept of 'Hellenization' or any sense of cultural or political dependence. He suggests instead that wine is simply incorporated into an existing structure within the society and that Mediterranean cultural practices and beliefs do not accompany the new drink and equipment. However, symbolic importance is attached to drinking and feasting in the society, and the imports support this assertion.

In comparison, a great quantity of wine amphorae have been found in the lower Rhône valley in the early Iron Age on all types of settlement site. In this area no wine straining and mixing equipment have been found. It seems here that wine was incorporated into existing traditions but that access to wine may have had implications for regional development.

Recent work is beginning to reveal a more complex picture during this period with finds of Marseille amphorae being found at a greater variety of sites. Excavations at Bragny-sur-Saône (Flouest, 1993) have exposed what appears to be a large community of artisans living there in the 5th century BC. The site is 20km north of Chalon-sur-Saône on the right bank of the river, 300m from the confluence of the Saône and the River Doubs and 1100m from the confluence of the River Saône and the River Dheune and thus occupies a high strategic location. It has produced a significant number of Mediterranean imports[6] including at least 30 individual examples of Marseille amphorae (**Fig. 10**). Interestingly, the site appears to be undefended and the excavator believes it may have served as some kind of entrepôt.

Another site, which widens the debate still further, is that of Lyon-Vaise which was a modest agricultural settlement near the River Saône on which Greek and Massaliote

imports have been found[7]. The implication is that the importation of wine was not restricted to either aristocratic or defended settlement sites during this period.

In the later Iron Age a second phase of wine imports reaches Gaul. This trade is predominantly Italian and is represented archaeologically by the appearance of Dressel 1 and the later Dressel 2-4 amphorae, manufactured and filled with wine on the Tyrrhenian coast of Italy (as described in Chapter 1.1).

3.2.1 The Distribution of Dressel 1 Amphorae in Gaul

The scale of the Italian wine trade in the 2nd and 1st centuries BC is unprecedented. Tchernia (1983: 92) attempted to estimate the quantities that may have been in circulation. He suggested that between 50,000 - 100,000 hl were being imported to Gaul per annum (but probably higher) which means that perhaps as many as 40 million amphorae were unloaded in Gaul during the course of the 1st century BC.

The enormity of the trade is reflected in the archaeological evidence. In the 19th century an antiquarian calculated that more than 24,000 amphorae had been retrieved from the Saône river bed by dredging operations at Châlon (on the edge of Eduen territory); the site probably contained a further 2-500,000 (Dressel 1) (Tchernia, 1983: 90). The largest published assemblage is from Bibracte (the capital of the Eduens) where 1000's of amphorae were found of which 94% were Dressel 1 (Laubenheimer, 1991).

Toulouse and Vieille Toulouse hold another very rich deposit of Dressel 1. Here "the labourers ... cart them away to clear the earth but despite such labours, repeated over and over again since time immemorial, their ploughshares are continually blunted by the impact of this pottery" Abbé Audibert (1764) (Tchernia, 1986: 80). By way of explanation, Tchernia suggested that Toulouse may have been a distribution point where the wine from amphorae was transferred into barrels for futher distribution into the hinterland. In the case of Bibracte, Goudineau & Peyre (1993: 141) argued that the quantity of amphorae was simply a matter of trade; the Italians exploited the region for minerals, agricultural products and slaves and in return they offered wine and fine bronze metalwork to the controllers of the routes between Marseilles and the north - the Aedui and their allies.

Tchernia proposed an explanatory model for the trade based on Mauss' potlatch system. In order to initiate the trade, Italian merchants employed a system of potlatch based on the Gaulish love of wine, as recorded by Diodorus Siculus (V.26). On the one hand wine was used

---

[6] For example, fragments of Attic vases, pseudo-Ionian pottery, Rhodian pottery, stamped decorated pottery from Golasecca (Etruscan), brooches with north Italian parallels and black turned pottery of the type found at Vix and Le Heuneburg (Flouest, 1993)

[7] See Bellon, C. Burnouf, J., Martin, J.-M., Verot-Bourelly, A. (1988) 'Une occupation du premier Age due Fer à Lyon-Vaise' in F. Audouze and O. Büschsenschütz (eds.) *Architectures des Ages de Métaux: fouilles récentes*, 2, Dossiers de protohistoire, Paris: Editions Errance, 55-66.

as currency by Italian merchants to acquire metals and slaves; on the other it was distributed by those in power to their dependants as largesse for the purpose of banquets.

It is now apparent that northern Gaul has a much wider distribution of Dressel 1 than early work on the subject suggested (Peacock, 1971; **Fig. 6** in this volume). Galliou's survey (1984) in north-western France first drew attention to the potential of regionally based studies when it revealed a large number of sites that had not been plotted before (**Fig. 11**).

The Lower Aisne valley has been the subject of a programme of excavation and survey (1983 to 1992) led by Colin Haselgrove (1990; 1996; 1999). The area shows a particular concentration of Dressel 1 but Haselgrove suspects this is due to over-representation rather than to other factors. In southern Picardy as a whole wine amphorae are very rare until 120 BC after the foundation of the southern Roman province, *Gallia Narbonensis*. Dressel 1A is represented in assemblages in the early 1st century BC; it is then replaced by Dressel 1B throughout the remainder of the century. Dressel 2-4 do appear in the record, but not apparently in great quantity. See **Fig. 12** for distribution map.

A recent study by Baudoux (1996) of north-east Gaul illustrates how Dressel 1 are the predominant import into this area in the Augustan period followed by a sharp drop in the 1st century AD attributed to the impact of the Roman army (see **Fig. 13** for distribution map).

Finally, the principal concentrations in northern Gaul have recently been plotted by Poux & Selles (1998)[8] serving to illustrate once again that wine was arriving in northern Gaul in significant quantities (**Fig. 14**).

These distribution maps serve as useful general comparanda for the British assemblage. However, it is likely that whilst the main concentrations in northern France have been located, these maps do not contain all the sites with perhaps only one sherd of Dressel 1. This is not the case in Britain where that is the extent of the evidence on the majority of sites.

3.2.2 Wine Amphorae in Mining Regions

In the rich metal mining areas of the Montagne Noire and Corbières in France, huge quantities of amphorae have been retrieved. The oppida of the Aude valley, particularly La Lagaste and Lastours-Fournes in the Montagne Noire have produced several thousand sherds of Italian amphorae. At the mines, Dressel 1 have been found around the shafts and even in the galleries themselves (Tchernia, 1983; 1986: 92). In Spain, Ampurias, and the mines of Sierra Morena, have also produced thousands of sherds. There is clearly a relationship between the mining

regions and the distribution of Dressel 1 (Domergue, 1990; 1991: Fig. 1).

Tchernia describes how the populations of the oppida and the mining regions are the main consumers of the huge trade in wine which develops in the course of the 2nd and 1st centuries BC in Gaul. He goes on to suggest that with no obvious technical reason why amphorae should be present in mines or why they should be transported there when empty, that this may be a case of 'a popular consumption of imported wine, a most unusual phenomenon in the history of wine-drinking'.

The model proposed by Tchernia to explain the mechanism by which wine amphorae appear in such abundance at mining sites is as follows. The ancient sources mention three categories of goods imported by Italy from Gaul - metals, slaves and livestock products (wool and hams). He suggests it is unlikely that the latter would be sufficient to account for this trade. Huge quantities of precious metals were extracted from the territory attributed to the Ruteni and Tabelli in the Basse-Pyrénées, one of the richest in amphorae finds. Tchernia, therefore, moots a direct relationship between the wealth created by the mines and the appearance of Italian wine, and this relationship is based on the fact that the mines are exploited by the local tribes and not Romans, either entrepreneurs or militia.

The model is based on the assumption that, as recorded in Diodorus Siculus (V.26), the Gauls had a passion for wine and, suggests Tchernia, that there was an element of potlatch. That is to say, wine played a valuable role in Gallic society as a bargaining tool due to its high value and obvious pleasure-giving capabilities.

In addition, using the high price obtained for wine in Gaul implied by Diodorus Siculus (V.26) and his own estimate of 100,000 Gallic slaves in Italy in the 1st century BC, Tchernia suggests that this burgeoning trade could account for the quantities of wine in circulation.

The slave trade may have accounted for between a tenth and a third of the goods exchanged for Italian wine according to Tchernia, but the scholar is right to point out that 'the merchants in question did not set off for Gaul for the purpose of selling an amphora of wine but in order to bring back a slave'. (Tchernia, 1983: 99)

To summarise, Tchernia suggests that wine was used by Roman merchants to acquire precious metals and slaves from the Gallic tribes who, themselves, played their part in organising this trade.

In Spain a similar phenomenon with regard to the presence of amphorae in mines has been recorded and is discussed by Claude Domergue (1990). The exploitation of mines in Iberia during the late Iron Age and Roman periods was extensive although it was dispersed and only concerned some districts (**Figs. 15** and **16**). By 138 BC, it is likely that the Romans controlled the mines of Sierra Morena and

---

[8] The find spots for Dressel 1 amphorae in northern Gaul are also listed in Roymans, 1990: Table 7.1.

this is definitely so by the end of that century. The mines at El Centenillo (Jaen) and Diógenes (Ciudad Real), both silver mines, produced large quantities of Dressel 1, supporting this fairly uniform pattern. Domergue believes that, contrary to Tchernia's model, the Iberian mines, for example, those at Sierra de Cartagena, were exploited by Italian and Roman entrepreneurs, not by Iberian chiefs.

Domergue (1991) makes three observations which have led him to re-define the relationship between mining and wine amphorae suggested by Tchernia.

1. Wine amphorae were found in huge quantities in the mines and settlements of the south of Spain; these were predominantly Italian Dressel 1. However, other vessels are represented - Lamboglia 2 (at Diógenes, Sortijón del Cuzna and Picatière) and Punic amphorae (Maña C1 and C2) were found at Sierra de Cartagena; oil amphorae have been found at Martyrs, Mazarrón and La Loba and fragments of Dressel 20 were retrieved from Martyrs and Dressel 7-11 from Peñón del Moro and Ermita de San Sebastián. Therefore the phenomenon is not solely concerned with wine.

2. In addition, 5th century Phoenician amphorae were retrieved from Filon Sud à Tharsis. Therefore, the presence of amphorae at mines is not exclusive to the 2nd and 1st century BC exploitation.

3. In the majority of cases where assemblages of amphorae fragments have been found they appear actually in the mine. Tchernia suggests that it is the miners who drink the wine but Domergue points out, why would they drink wine in an already dangerous working environment?

With these points in mind, why are wine amphorae found in mines? Domergue has examined the options:

-   Roman entrepreneurs bring wine to the workers[9] for whom it is part of their diet.[10] This idea is reinforced by the presence of Campanian pottery (bowls and plates) which accompany Dressel 1, thus intimating an element of domesticity. However, there is no continuation reflected in the distribution of Dressel 2-4, Haltern 70 or Gauloise 4/5 etc.

-   amphorae were used for another purpose, perhaps bailing water out of the mines. The amphorae may have been supplied as empty containers from the commercial centres of southern Spain. They became defunct when miners began to be supplied with special tools eg. pumps, water wheels and other types of buckets which would explain their demise in the mines post-1st century AD. However, bronze buckets have been found in the Iberian mines, for example, at Mazarrón. Rope buckets have also been found, although these are rare, only 20 are known from the mines of Sierra de Cartegena and Mazarrón. These were lined with pitch to make them impermeable.

-   alternatively, there is evidence that amphorae were used to store minerals; at Coto Fortuna (Murcia), for example, a concentration of lead sulphide (with silver) was found at the bottom of a vessel. M. Mangin[11] also noted the use of amphorae for the storage of minerals in the metal workshops at Alesia.

The most convincing explanation however, is that amphorae were used in the mines to hold drinking water for the miners. The vessels would have been propped up against the gallery walls - although usually found in fragments, they have been found intact in the deep shafts of El Soldado (Cordoba) and even at 160m depth underground in the shafts of Santa Bárbara. (**Fig. 17** shows a scene depicted on a painted plaque from Penteskouphia, Corinth. It depicts a scene in a mine where workers are extracting ore or clay in the middle of the image stands a suspended 'amphora' or water container.) Workers may have also carried flasks. A gourd flask has been found at Majarrón (Murcia) which measured 42cm in diameter and 17cm high; it would have contained about 12.5 litres of liquid.

In addition, it should be mentioned at this point as a further alternative that one of the techniques employed in the southern Spanish mines was that of attacking the rock with fire and vinegar[12]; even cold water could also be effective. This may provide an alternative explanation as to the presence of amphorae below ground.

To summarise, the most likely scenario would appear to be that the amphorae have been re-used. Domergue envisages that Dressel 1, for example, would have been imported to the ports on the coast and their wine decanted into barrels or skins for distribution. Empty amphorae were taken to the mines on pack animals returning to collect the minerals. In no respect was this a direct exchange of wine for metal.

3.2.3 Wine Amphorae and Accoutrements in Burials

Throughout Gaul there are examples of burials containing wine amphorae and/or bronze drinking sets. There are two useful surveys of this material: one which examines the rich

---

[9] Slaves also worked in the Iberian mines; slave chains weighing a staggering 2700 kg were found at the mine of Riotinto (Huelva) (Domergue, 1990).
[10] Cf. Roman army provision of wine for soldiers; Cato, *de Agric.*, 25 - reference to workers of vineyard being given .75 l of wine a day, albeit the owner of that vineyard (Domergue, 1990).

[11] Reference - Mangin, M. 'Caractères et fonctions de la métallurgie du fer à Alésia' in *Mines et fonderies antiques de la Gaule* (Table ronde CNRS, Université de Toulouse-Le Mirail, 21-22 novembre 1980) p.240 Paris (1982) - in Domergue (1991)
[12] 'ignis et acetum' as recorded by Pliny, *Natural History* 33, 71-72.

burials throughout the country so by default covers those of interest here, by Ferdière & Villard (1993) (**Fig. 18**) and a second survey listing the findspots of imports in northern Gaul by Roymans (1990: Table 7.1; Table 7.3).

For the purposes of this study attention is drawn to two aspects of the record on the continent. Firstly, the group of rich tombs in central France, known as the Fléré-la-Rivière group (Ferdière & Villard, 1993) and a comparable, recently excavated, assemblage[13] from Antran (Vienne) (Pautreau, 1999) which provide an opportunity to examine the potential relationships between the grave goods. Secondly, the tomb at Clemency (Luxembourg) (Metzler, Waringo, Bis, Metzler-Zens, 1991) which has provided additional insight into the treatment of amphorae.

The burial at Fléré-la-Rivière is one of a group of seven rich tombs in Berry in central France. The group consists of Fléré itself (Indre), Châtillon-sur-Indre (Indre), Dun-sur-Auron (Cher), Berry-Bouy (Cher), Ménestreau-en-Villette (Loiret), Primelles (Cher) and Neuvy-Pailloux (Indre). They range in date from the middle of the 1st century BC (Dun-sur-Auron) to the middle of the 1st century AD (Neuvy-Pailloux) but the majority are Augustinian in date.

Table 3 illustrates a change in the type of bronze vessels from the early tomb (Dun-sur Auron) to the latest (Neuvy-Pailloux) and serves to highlight the similarities in composition between four of the graves - Fléré-la-Rivière, Châtillon-sur Indre, Berry-Bouy, Neuvy-Pailloux. Here, intact wine amphorae (Pascual 1) accompany bronze vessels.

A similar assemblage from Antran, also dating to the Augustan period contained, amongst other objects, seven Pascual 1 amphorae and an elaborate set of bronze vessels including an oenochoe (Eggers 124), a patera (Eggers 150), a strainer, a ladle and three buckets with bronze fittings.

A rich burial was excavated at Clemency in south-west Luxembourg in 1987 (Metzler, Waringo, Bis & Metzler-Zens, 1991). It contained 10 Dressel 1B amphorae, two of which were probably deposited complete; the remainder were scattered in fragments on the floor of the chamber. The tomb did not contain a drinking service similar to later graves, for example, Fléré-la-Rivière, but it did contain one bronze basin and a large collection of ceramic bowls.

Of particular interest at Clemency, however is the presence of between 20 and 30 Dressel 1B amphorae outwith the funerary chamber. The sherds from these vessels were evident in two places. A pyre site was found outside the funerary enclosure (marked D on the plan); fragmented remains of amphorae suggested that the vessels may have been inclined against the fire because there was evidence

for burning on some sherds but not on others, from the same vessel. In addition, an area marked E on the plan, consisted of an area 'paved with amphorae'. It may be that amphorae had been removed from the pyre and systematically broken here. The presence of amphorae on ritual sites is discussed below but it is evident that at Clemency they constituted an important part of the funerary ceremony in advance of grave good deposition in chamber itself (**Fig. 19**).

3.2.4 Wine Amphorae at Ritual Sites

Amphorae sherds have been found at some of the Belgic sanctuary sites, for example, Estrées-Saint-Denis and Chilly (Roymans, 1990: 148-150). Matthieu Poux has been working in this area and is drawing together a convincing body of evidence for the ritual deposition of wine amphorae in ditches. In addition to the above two sites, he has been examining the evidence at Ribemont-sur-Ancre (where sherds of Dressel 1 are particularly abundant), Montmartin (Oise), Corent and Muron (Auvergne). The relationship between amphorae sherds and votive offerings is particularly clear at Ribemont-sur-Ancre where a deposit (dated to the middle of the 1st century BC) of several hundred amphorae sherds was made in one of the branches of the enclosure ditch. The deposit was associated with metal offerings, animal (particularly pig) and human bones. The amphorae carried traces of burning.

Recent excavations at Corent (V. Guichard & M. Laughton, forthcoming) have revealed a vast gallo-roman complex. A large quadrangular area paved with amphorae sherds has been found with abundant votive objects, for example, mutilated weapons, brooches, coins and human skulls and also the remains of animals. It is not clear yet whether the large sherds of amphorae were simply laid down to form a pavement (cf. Clemency) or whether they held greater significance (Poux, 1999).

Poux has also examined the taphonomy of the amphorae deposits in the ditches at the site of the Usine à Gaz, Bâle (1997: 147-172). Amongst the deposits were patterns which seemed to indicate the use of amphorae in a ritual or funerary way in ditches on this site. He suggests that some vessels had been consciously manipulated after consumption and before deposition. Some had been the subject of deliberate breaking or burnt while still whole vessels; some sherds had been exposed before burial to fire and weathering or had been re-used as tools. In ditch 145/230 entire amphora bodies and large sherds were arranged in a circle, some of them appeared to have been deliberately cut and careful selected. In ditches 255 and 284, amphorae sherds were concentrated at particular, precise points in the lower levels of the fill. Poux argues that it is difficult to explain these phenomena in terms of normal domestic debris. In addition, these deposits are associated with deposits of human bone and specific objects.

---

[13] The excavator describes Antran as an assemblage rather than a burial site which it obviously resembles because no evidence of an interment was found during the excavation (Pautreau, 1999: 30).

Some of the characteristics are reminiscent of the 'amphorae pavement' at Clémency where the sherds appear to have been the subject of meticulous sorting before deposition. There may be similarities with the treatment of amphorae in the ditches of the Sarra plateau at Lyon[14]. The funerary shafts of Toulouse may also bear comparison (Fouet, 1958).

Bronze vessels have also been found on some Iron Age cult sites and early temple sites, for example, the patera (Eggers 130) found at Sainte-Eulalie-de-Carnon (Aveyron), the bronze strainer and vessel at Triguères (Loiret) (Horne & King, 1980) and the fragment of a Kelheim jug at Pierrefonds, Mont Berny (Roymans, 1990: 157) although they do appear to be rare.

---

[14] Briefly described in Metzler et al., 1991: 82-84; B. Mandy et al. (1989) 'Les fosses du plateau de la Sarra' in C. Goudineau *Aux origines de Lyon* p.37-95

PART II

Wine in Britain in the Late Iron Age: a consideration of the evidence and its contexts

As described previously, Peacock's model, first proposed in 1971, has tended to dominate the study of imported wine in the Iron Age. This exotic commodity has signified primarily the wealth, prestige and active international connections (either economic or political) of those on whose settlements it has been found or in whose graves it has been offered. Archaeologically, the status of an individual is reflected in a burial by their accompanying grave goods, that of a society in the content of their rubbish. Realistically, this is only true if the commodity means something special either to the individual or to the society concerned. As first intimated in Chapter 1, in order to examine the evidence anew, the author has considered the archaeological contexts in which wine is found.

Part II of this study is divided into four chapters. The first deals with the appearance of the wine amphorae Dressel 1 and Dressel 2-4 on settlement sites along the south coast and in the south-east of Britain. It explores the distribution and concentration of these carriers and examines the evidence for imported bronze vessels.

The second chapter describes and assesses the evidence for the association between Dressel 1 amphorae and the production of salt in the same areas.

Chapter 6 deals with the appearance of wine amphorae in burials. The data to be examined, for the most part, comes from south-east Britain during the second wave of wine imports. Wine amphorae are deposited as part of grave good assemblages thus throwing open a new avenue of interpretation, that of ideologies and beliefs, which may be associated with wine drinking. As described in Chapter 2, the use of wine in the classical world was rich in subtleties, from social drinking to its use in funerary libations and ritual: its identity and appearance is never straightforward. The burials in which wine amphorae appear and in some cases imported bronze vessels, which may be part of wine services, are examined in some detail.

Finally, Chapter 7 assesses the evidence for the use of wine in the British Iron Age at ritual and ceremonial sites.

Further analysis, conclusions and discussion are advanced in Chapter 8.

The Evidence for Wine on Settlement Sites

Amphorae, in particular Dressel 1 and Dressel 2-4, provide the main source of evidence for wine on settlement sites. Imported bronze vessels have been found but they are noticeably rare.

4.1 Presence of Wine Amphorae

There are 58 findspots of sherds of Dressel 1 or Dressel 2-4 which have been identified as coming from settlement or probable settlement sites; these are listed in the attached database (see **Fig. 20** and **Appendix 1**). This number does not relate to the same in settlements. The gazetteer has been compiled using individual accounts so in a few cases, for example, sites such as Heybridge, Braughing, Sheepen and Canterbury several sherds have been retrieved from different excavations but they may well relate to the same Iron Age settlement.

The largest assemblages have been retrieved from Hengistbury Head, Hampshire (predominantly Dressel 1A), Heybridge, Essex (predominantly Dressel 1B) and Sheepen, Colchester, Essex (predominantly Dressel 2-4) and these are discussed individually below. Maiden Castle (Hampshire), Braughing (Hertfordshire) and Canterbury (Kent) are the only other sites with more than one type represented[1] which makes a total of 6 sites where any likelihood of continuity of supply could be inferred.

4.1.1 Hengistbury Head, Hampshire

Hengistbury Head has been the subject of four major excavations - Bushe-Fox, 1911-12; St. George-Gray, 1919-24; Peacock, 1970-71 and Cunliffe, 1979-85. Between them they have produced nearly 1,400 amphorae sherds of which 69% are Dressel 1 (Dr.1A 8.4%; Dr.1B 1.5%; Dressel 1 sp. 58.1%[2]). The other types present are Pascual 1 (Spanish wine) 3.6%; Dressel 2-4 (probably wine) 0.7%; Dressel 20 (olive oil) 24.4%; Camulodunum 185A (defructum) 1.8% and Camulodunum 186 sp (fish products) 0.1% (Cunliffe, 1987).

Cunliffe recognised two phases within the late Iron Age, 'LIA1' - 100-50 BC and 'LIA2' - 50 BC - AD 50. In the first phase he observed an association between Dressel 1A, wheelmade vessels from Armorica, decorated wares from south west Britain (Glastonbury wares), a range of decorated wares of probable local origin and handmade vessels in local MIA tradition.

The scant evidence for imported bronze vessels at Hengistbury Head is discussed below and it should be noted also that fine wares did not begin to be imported here until later in the 1st century BC when Dressel 1A was already in decline. This coincides with the beginning of importation of Spanish wine and fine table wares from the Santonge region of western France, in addition to the emergence of Durotrigian wares. The phenomenon of the decline of Italian wine has been discussed by Peacock (1971) and Sealey (1985) with reference to the Sheepen site at Colchester (see below). It seems unlikely therefore, that wine was arriving at this site accompanied by a special service.

There is a lack of evidence indicating permanent settlement during the phase of imported amphorae and pottery and a concentration of industrial activity at the site. There is also an indication, via the composition of the seed and bone assemblages that the site did not appear to be associated with agricultural production (Fitzpatrick, forthcoming).

There is some evidence for redistribution in the hinterland. A minimum representation of four Dressel 1/Pascual 1 type amphorae and five Dressel 2-4 were retrieved from Maiden Castle, Dorset (Sharples, 1991: 203-205) and six vessels (three of which are Dressel 1A) were found at Danebury (Hampshire). Fragmentary finds from Gussage All Saints and Lake Farm, Wimborne (both inland Dorset) are completely outnumbered by the increasing numbers of Dressel 1, particularly Dressel 1A being found along the south coast. Weymouth, Poole, and most recently the Isle of Wight, have produced evidence of Dressel 1A amphorae. The distribution now also extends further east to Pulborough, West Sussex (unpublished) and further west to Bucknowle Farm, Corfe Castle, Dorset (unpublished) (Fitzpatrick, forthcoming) emphasising this coastal distribution.

Hengistbury Head was one of many places along the south coast that received imports from Armorica. Hearne & Cox (1994) suggest that Poole Harbour replaced the activity at Hengistbury Head in Cunliffe's LIA2 (50 BC - AD43). This change is identified in the relative proportions of Dressel 1/Pascual 1 which make up 3% of the assemblage at Hengistbury Head and 83% on the Ower Peninsular (to the east of Hengistbury).

No single whole amphora has been found at Hengistbury Head. This led Cunliffe to suggest that the carriers may have been opened at this point and the wine redistributed by barrel as suggested by André Tchernia (1986) as an explanation for the huge quantities of broken Dressel 1 in Toulouse. This would also explain the scarcity of contemporary amphorae in Hengistbury Head's

---

[1] This does not include those sites which have for example, a Dr.1 fragment and Dr.1B fragment - Dressel 1 simply means it has not been possible for the finder to say whether the vessel is Dressel 1A or 1B.

[2] Dressel 1 sp. (where it has not been possible to say Dressel 1A or 1B).

hinterland. However, there is no firm evidence to confirm this, in the form of barrels, for example.

To summarise, at Hengistbury Head wine arrived in Dressel 1A, Dressel 1B and Dressel 2-4 amphorae, over what may be a period of 150 years or, as is more likely, over a much shorter timespan. Its appearance is likely to be associated with traders from the northern Gaulish coast who may even have settled in this area. Cunliffe did suggest that the level of foreign goods implied an actual Armorican presence at Hengistbury, perhaps following their rebellion in 56 BC (Cunliffe, 1987:342). This occupation could have been on a seasonal basis as is intimated by Caesar's remarks made on crossing the Channel:

> "Only a small part of the summer was left, and in these regions, as all Gaul has a northerly aspect, the winters are early; but for all this Caesar was intent upon starting for Britain."
>
> (Caesar, *The Gallic War* IV.20)

Dressel 1A vessels did not appear in the first instance with fine wares or bronze vessels, but with wheelmade vessels from Armorica suggesting that no special service was supplied with the wine. There is also no evidence to suggest that wine was imbued with anything other than domestic value at this site.

4.1.2 Isle of Wight

To date 35 sites have produced Dressel 1 or Dressel 2-4 amphorae on the Isle of Wight; of these 8 have produced Dressel 1A, 6 with Dressel 1B, 5 with Dressel 1/Pascal 1, 32 with Dressel 1sp. and 23 findspots of Dressel 2-4. (See **Fig. 21** for distribution maps).[3] The majority of finds appear to have been made on rural settlement sites with further examples from underwater and inter-tidal locations (Trott, *pers. comm.*).

Two sites have produced a considerable number of sherds. Bowcombe, the site of a later Roman complex, contains a ditch with cremation urns and fragments of Dressel 1A vessels. Recent fieldwork has added evidence for at least another 10 amphorae. Yarmouth Roads, thought to be a wreck site by Peacock (1984: 38) may now be reclassified as an anchorage or the site of a quay (Trott, *pers. comm.*) but the site remains unpublished.[4] At least 21 Dressel 1A have been retrieved from this site, where other related

material consists of Durotrigian and Armorican pottery and a stone anchor (hence Peacock's initial suggestion).

Sixteen of the find spots contained evidence for only one amphora, often only a sherd and there are 3 examples of amphorae seemingly deposited intentionally in enclosure ditches (see Chapter 7.1). Knighton and Freshwater Bay have been provisionally interpreted as rural settlement sites as have Grange Chine and Redcliff but these have also produced evidence for salt production (see Chapter 5).[5] Dressel 1A have been dredged from the sea floor at Ryde Middle Bank and in the Western Solent. Finally, there is also evidence for two burials containing amphorae, some considerable distance from their core distribution. These are potentially very important and discussed in Chapter 6.

The settlement sites with Dressel 1A are contemporary with Hengistbury Head during Cunliffe's LIA1 (100-50 BC) phase. As the author writes it is not possible to present an in-depth analysis of the finds on the Isle of Wight. However, even from the little information available it is apparent that a) the Isle of Wight was very much part of the coastal activity in the early/mid 1st century BC, if not a focus of it, as the arrival of Dressel 1A shows; and b) there is evidence to suggest that Dressel 1B and Gallo-Belgic pottery were arriving on the island during Cunliffe's LIA2 phase. This is unusual in itself (see **Fig. 3**[6]) but even more intriguingly there are two potential burials with Dressel 1B at Packway, Newchurch and Newport Goods Yard. This practice has previously been confined to the territory of the Trinovantes and Catuvellauni (see Chapter 6).

4.1.3 Heybridge, Essex

This site has long been recognised as an important late Iron Age/ Roman settlement since E.A. Fitch[7] a local antiquarian, reported finds of pottery, imported wares, coins and metalwork. These were discovered in 1887 due to work on the extension of a railway line at Langford Junction. The modern town of Heybridge is situated on the northern bank of the River Chelmer, opposite Maldon in Essex (see **Fig. 22**).

The site at Elms Farm, Heybridge has been the subject of a major excavation project in advance of development. There is evidence of earlier occupation, a small farmstead in the MIA period, but the first major use of the site began in the late pre-Roman Iron Age (LPRIA) in about 50 BC. These deposits were severely damaged by deliberate re-modelling in the 1st century AD but enough evidence remains to confirm a late Iron Age occupation of the site, and more specifically, that this was a site with a religious focus. Two late Iron Age shrines were found under the

---

[3] The finds from the Isle of Wight are only just beginning to reach wider attention; many of them have only been made recently and the bulk are unpublished. The information presented here was provided through personal communication with Kevin Trott, who has been working on the material, and who also kindly sent a copy of his forthcoming article on cross-Channel trade and the Isle of Wight together with other papers including a gazetteer of findspots.

[4] 'Yarmouth Roads' Collection to be published as part of Wootton Haven Intertidal Survey funded by English Heritage, 2000 by D. Tomalin (Trott, K. pers.comm.).

[5] These sites have yet to be published in full.

[6] Not all the findspots now known on the Isle of Wight of Dressel 1 and Dressel 2-4 and included in Appendix 1 and Gazetteer 1 are shown on distribution maps **Fig. 3** and **Fig. 4**.

[7] Reported in E.A. Fitch *Maldon and the River Blackwater* (1905).

later Roman temple. The evidence for domestic occupation is less conclusive and consists of fragmentary hut circles, 5-10m in diameter, in Area L. The deliberate re-modelling referred to above, meant the creation of zones of activity which were clearly defined - areas of domestic, industrial and ritual activity, have been identified (see **Fig. 23**).

The amphorae at this site are very important and actually key to this study - Heybridge is a site which appears to combine all the elements of wine importation in the later Iron Age on one site. It is a salt producing area, as evidenced by the excavations at Osea Road, Heybridge (de Brisay, 1975) (see Chapter 5), a settlement site as described by Atkinson & Preston (1998), a religious site and most recently a small late Iron Age cemetery has been excavated in Area W. For more discussion of these finds see Chapter 6.

The site as a whole has produced at least 42 Dressel 1 amphorae, the majority of which are Dressel 1B (Steve Preston *pers.com*). 200 contexts have produced amphorae, although in many cases the evidence is a single sherd. The site has produced only one rim of Dressel 1A (unstratified) to date, but overall the Dressel 1 assemblage is dominant and outweighs that of Dressel 2-4 amphorae which are also present. The imported pottery in the late Iron Age and early Roman phase makes up 16.7% of the total assemblage, amphorae 16.1%, local pottery 65.6% and residual 1.6%.

Apart from the fact that amphorae were re-used in a cobbled surface in Area M, the author has no further details of the location of wine amphorae in domestic contexts throughout the site. All that can be noted at this point is that Heybridge has produced the single largest assemblage of Dressel 1B amphorae.

4.1.3 **Sheepen, Essex**

This Iron Age site lies to the north-west of Colchester and was occupied from AD 5; the amphorae from this site were dealt with in a thorough report, separate from that of the excavation (Sealey, 1985). A wide range of finds were represented, of which those containing wine included Dressel 1, Dressel 2-4 and Camulodunum 184.

Of the 676 stratified amphora sherds (representing about 127 vessels), 93.4% came from deposits dating from AD 43 to Boudica's uprising and subsequent sack of Colchester in AD 60-61. The remainder include the Dressel 1 amphorae.

Dressel 1B is represented by a surviving 12 sherds of an original 46 from Hawkes & Hull's excavations (1947), and a minimum of 5 vessels from the 1970 excavations. This created a problem in that when first excavated it was thought that the site was occupied from AD 10 (due to the fact that between 85 and 90% of the coins from Sheepen are of Cunobelinus) and that Dressel 1B ceased to be produced around 10 BC thus creating a 20 year gap. This gap was slightly reduced by Sealey when he re-dated the

start of occupation on the site to AD 5. Since Sealey's report the production of Dressel 1B has extended to the turn of the 1st century BC potentially reducing this particular problem still further.

It seems likely that the Dressel 1 amphorae at Sheepen could have been brought there for re-using (as suggested by Sealy). More specifically, the excavations at Camulodunum have produced briquetage and the Dressel 1 could be related to that aspect of the site (see Chapter 5).

A total of 44 Dressel 2-4 vessels were represented at Sheepen. These amphorae were analysed petrologically and found to come from 19 different sources reflecting a complicated pattern of supply. This was indicative, argued Sealey, of the rapid increase in viticulture as a profit-making venture, encouraged under the Julio-Claudians in Italy (*ibid*.: 127-129). This may even have been the case in Britain represented by the short-lived workshop at Brockley Hill which made Dressel 2-4 amphorae possibly to contain locally produced wine (Castle, 1978).

4.1.4 **Braughing, Hertfordshire**

The Iron Age settlement at Braughing is now thought to cover at least 100 ha with the earliest centre probably in the Gatesbury area. It is situated in the Rib valley just north of Hertford. In the late 1st century BC, the area occupied expanded rapidly to surround Wickham Hill and cover the valley bottom. The site has been the subject of several excavations beginning with discoveries of finds made in the 1860s during railway construction. Extensive road building in the area led to the excavations at Ermine Street (Potter & Trow, 1988), Skeleton Green and Gatesbury Track (Partridge, 1981) and minor development to the finds at Wickham Kennels (Partridge, 1982) (see **Fig. 24**).

It is recognised as one of the most important settlements in south-east Britain from about 50 BC to c. AD 25 with rich assemblages of coins (most particularly Tasciovanus) (Haselgrove, 1988), imported amphorae and finewares[8]. Thereafter its importance as a regional centre appears to have diminished, possibly replaced by Verulamium, until its fortunes were revived after the Roman Conquest.

Dressel 1, 1B and 2-4 are represented by sherds at Ermine Street (Williams, 1988: 119). They were found in LPRIA domestic rubbish pits (C5, C36 and B50) with Gallo-Belgic wares, coins, glass and Arretine ware. The bulk of the assemblage (52.4%) consists of body sherds which could be either Dressel 1 or Dressel 2-4, so it is not possible to distinguish a dominant type. Sherds of Dressel 20 appear in some quantity on the site, making up 33.9% of the assemblage by sherd count.

---

[8] Gaulish ceramic imports (Gallo-Belgic, Central Gaulish and North Gaulish ware) support the intensive occupation of this site between c. 50 BC and AD 85. The Gallo-Belgic wares decline earlier c. AD 25 (Potter & Trow, 1988: 110).

The site at Gatesbury Track produced Dressel 1A and 1B amphorae but no Dressel 2-4 endorsing the view that this is the earliest part of the site (Partridge, 1980). Excavations at Skeleton Green on the west side of Wickham Hill produced sherds of Dressel 1 and Dressel 2-4. although the excavator considered the Dressel 1 on this site were likely to be residual as they were found in a context dated c.25-40 AD (Partridge, 1980). Dressel 2-4 made up 24.4% of the assemblage and was found in several contexts.

There is possible evidence for ritual deposition of amphorae at Braughing in the late Iron Age ditch (F1) at Station Road, Puckeridge and at Gatesbury Track (see Chapter 7); there is also one burial which contains a bronze bowl described in Chapter 6.

4.2 Presence of Bronze Vessels

The evidence for imported bronze vessels on settlement sites is very slim. Along the south coast, only two handles of vessels have been retrieved, these were from excavations at Hengistbury Head. Firstly, a silver/gold handle (70:30) of a strainer (Bushe-Fox; No.96 Cunliffe, 1987); it is Y-shaped and was attached to a type of strainer widely known on the continent (see **Fig. 25**). It is of a type with a date range running from the end of the 2nd century BC to the reign of Tiberius according to Guillaumet (1991)[9]. Of the 24 examples studied by Guillaumet the smallest measured only 7cm in diameter and the largest 13.4cm (see **Fig. 26**). Their size intimates that perhaps only a cupful or beaker of liquid at a time was strained suggesting personal rather than communal use.

The distribution of these vessels appears to follow closely the river systems and it would seem that the example from Hengistbury Head will have come directly from northern Gaul rather than representing coastal maritime trade from the west.

These vessels are made in two or three pieces and have generally been found on settlement sites rather than in burials; so far none have been found complete. They are made of a pierced basin of sheet metal, and a cast or beaten bronze handle. It has been very difficult to isolate their source and Guillaumet leaves the question of where they were made open due to the prevalence of copying. This find is important for two reasons; it is the only strainer with a continental provenance found in Britain and it was found on a settlement site.

The second vessel was represented simply by a flat bronze handle (Bushe-Fox; No.48; Cunliffe, 1987) which may be a patera handle of domestic type.

In the south-east, the extensive excavations at Braughing have only produced two bronze bowls, from separate

interventions. The fragment of a bronze vessel with a simple turned over rim came from the site of Gatesbury Track (SF NO.3 F30) (Partridge, 1980) and a further fragment of a rim of a bronze vessel which had been tinned came from the Iron Age ditch (F1) at the Station Road site at Puckeridge, Braughing (SF No.91 (F1(2)). From the same feature, although in a different context (F1(5)), SF No.70 was retrieved. It appears to be the waste from the manufacture or repair of a bronze vessel (Partridge, 1980). There is evidence from bronze vessels found in burials of re-working or repairs, not least the converted strainer from Grave 1, Welwyn Garden City (Stead, 1967). The excavator does not indicate whether he believes these two bronze bowls are imported or not.

A copper-alloy ewer was retrieved from the topsoil in Area A2 of the Elms Farm excavations at Heybridge (Atkinson & Preston, 1998) (see **Fig. 27**). The post-excavation is on-going and the ewer is as yet unpublished, however from this photograph it appears not dissimilar to jugs of the Kjaerumgaard type, two examples of which have been found in burials (Welwyn and Aylesford, see Chapter 6). However, it may be a Wheeler B4 which has a slimmer neck and is dated to around the mid-3rd century AD.[10]

Discussion

It is immediately apparent that the character of the sites along the south coast differs greatly from those in the south-east of Britain. Finds from sites such as Hengistbury Head, Poole and the Isle of Wight do not appear to accompany the intensive and extensive occupation of those in the south-east. Braughing in the south-east, in particular, exhibits indications of political centralisation in the late 1st century BC, even producing evidence for coin minting, in the early 1st century AD and may have been located on the border of Trinovantian and Catuvellaunian territories as suggested by the coin distributions (Trow, 1988: 157-158).

The assemblages in both south and south-east Britain have the following in common. Firstly, no single amphora has been found on a settlement site in its entirety; only fragmentary remains have been retrieved. Secondly, it is likely that the amphorae assemblages on settlement sites are not accompanied by imported bronze vessels.

---

[9] Guillaumet's original inventory for these finds numbered only 48, the total has more than doubled and in 1991 consisted of 105 finds (Guillaumet, 1977).

[10] Correspondence with Mark Atkinson (Elms Farm Project Manager) just prior to publication suggests that the ewer is probably 2nd century AD and appears to be a structured deposit made in the 3rd century.

The Presence of Amphorae on Salt Production Sites

This chapter presents the evidence for the association between Dressel 1 sherds and the salt production industry in southern Britain. This commodity was manufactured in the marshes of the Dorset/Hampshire/Sussex coast and those of Essex in the later Iron Age.

There are two separate facets in the relationship between Dressel 1 amphorae sherds and salt production which require consideration. Firstly, the appearance of amphorae sherds on salt production sites. Secondly, the co-occurence of sherds and *briquetage* on non-production sites, situated not only along the coast, but also inland.

The maps below showing the location of salt production sites in Dorset, Hampshire and Sussex and Essex were both produced some time ago, in 1975. However, the relationship between them and the present day distribution of Dressel 1 (**Fig. 3**) can still be seen clearly.

5.1 Dorset, Hampshire and Sussex Salt Marshes

Along the south coast, the marshes of Poole, Portsmouth and Chichester harbours were exploited in the late Iron Age for salt (**Fig. 28**). Some of the earliest evidence comes from Gaulter Gap on the south coast of the Isle of Purbeck (Dorset) dated to the mid-2nd century BC (Farrar, 1975) but the industry as a whole in this area appears to have suffered a steep decline after AD 100.

It has been suggested that salting was a summer occupation; there is even some botanical evidence to support this implying that *briquetage* were used in the more advanced stages of salt production in August (Bradley, 1975; see **Fig. 29**). Salt-winning was conducted away from settlements on the shoreline and as Bradley noted it was likely to have been part of the seasonal cycle of industrial activities rather than a specialist occupation and it remained so until its decline at the end of the 1st century AD.

The decline in salt-winning does seem to coincide with the arrival of the Romans. One possible explanation may be that salt began to be brought in from elsewhere in the country or even from places like Zeebrugge (West Flanders) or Raversijde (near Ostend, West Flanders) on the Belgian coast. Here salt making continued into the Roman period with new technology involving complex wooden structures and artificial heating in small ovens. The *briquetage* element of production remained only in the salt-cake moulds (Thoen, 1975). Two inscriptions discovered at Rimini are dedicated by the *Salinatores Civitatis Menapiorum* and the *Salinatores Civitatis Morinorum CIL XI 390/1* to L. Lepidius Proculus (a centurion of the Legio VI Victrix in Novaesium (Neuss))

for services rendered to salt commerce. The inscriptions were written during the reign of Vespasian (69-79 AD).

Bradley noted that there was a clear relationship between the overall distribution of early amphorae (Dressel 1A), Armorican coins and salt production in his study of the Hampshire and Sussex coast. More recent work on the Isle of Wight continues to support this simple correlation. The cliff-top site at Redcliff contained a u-shaped gulley in which lay a rich deposit of Belgic wares with *briquetage*, 1st century AD Samian ware and fragments of Dressel 1 amphorae (Tomalin, 1979). The site is thought to be associated with a timber structure, as yet uninvestigated and is provisionally classified as a rural settlement. At Grange Chine, fragments of Dressel 1A have been recovered from two late Iron Age coastal salt-working floors. A single sherd of Gallo-Belgic fine ware was also retrieved. On-going excavations at Newchurch have so far produced at least 10 Dressel 1A amphorae in association with *briquetage* vessels, clay loom weights and copper-alloy binding associated with a scabbard (Trott, forthcoming). The site at Newchurch is a ditched enclosure and these finds came from the outer enclosure ditch.[1]

5.2 Essex Salt Marshes

The earliest evidence for the production of salt on the Essex coast is at Mucking in the form of a pit containing *briquetage* dating to the late Bronze Age. There is also evidence of Middle Iron Age production from Gun Hill, West Tilbury. In the late Iron Age period, however, this area appears to have hosted a major industry leaving behind debris in the form of 'Red Hills'.[2] In 1975, 175 Red Hills had been identified although it is likely there are many more (de Brisay, 1975; see **Fig. 30**).

Salt production in Essex does appear to show a correlation with the importation of wine amphorae, similar to the Hampshire/Sussex salt marshes. Osea Road, Heybridge (de Brisay, 1975; Rodwell, 1976; Fitzpatrick, 1985) and South Benfleet, Benfleet Creek (Rodwell, 1976; Fitzpatrick, 1985) (both in Essex) are salt production sites with no evidence for settlement. One Dressel 1B rim was recovered from Osea Road (unstratified) and one Dressel 1 or Dressel 2-4 sherd was recovered from South Benfleet. The Linford Quarry site at Mucking (Rodwell (1976); Fitzpatrick (1985); *Antiquaries Journal*, 57) and Gun Hill,

---

[1] The evidence from this site is also discussed in Chapter 7.

[2] The 'Red Hills' of Essex are the industrial debris from a process of making salt by evaporating sea water in clay-lined tanks. Subsequently the brine is crystallised in rough coarse pottery containers over a gentle heat caused by brushwood fires. The remains of these crude containers are known as *briquetage* and the combination of their disposal and burnt clay leaves a reddish deposit.

West Tilbury (Rodwell, & Drury, 1973; Rodwell, 1976; Fitzpatrick, 1985) are settlement sites although they have also produced evidence for salt production in the form of *briquetage*. One Dressel 1 burnt handle fragment was retrieved from Mucking and a single body of Dressel 1 or Dressel 2-4 was found in a ditch (F1) at Gun Hill along with several other types of amphorae (see Chapter 7.1).

Warwick Rodwell (1979) suggested that during the late Iron Age the production of salt changed from purely a local concern into an export industry.[3] Rodwell argued that a more extensive industry was controlled by the newly empowered post-Caesarian Trinovantes tribe based at Camulodunum. Kelvedon, Ardleigh, Great Chesterford and Camulodunum have all, despite being inland, produced evidence of *briquetage*. The presence of imports, for example, the sherd of Dressel 1B found during the excavation of the Red Hill at Osea Road, Heybridge and possible imported pottery from Goldhanger X, might indicate a two-way relationship between the two types of site. The industry fell into decline in the 1st century AD and very little early Roman pottery is found in the Red Hills. The industry moved to a new area, that of south Essex and north Kent around Canvey Island in the 2nd century, now argued Rodwell, under Roman control.

One factor not considered by Rodwell with regard to Essex, might be a change in the water level. Charles Green in 1961 reported that there was evidence that the Thames estuary now lies at least 15' lower than in the early Roman period. He suggested that the Red Hills of Essex appear to have come to an end at the time of the highest waterline or maximum submergence, perhaps making this stretch of the coast non viable. This might explain the emergence of the extensive Romano-British salt panning in the marshes of northern Kent which thrived in the 2nd century AD (Miles, 1975).

An idea put forward by J.A. Alexander (1975) may still have some resonance. Using ethnographical and archaeological research conducted in Africa, he proposed the following model. The Essex coastline, well-suited to salt production provides salt for the deficient heartland - Hertfordshire, south Cambridgeshire and possibly Bedfordshire. Due to the difficulties of travelling overland, routes are carved upstream where possible, and trans-shipment points to the Icknield Way and beyond develop, for example, Braughing and Great Chesterford. The definition of the Trinovantes tribal area by the coin distribution suggests that they may be holding a salt-trading network defined by kinship and trade relations. Importantly, Colchester, the base of the Trinovantes, becomes an attraction to continental traders who attach themselves to a well-developed salt trading network with the interior.

Braughing and Great Chesterford have both produced a number of imported goods, not least the Chesterford bucket (Fox, 1923; Fitzpatrick, 1985). Wine amphorae have been found at both sites: the Gatesbury Track site at Braughing has even produced Dressel 1A, 1B and 2-4 vessels (Partridge, 1980) which would support Alexander's hypothesis.

The idea of wine amphorae being distributed via an existing salt-trading network helps to elucidate how the vessels were actually transported. However, although this network may have been extensive there is no evidence to support heavy traffic.

Another example of salt trading providing a conduit for imported goods may exist in Cheshire. This area supported a salt production industry in the 1st millennium BC also characterised by *briquetage* and the mechanism described above may explain the presence of a *Massaliote* amphora (5th century BC) in the Grosvenor Museum, Chester which was dredged from the River Dee in about 1900 (Matthews, 1999: 177).

Discussion

Who controlled salt production? Unlike the scenario put forward by Domergue (see Chapter 3) for the Iberian mines, it is clear that salt production in both areas during this period was not run by the Romans prior to invasion, but rather was in the hands of the local community. The difference in production evident in the salt marshes of the Belgian coast and that of the Essex and Hampshire/Sussex coasts shows that if there had been an element of pre-Conquest imperialism it is likely that methods would have improved and output increased. It is also likely that if this had been the case the number of imports distributed on the 'salt route' would have increased. In response to the model put forward by Rodwell the number of imports on salt production sites themselves does not warrant the hypothesis of a two-way relationship but that is not to dispute the possibility of the secondary use of this trade network.

What was the purpose of the wine amphorae on these industrial sites? Referring once again to the evidence from the Gallic and Iberian mines, there are two possibilities. Firstly, that the salt producers were drinking the wine themselves, and secondly, that the amphorae were actually used in the process, either as containers for water or for storage of minerals.

There is a British example of the re-use of imported containers in salt production. A Roman brine kiln has been excavated at Middlewich (*Salinae*) and dates to as early as AD 80 (Bestwick, 1975). Two Dressel 20, and holes for three other similar amphorae, were used as brine containers for storage; all five vessels had been buried in the floor and packed in position using clay and stones. One vessel was inscribed with grafitti - AMVRCA - 'waste from

---

[3] In a recent review of salt production in Iron Age Britain (Morris, 1994) the premise that prior to the pre-Conquest period production was not controlled by a central power, was sustained.

brine'(although the translation is somewhat controversial and may refer to the original contents, 'crushed olives').

The author believes that the fragments of imported amphorae found on salt production sites indicate a secondary use of the container itself and do not bear any relation to the original contents.

Was salt exchanged by local communities for wine? This is a much more complex question. It is possible for merchants to use trade networks created by one product to sell another without there being a direct link with the original product. It may also be the case, as discussed above, that the presence of amphorae on production sites bore no relation to their contents as may be the case in the Iberian mines. However, on a national scale there is a clear relationship between salt production and the distribution of Dressel 1 amphorae and it is certainly possible that salt could have provided the mechanism for distribution for the imports of the 1st century BC/1st century AD. Whether it was as direct currency or simply lent its existing transport network is unclear. It must be remembered that there are other salt producing areas, for example the silt fens in Lincolnshire (Simmons, 1975) which were exploited in the late Iron Age and then later by the Romans where there is no extensive evidence for exotic imports.

The Treatment of Amphorae and Bronze Vessels in Burials

The appearance of wine in burials in south-east England has generated much interest, particularly since Ian Stead's excavation of Welwyn Garden City in 1965 (Stead, 1967). In this paper Stead defined the series of graves containing wine and recognised two chronological phases based on the presence or absence of Gallo-Belgic pottery[1]. The author has revised the grouping slightly and has identified three phases in the light of recent excavations:

Phase One (pre-15 BC)
Welwyn A, Welwyn B, Hertford Heath, Welwyn Garden City, Baldock, Old Warden

Phase Two (post-10 BC, turn of the century)
Dorton, Lexden C, Mount Bures, Elms Farm (Heybridge), Newchurch(?)

Phase Three (Conquest)
Snailwell, Stanfordbury A, Stanfordbury B, Folly Lane, Stanway

The concern of this study is to examine the treatment of wine and bronze vessels in these graves. For this purpose the material relating to the pre-Conquest and immediately post-Conquest period will be under review. It is acknowledged that the phenomenon of wine burial does not cease in the 1st century and that there are examples in the 2nd century of very similar graves, especially with regard to the grave good assemblage, and even the 3rd century, for example, the Holborough barrow.[2]

6.1 Presence of wine amphorae in burials

The evidence for wine in burials has generally been restricted to an area bordered by the Thames to the south, the River Great Ouse to the north and the River Stour to the east in the south-east of Britain (see **Fig. 31**). The possibility of a burial containing a Dressel 1B amphora has, however, recently arisen on the Isle of Wight extending the distribution for the first time to the south coast.[3]

There are four conditions in which amphorae appear in graves: they were either buried complete, with the neck removed, deposited in fragments or they served as the cremation container. These various states do not fit neatly into a chronological framework although graves with complete amphorae tend to be earlier than those with fragmented amphorae. Examples are set out in **Table 4**.

The treatment of amphorae may indicate the role that wine played in the funerary ceremony. If an amphora is complete in the grave - are its contents the preserve of the afterlife? If its neck has been broken, can we assume the wine has already been drunk? Because so many of these graves have been rescued or excavated many years ago little work has been done on analysis of the contents of the amphorae to support either of these contentions. Current work has shown, however, that the role of wine in the ceremony itself is not restricted to mere deposition as a grave good.

6.1.1 Elms Farm, Heybridge

Potentially one of the most revealing sites with regard to the use of amphorae in burials is Heybridge in Essex.[4] A linear cemetery consisting of a series of late Iron Age graves has recently been excavated. Dressel 1 amphorae sherds form part of the assemblage from the site although they are usually badly degraded and very small in size. The features in which they occur are now recognised as under-pyre 'vents' into which debris from a pyre has fallen and been preserved *in situ*. In one example 49 sherds were found, all very small and badly burnt. The pyre-sites are similar to those seen at Westhampnett (Atkinson, *pers.comm.*; Fitzpatrick, 1997). In no cases have amphorae been used to contain the remains.

About 400m to the south-west of the cemetery lies a pit (Pit 15417) containing similar and contemporary redeposited debris from a pyre; the excavator believes that this deposit may be selective and not simply the result of surface clearing. It has been dated to about 10 BC and contained Dressel 1B amphorae, Gaulish platters, flagons and cups, all broken and burnt before burial (Atkinson & Preston, 1998; Preston and Atkinson, *pers.comm.*). The nearest parallel is probably the site at Clemency (Metzler et al, 1991) although the treatment of the finds also has much in common with the evidence from Westhampnett. Both Pit 15417 and the cemetery are important as they contain

---

[1] Phase I: Welwyn A and B, Welwyn Garden City, Hertford Heath; Phase II: Mount Bures, Snailwell, Stanfordbury A and B (Stead, 1967: Table III)

[2] See for example the burials at Welshpool and Riseholme (Boon, 1961).

[3] Newchurch: a single Dressel 1 type amphora was recovered from the plough soil during an amateur investigation of an Iron Age grave. Gallo-Belgic wares were associated with the find. Newport Goods Yard: finds were reported in 1869 during railway construction of early Roman amphorae and cremation urns with associated ditches and bone (human?) filled pits observed (Trott, forthcoming; *pers.comm.*).

---

[4] All information on the cemetery and burial at Elms Farm, Heybridge has been kindly provided through correspondence with Mark Atkinson and Steven Preston, Field Archaeology Unit, Essex County Council and is in advance of publication.

evidence for part of the funerary ceremony and in particular for the role of wine amphorae.

6.1.2 Folly Lane, St. Albans

The recently excavated site at Folly Lane (Niblett, 1999) consisted of a ceremonial enclosure within which lay a funerary shaft and a separate burial pit and pyre site (see **Fig. 32**). The site is dated to the middle of the 1st century AD and its complexity is unprecedented. Sherds of at least four amphorae (Dressel 2-4) were found in the shaft itself, perhaps the remains of a feast(?); they were unburnt. The separate burial pit contained burnt amphorae sherds (1428g), which would have represented at least two vessels, amongst other molten debris indicating that they had been part of the pyre. The sherds were in amphorae Fabrics 3 and 4 (Niblett, 1999: 194); Fabric 3 was found in the turf filling of the funerary shaft but Fabric 4 was found only in the burial pit (see **Fig. 33**). This indicates that additional amphorae were added to the pyre, not just those which were part of the feast in the funerary shaft.

At this site, potentially at Heybridge, possibly at Lexden C and at the much earlier burial at Clemency, the role of wine is clearly more complex than that of a static grave deposit. Returning to the evidence cited in Chapter 2.4.5, is it possible to determine from where these new practices may have come? The major difference between all the tombs in this survey and those in Republican Rome is the lack of a cinerary urn. There are exceptions, but the majority of late Iron Age graves in Britain in the 1st century BC/1st century AD contain apparently unenclosed cremations (see for example, King Harry Lane (Stead & Rigby, 1989) or Westhampnett (Fitzpatrick, 1997). This immediately distinguishes them from a *bona fide* Roman model. However, the use of wine on a funerary pyre appears to be a Roman custom (Folly Lane and possibly Heybridge); as does the practice of burying masks with the dead (Welwyn, Grave A and possibly Folly Lane (Niblett, 1999: 157)).

6.1.3 Amphorae as Cremation Urns

There is one other circumstance where amphorae appear in burials and that is when the vessels themselves are re-used as cremation urns. Dressel 20[5] were quite commonly used for this purpose in Roman Britain according to Callender (1965); examples include Earl's Colne and Colne Engaine (**Fig. 34**). However, there are also examples of lone Dressel 1 amphorae which are thought to have been used in this way, amongst them Aston Clinton (Buckinghamshire) and Lindsell (Essex) where amphorae have been found containing ashes. At Foxton and Lord's Bridge in Cambridgeshire pottery was also found within the vessel. In this instance it is possible that the wine amphorae held special significance but because there are many examples where Dressel 20 are used it would be hard to prove. It is perhaps pragmatism rather than any ritual association

which causes amphorae to be used in such a way. A similar re-use can be seen below showing graves marked by amphorae at the Isola Sacra cemetery, north of Ostia (**Fig. 35**).

6.2. Bronze drinking vessels as grave goods in burials

The evidence for bronze drinking vessels in burials with wine amphorae is restricted to one area, which is centred on Hertfordshire. This region coincides with what roughly may be defined as the territory of the Catuvellauni whose capital was latterly at Verulamium (St. Albans) (see **Fig. 36**).

Using the assemblages found on the continent which are described as drinking services (see Chapter 3.2.3) as examples of what may be found, the evidence from south-east Britain is summarised below.

6.2.1 Paterae and Oenochoe

Four particular types of bronze vessel have been found in Britain within grave assemblages which can be identified and compared with their continental distribution. It should be noted that these vessels are not always whole, sometimes they will be represented by only a handle.
Kjaerumgaard jugs (Eggers 122)

Aylesford (Grave Y) and Welwyn (Grave A) contained bronze jugs of Eggers 122 or Kjaerumgaard type (Boube, 1991) (see **Fig. 37**). These vessels vary in height from 16.4cm (Welwyn A) to 28cm (Siemianice, Poland); the average height of the measurable known examples (10 out of 12) is about 20cm. They were produced from 25 BC to AD 25 (Boube, 1991). Boube surmises that these vessels were originally produced in Italian workshops and that their distribution is related to the military expansion towards these regions in the Augustan period. However, that distribution markedly lies outwith the boundaries of the Empire which in turn suggests a different mechanism of distribution to that of the Roman army (see **Fig. 38**).

Aylesford type paterae (Eggers 130)

The patera at Aylesford gave its name to a distinctive type of shallow bronze pan with a wide distribution on the continent (Eggers 130; Werner Form B) (**Fig. 39**). It is the latest of three types of this saucepan produced in Italy in two phases from 125-70 BC (LT D1) and from 70 - 30 BC (LT D2).

The distribution of these vessels is particularly concentrated in northern Italy and the Alpine region with a further concentration in south west France in the mining region[6] (**Fig. 40**). These pans measure between 25.4cm

---

[5] Dressel 20, also known as 'globular amphorae' contained olive oil.

[6] The author has not yet had the opportunity to investigate this interesting distribution in connection with the prominence of Dressel 1 in the same region.

(Galerie Arete 452, Switzerland) and 60cm in total length (Gautzsch, Germany) with the diameter of the pan itself varying from 13.8cm (Bourg-sur-Gironde, France) to 31cm (Gautzsch, Germany). They are distinguished by long slender handles which terminate in a depiction of a bird's (traditionally recognised as a swan) neck and head.

These vessels were made in the 1st century BC but disappear from the record in the first years of Augustus' rule and appear to have been replaced by other sorts of vessel; four have been found in Britain:

> Aylesford, Grave Y
> Welwyn Grave B
> unknown provenance, Ashmolean Museum, Oxford, no. Inv. 1932.435
> unknown provenance, Coll. Wellcome, London No. R11415/1936[7]

Bronze Patera (Eggers 155)

This type of patera has a distinctive handle which terminates in a ram's head. They are found on the continent as demonstrated by the finds at Antran (**Fig. 41**) and Fléré-la-Rivière (**Fig. 42**) and well beyond the Roman frontier as demonstrated in Eggers' distribution map (Eggers, 1951). There are six finds from Britain known to the author, two in burials, two in hoards and two unprovenanced.

The two examples from burials were found in the Warrior's Grave at Stanway dated to the AD 50s (Crummy, 1997) and the grave at Welshpool (Boon, 1961) dated by the excavator to AD 150-200.[8] The hoards at Santon Downham and Crownthorpe both contained this type of patera amongst their assemblages. Finally, little is known about the recovery of the examples from Biggleswade (Kennett, 1969) and Stanfordbury (Smith, 1911) so they must remain as isolated finds.

Bronze Trefoil Lipped Jug (Eggers 124; Werner K)

Five examples of this type of jug have been found in Britain. Three are from graves; the Warrior's Grave at Stanway, Colchester (CAT Web Site), Winchester, Grave II (Biddle, 1967), Stanfordbury Grave A (Smith 1911-12), a fourth from the hoard at Santon Downham (Fox, 1923) and one from Borden (unknown context; Hutchinson, 1986: Me-130). Many examples have also been found in Gaul, for example, at Antran (Pautreau, 1999: 33-35) (**Fig. 43**), Fléré-la-Rivière (**Fig. 44**), Berry-Bouy and Neuvy-Pailloux (Ferdière & Villard, 1993). They are distinguished by the lip and the decorated terminals of the handle which usually depict the bust of a woman at the top

and a mask in raised relief at the base. Toynbee (Biddle, 1967: 241-2) suggests a Campanian origin for these vessels; they were manufactured in the 1st century AD (Augustinian/Claudian: Ferdière & Villard, 1993: 50).

Strainers

There are only three examples from burials in Britain and none of these compare with the ladle/strainers found in similar graves on the continent. These are the bronze spouted strainer bowl from the Doctor's Grave at Stanway (which contained *artemis*[9]; Sealey, *pers.comm.*), the fragment of a strainer from Burial 325 at King Harry Lane and an earlier version in Grave 1 at Welwyn Garden City which was made from a converted bronze bowl (imported).

Buckets

These are found in the earlier series of graves in the 1st century BC, for example, Welwyn Garden City, Hertford Heath and Baldock but tend not to be deposited in the 1st century AD. Examples have also been found with no evidence for wine at Harpenden, Alkham and Marlborough. These are likely to illustrate the continuation of an older custom.

6.2.1 The Function of Imported Bronze Vessels in Burials

Feugère & de Marinis (1991) noted the association between paterae with swan's neck handles (Eggers 130, as described above) and jugs. These vessels actually usually appear with a specific vessel: the bronze jugs of Kelheim or Kjaerumgaard (Eggers 122) type. This is the case at Aylesford (Tomb Y) and (Welwyn Tomb B); the relationship is also noted at Chatillon-sur-Indre (Indre).

The relationship between Eggers 124, the trefoil lipped jug and Eggers 155, a patera with a handle usually terminating in a ram's head[10] is noted by Nuber (in Pautreau, 1999: 37) for Britain, Germany and Belgium but the recent survey of central France (Ferdière & Villard, 1993) and the burial at Antran have extended the distribution to the west. In Britain, they have been found in the Warrior's Grave, Stanway (Crummy, 1995;1997), Grange Road II, Winchester (Biddle, 1967), the Santon Downham hoard (Fox, 1923) and possibly at Stanfordbury Grave A (Smith, 1911-12) and Welshpool (Boon, 1961). In France, examples have been found at Antran (Pautreau, 1999),

---

[7] Cited in Hayes, J.W., *Greek, Roman and Related Metalware in the Royal Ontario Museum*, p.73, Toronto (1984)

[8] The dating for this grave is probably due for re-examination. It contains a number of objects dated firmly to the 1st century AD which were classified by the excavator as heirlooms.

[9] 'His jaws are fixed, and he is unable to open his mouth ... Grind wormwood [*Artemisia absinthium*], bay leaves, or henbane seed with frankincense; soak this in white wine, and pour it into a new pot; add an amount of oil equal to the wine, warm and anoint the patient's body copiously with the warm fluid, and also his head ... also give him a very sweet white wine to drink in large quantities.' on tetanus, Hippocrates of Cos, *Internal Affections*, pt.52

[10] Similar paterae are also occasionally found with handles terminating in another animal, for example, the patera from Berry-Bouy (Ferdière & Villard, 1993: 132).

Fléré-la-Rivière, Berry-Bouy and Neuvy-Pailloux (Ferdière & Villard, 1993).

These vessels (Eggers 122/Eggers 130 and the later Eggers 124/Eggers 155) are either found in isolated contexts about which little is known, or in tombs. They are not found on settlement sites. It is suggested therefore, that bronze vessels such as these were made to be deposited in tombs as grave goods and that they were imported to Britain solely for that reason. This hypothesis could also apply to other grave goods. The burial pit at Folly Lane, for example, contained nine items of horse equipment. Among these was a locally made bridle bit which Foster suggested, due to its lack of wear, may have never been used and made specially for depositing in the grave (Foster, 1999: 136).

If these vessels were imported as grave goods - were they intended for use as a wine service?

Feugère & de Marinis (1991: 108) suggest that Eggers 130/ Eggers 122 were not part of a drinking service as had been suggested by Werner and Bolla amongst others. Due to their consistant appearance with jugs in graves they argue that these vessels were used for washing. The phenomenon is interpreted as a clear sign of adoption of Roman manners by the Gaulish aristocracy and this is recognised as part of a successful Roman strategy towards consolidating loyalty in the new province. They argue that where amphorae are present, more often than not, the drinking service is provided by ceramic vessels. Might the same be applied to the later series of vessels, Eggers 155/Eggers 124?

Does the position in the grave help to throw light on this matter? In the Warrior's Grave at Stanway the patera and jug were deposited with the pottery service, sharing the centre of the grave with the unenclosed cremation; the amphora lies propped up against the side of the tomb (see **Fig. 45**).[11]

At Antran, the patera and jug are deposited on the north-west side of the tomb amongst the seven Pascual 1 wine amphorae (**Fig. 46**).

The bronze patera, jug, basins and strainer at Fléré were placed at the foot of the body near the 13 Pascual 1 amphorae stacked against the side of the tomb. Amongst the amphorae remained the bronze *simpulum*, two goblets and a bowl. At Berry-Bouy the service was placed away from the amphorae near the cremation in the centre of the tomb and at Neuvy-Pailloux, the drinking service was placed near the stack of 57 Pascual 1 amphorae.

The evidence is spatially inconclusive although the bronze vessels do appear to be placed near the amphorae more often than not.

An additional thread lies with the iconography of the bronze vessels. The later series, identified above (Eggers 150 and 124) are decorated with Bacchic imagery according to Hutchinson's directive (Chapter 2.4.4). The ram's head[12] decorating the terminal of the patera handle and the maenad or tragic mask on the base escutcheon of the trefoil jugs could be seen in this light. Could these vessels provide very early evidence of the Bacchic cult in Britain? This would imply almost certainly that these accoutrements were intended to be used in conjunction with wine.

---

[11] This site has not been published yet; the amphora is referred to as 'from Pompeii' - it may be a Dressel 2-4 but this is not confirmed.

---

[12] The ram's head is not exclusively Bacchic; see for example, two stone altars from the Roman temple site at Uley, Gloucestershire which show Mercury with a cock on his left side and a ram by his right (Henig, 1980). Caesar writes about seeing "images of Mercury" (BG, VI,17) in Britain.

The Appearance of Wine on Ritual or Ceremonial Sites

The easiest way to demonstrate that wine may have held more than domestic meaning to the people of later Iron Age Britain would be to present evidence of its use in their sanctuary sites. An attempt to do that follows but the evidence is by no means clear cut.

7.1 Sacred Enclosures

It is a possibility that similar enclosures to the large, well-documented sanctuaries of Belgic Gaul, for example, Ribemont-sur-Ancre (Brunaux, 1996: 77-90) and Gournay-sur-Aronde (Oise) (Brunaux, 1985), may be found in southern Britain in the period immediately prior to the Roman Conquest. These have been assimilated with a group of generally more extensive sites termed *Viereckschanzen* after rectilinear enclosures thought to have a ritual function recognised in Bavaria (Webster, 1995: 453 for background).

The Belgic examples share two distinguishing characteristics - groups of artefacts deliberately deposited (for example, weapons, animal and human bones and jewellery, often intentionally broken) and a ditched and/or palisaded enclosure (Webster, 1995: 458).

The following sites hold the potential for further investigation with these characteristics in mind.

The site at Oram's Arbour, Winchester is an Iron Age sub-rectangular enclosure measuring over 400m in length with an entrance in the west. A section of the southern ditch was excavated which appeared to be partly deliberately refilled. From the lower fill, a Dr.1B rim was retrieved amongst 'a few sherds and flakes of Dressel Type 1 amphorae' (Biddle, 1975) (**Fig. 47**).

The most substantial evidence for the practice of deposition in ditches comes from the excavations at Station Road, Puckeridge which is part of the large Iron Age complex at Braughing (Partridge, 1980). F1 is a late Iron Age enclosure ditch which has been traced for 75 metres through housing. Of the section excavated, a total of 42 sherds of wine amphorae have been retrieved (Dressel 1 and Dressel 2-4) which represent at least six amphorae.[12]

Other finds in the ditch included the remains of fourteen individual animals; ovicaprid dominates the assemblage of Groups 1 and 2 (the layers in which the amphorae were found). No bones are articulated and some show fine knife cuts which led the excavator to suggest that these remains had been ritually exposed. In addition, the ditch produced

Gallo-Belgic wares (*terra rubra* butt beakers, a pedestal bowl and beaker, platters in *terra rubra* and *terra nigra*), coarse pottery and three sherds of Samian. Thirteen brooches were found of the Colchester and Hod Hill types, an iron strip brooch, a Rosette brooch (turn of 1st century AD - c. AD 25-30) and three large iron examples, apparently derivative of a Nauheim type (in common use until AD 75 but probably pre-Conquest).

There were also two human burials within the ditch. These were both similar to burials at King Harry Lane but of a later date (c. AD 50-60 and AD 45 +) and were simple cremations accompanied by a flagon each with other pottery.

The amphorae do not appear to be associated with either of the burials nor was it recorded that there was any evidence of burning within any of these deposits. However, the combination of the deposits of amphorae sherds, imported pottery, the brooches (in particular) and the deposition of burials in the ditch of this large enclosure, highlight this site as a possible candidate for ritual status.

The large ditch at Gatesbury Track, Braughing (F7) crossing Wickham Hill from east to west produced Dressel 1B in all levels and Dressel 1A in an early level (Partridge, 1980). A second ditch (F41) also contained Dressel 1B sherds and may have been the north-east end of the same enclosure as defined by F7. The only imported wares in F41 were Dressel 1B sherds; there was evidence of burning in F41 but not directly related to the amphorae sherds. The site produced a total of 198 amphorae sherds of which Dressel 1 made up 63.4% and Dressel 2-4 only 0.7%. It also produced Gallo Belgic wares 3:1 (*terra rubra: terra nigra*) which were all dated to the last decade of the 1st century BC; no finds appear to post date AD 25.

Finally, a much smaller example is that of Gun Hill, West Tilbury where an Iron Age sub-rectangular enclosure ('A') produced an unstratified Dressel 1 sherd in the southern arc of its ditch (F1) (**Fig. 48**). The enclosure dominates the summit of a hill with a single south-east facing entrance. Its construction is dated by the excavators to the middle of the 1st century AD (Phase 5); there is no suggestion in the report that this could have been a ritual site (Rodwell & Drury, 1973). However, there was evidence that the ditch had been partly deliberately refilled (as at Oram's Arbour) and for a gateway to be built formed by 2 posts. Within the enclosure were two large pits, 44 and 45 which contained a large post-setting which the excavators felt was unlikely to be a building (Rodwell & Drury, 1973: 54). If this arrangement was not a building, what was it?

In the next phase (5B) sherds of Dressel 20 amphorae were found in the northern section of ditch F1 in a charcoal layer and inside Kiln 1. This was described by the excavators as

---

[1] Fitzpatrick (1985) noted that a palmette on one of the Dressel 1 amphorae is paralleled at Basel-Gasfabrik by a Dressel 1A amphora, and also at Roanne, *contra* Peacock's report (Partridge, 1981)

part of a Romano-British industrial area. An oven with an accelerated radiocarbon date of 2055 ± 45 B.P. was cut into the southern face of the ditch surrounding the ceremonial enclosure at Folly Lane (Niblett, 1999: 22-23).[2] The excavator suggested that this oven may have been used in the funerary ceremony, perhaps for food preparation? Ovens were found in the precinct of the temples in *insulae* VII and XV of the Roman town of Verulamium (*ibid*: 99) suggesting they may have held some associated function.

In any comparison of the sites described above with the large sanctuary complexes in Belgic Gaul, one of the most immediate enquiries is - where are the weapons? These artefacts played a very important role in enabling the distinction between ritual and non-ritual to take place, not least because of the quantity in which they were found but also the nature of their deposition. Deposits at Gournay-sur-Aronde, for example, produced 2,000 metal finds, many of which were deliberately damaged swords and scabbards (Brunaux *et al*, 1985).

None of the British sites cited above have produced weapons and yet this may be a peculiar characteristic of the territory because weapons are not a main feature in any of the rich burials in the south-east of Britain. Late Iron Age burials on the continent often feature weapons, particularly swords, within the assemblage, for example, Mailleraye-sur-Seine (Seine-Maritime) (Lequoy, 1993), Tomb B at Goeblingen-Nospelt (Metzler, 1984) or Fléré-la-Rivière (Ferdière & Villard, 1993).

7.2 **Shafts**

The use of shafts as foci of religious activity is well attested on the continent, for example, those from Aquitaine (Fouet, 1958) which contained large quantities of Dressel 1 amphorae. The enclosure at Folly Lane (Niblett, 1999) contained a shaft which had been used to house a structure used in the funerary ceremony but not for the burial itself. It was then deliberately refilled at the same time as the cremation was placed in a separate pit. On the floor of the shaft were sherds of wine amphorae (Dressel 2-4) and other ceramic vessels considered by the excavator to be the remains of a funerary meal. This has a completely different character to the 24 votive shafts found in a different part of the site at Folly Lane and which date to the 2nd century AD. This concurs with Webster's (1995) observation that shafts used for ritual purposes generally post-date the Roman Conquest. Of the seventeen sites in Webster's catalogue (1997)[3] only Shaft 3 at Bekesbourne in Kent contained an amphora (accompanied by two urns) but this has not been diagnosed as pre-Roman.

7.3 **Temples**

There are two temple sites which are potentially relevant to this study. Unfortunately, details are limited with regard to both sites, however, what is known is summarised below.

7.3.1 **Hayling Island, Hampshire**

The temple at Hayling Island (Downey, King & Soffe 1980; King & Soffe, 1994) was excavated as part of a research programme instigated in 1976. The site was originally located by aerial photography. It consists of a circular timber building with an entrance facing east within a trapezoidal shaped courtyard, and was found beneath a later stone-built temple. The temple was in use from the mid-1st century BC to mid-1st century AD (**Fig. 49**). A large pit in the centre of the building had been backfilled with brickearth and a variety of objects including pottery, bones, brooches, coins and a piece of a speculum mirror were included in the deposit. In the main courtyard were found horse and chariot fittings, spearheads, belt hooks, two triskele straplinks, brooches, finger rings, bracelets, glass, amber beads, two bronze tankard handles, currency bars, and most importantly, amphorae (King & Soffe, 1994: 115)[4]. Most of the pottery appeared to serve as food containers and the animal bones were almost exclusively sheep and pig unlike contemporary settlement sites (cattle). There were also the remains of human bones. In specially set aside areas of the courtyard large assemblages of coins were found which were probably votive offerings. Many of the objects within the courtyard showed signs of having been bent or deliberately broken before disposal (cf. Gournay -sur-Aronde).

A stone building was constructed on the same site in AD 60-70 (as at Heybridge). With the new building came a change in the type of votive objects deposited, most significantly there was a reduction in the number of weapons deposited. Downey, Soffe & King (1980) suggested this was due to the *Lex Julia de vi publica* banning civilians from carrying weapons. However, what may be more signficant in a British context is that weapons were being deposited at all.

7.3.2 **Heybridge, Essex**

Heybridge contains evidence for an early religious focus in the form of two late Iron Age shrines. One is circular with an internal diameter of 5m (A) and the second, adjacent structure, was 4.5m square with a central pit (B) (**Fig. 50**). These were located in Area J (see **Fig. 23**) on a gravel rise. During the immediate post-Conquest period these shrines were levelled and a temple complex consisting of four rectangular structures, one inside the other, was built. The excavators believe, at this stage, that this was one single structure, not one building successively enlarged; it directly overlaid the circular IA structure (C). The finds have not

---

[2] The large ceremonial enclosure at Folly Lane (Niblett, 1999: 17) is not included in this group because it appears to have been purpose-built to contain the rich burial in its centre in the middle of the 1st century AD.

[3] 'Appendix. Wells and shafts with putative Iron Age fills' (p.141-143)

---

[4] Unfortunately, the author has been unable to obtain any further information about the amphorae from the excavators.

assisted in the interpretation of these buildings as being part of a temple complex; the interpretation is based on morphology, and the circular *cella* within a rectangular enclosure is closely paralleled at other sites, for example, Hayling Island (Atkinson & Preston, 1998: 97-8). As yet therefore, there is no direct evidence that amphorae were associated with these buildings, either in the LPRIA or post-Conquest phases, but Dressel 1A, 1B and 2-4 have been found at Heybridge.

7.4 The Appearance of Imported Bronze Vessels in Hoards

There are no known, as yet, examples of bronze vessels being found on ritual or ceremonial sites in Britain. However, evidence may well come to light in the future. In northern Gaul, for example, at Pierrefonds, Mont Berny a fragment of a Kelheim jug was found at what may be a cult place (Roymans, 1990: 157).

There is, however, evidence in Britain for imported bronze vessels being deposited in hoards during the late Iron Age. Two examples with much in common are Crownthorpe (Norfolk) and Santon Downham (Suffolk). The hoard from Crownthorpe contained a copper alloy bowl[5] together with a patera with handle terminating in a ram's head and an animal-spouted strainer bowl, perhaps similar to the example from Felmersham.[6] The objects remain unpublished. The hoard at Santon Downham, found in 1897, consisted of a fine bronze jug with trefoil spout, bronze handle of a patera with animal head terminal (mid-1st AD), a large bronze cauldron, fragments from two buckets or tankards and harness ware (including red champleve enamel work) (Fox, 1923). Both hoards contain paterae terminating in animal heads and trefoil jugs; this is a combination often found in burials and is discussed further in Chapter 6.2.

In northern Britain there are examples of bronze drinking vessels being deposited in hoards, for example the assemblage found at Ruberslaw (Roxburghshire)[7] which contained a silvered jug handle, bowl and paterae. Other examples include a colander and patera from Lanark (unprovenanced) and a hoard from Helmsdale[8] which consisted of two colanders and seven shallow basins or bowls, including a punched bowl with a rosette in the

middle (Robertson, 1970). However, these finds are from the 2nd century AD and later.

A further example of ritual deposition is the Ardleigh cauldron pit (Erith & Holbert, 1974; Sealey, unpubl.). Here a pottery cauldron was deposited in a deliberately cut pit with three pottery spouted strainer bowls in about AD 45. Sealey argues that this assemblage would have been used to serve a local drink such as beer or mead and extends this assertion to include the bronze versions, for example, the animal spouted strainer bowls from Felmersham (Kennett, 1970) (**Fig. 51**) and Crownthorpe (unpubl.) found in hoards (see Chapter 6.2)[9].

---

[5] The bowl is comparable to that found in a burial at the Ermine Street site at Braughing, although it is twice the size (Partridge, 1980).

[6] Kuhlicke (1969) suggests that the finds from Felmersham Bridge may also constitute a hoard.

[7] Curle, A.O. (1905) 'Description of the fortifications on Ruberslaw, Roxburghshire and notices of Roman remains found there' *Proceedings of the Society of Antiquaries of Scotland* 39: 219-232

[8] See Spearman, R.M. (1990) 'The Helmsdale bowls, a reassessment' *Proceedings of the Society of Antiquaries of Scotland* 120: 63-77

[9] See also May, J. (1971) 'An Iron Age Spout from Kirmington, Lincolnshire' *Antiquaries Journal* 51

Conclusions

In the introduction the author posed four questions to ask of the evidence. These are now treated in turn.

Does the appearance of imported wine into later Iron Age Britain constitute a trade?

The number of findspots of the hardy Dressel 1 is increasing all the time, with only recently the largest deposit of Dressel 1B being found at Heybridge. However, nationwide only about 450 Dressel 1/Dressel 2-4 containers have been retrieved, which over a potential 150 year span is still less than the cargo of one shipment. The wreck of Grand Congloué 2 in the bay of Marseilles held between 1,200 and 1,500 Dressel 1 vessels alone (Laubenheimer, 1990: 69). A brief comparison also with the quantities of amphorae in circulation in Gaul may bring into question the relevance of the term 'trade' to this discussion.

It is apparent, however, that the dynamics governing the commodity's distribution differed between the south-east of Britain and the south coast. The importation of Dressel 1A is now plotted along the south coast with a particular concentration around the Isle of Wight. At this early stage, there is little evidence to suggest anything other than a secular use for wine. Apart from the one fragment of strainer at Hengistbury Head no special wine drinking vessels appear to accompany Dressel 1A and there are no recorded burials of the type found in the south-east of the country. However, once the excavations at Hayling Island are finally published and the record from the Isle of Wight becomes clearer it may be that the picture along the south coast does become more complicated.[1]

If economic bearing can be brought to the introduction of wine in Britain then it must have been an exchange conducted on a small scale. In certain circumstances the appearance of wine amphorae may even have been a secondary use for the vessel as suggested in Chapter 5.

Is it possible that wine held a ritual significance to the people of later Iron Age Britain?

By the mid/late 1st century BC in south-east Britain, the evidence for wine suggests that it may have taken on additional or new meaning with wine amphorae being used in different ways. They appear in burials as a grave good and later their treatment appears to be an important element of the funerary ritual (for example, Folly Lane and Heybridge). There is also evidence to suggest, although this is not substantial at the present time, that amphorae may appear in ritual deposits in ditches. The presence of wine at shrines is likely although, as with the previous observation, concrete evidence is lacking. The publication of the recent finds at Heybridge, Heathrow, Hayling Island and Stanstead will hopefully throw more light on this aspect.

Were wine sets consisting of elaborate bronze vessels, such as flagons, paterae and ladles such as those found at Fléré-la-Rivière/Antran group?

Some bronze vessels are found in the archaeological record in Britain as were described in Chapter 6. However, none of the British graves exhibit the degree of wealth found in examples on the continent or the range of imported vessels. There are no ladles or strainers such as those found in the Fléré-la-Rivière/Antran group. In one case only is the standard drinking set encountered in the Classical World detected; this is the grave at Welwyn Garden City (Stead, 1967). It is the only example with a strainer but this was part locally made and is not in the tradition of those on the continent.

The decorated bronze buckets form an interesting group (see **Table 5**). They are a key feature of the 1st century AD drinking assemblages found in rich burials in Gaul (see **Fig. 52** for example from Antran). This table illustrates the variety of contexts in which buckets have been found in burials in south-east Britain. There appears to be an association between the use of buckets decorated with indigenous iconography in burials without wine amphorae but this is not exclusively so. The author believes that the presence of decorated buckets reflects a different tradition, elements of which are mixed with the new customs, as seen at the earliest grave in the sequence at Baldock. The use of buckets, as strainers, is not a straight forward transference from one culture to another.

It is only the patera and jug which appear consistently together that make up a distinct set. The author believes these were used for serving wine on the basis of the descriptions of wine services in the ancient sources (Chapter 2.2) and the possibility of the use of Bacchic imagery in the later set (Eggers 124/Eggers 150). It is also likely that they were exclusively made for funerals.

With regard to wine, how similar are the circumstances of its discovery to those identified in Gaul?

Recent work by Metzler and Poux is beginning to change the way that amphorae are observed in northern Gaul. There are many links to be made between the treatment of amphorae, particularly with regard to burials and ditch deposits in the evidence from northern France and Britain. In addition the series of graves typified by Fléré-la-Rivière

---

[1] There are already intimations that the Isle of Wight record is quite complex - a possible burial at Packway, Newchurch for example, together with possible ditch deposits with gallo-belgic pottery. There are also finds associated with briquetage (Trott, forthcoming).

in central France holds many similarities with British examples.

Brunaux has described the new forms of religious expression being observed in north-eastern France such as the Belgic sanctuaries and the evidence for a Druidic religion developing in Gaul between the 3rd and 1st century BC (Brunaux, 1996). It may be possible to identify elements of this expression in Britain as Fitzpatrick has attempted to do for the cemetery at Westhampnett in Hampshire which was in use from 90-50 BC (Fitzpatrick, 1997). The most important aspect is the adoption of cremation, but this coupled with formal cemeteries and similar treatment of grave goods all begin to make a coherent picture (see **Fig. 53**[2]). Even once cremation is adopted a considerable variety is detected in the grave good assemblage.

It is more than likely that wine played a part in this expression, although to what extent is not yet clear. The results of the excavations at Heybridge will probably be the turning point in this avenue of enquiry.

The author concludes by saying that this is an exciting time to be studying the Iron Age. There is a lot of new evidence from excavations, the results of which are not yet fully known, but which are likely to add immensely to our understanding of this period.

---

[2] The shrine at Heybridge can now be added to this map.

Further Work

It is felt that further work on the salt industry would be very valuable especially with regard to a) its extent geographically, b) which factors caused the industry to move from one area to another, and c) whether the industry was centrally controlled or whether it was, as Bradley (1975) suggested, simply another task in the agricultural calendar for individual communities. In this respect also, it is felt that the relations between the salt mines of Hallstatt and the evidence for wine would bear further analysis.

The author also considers that the use of wine in the early Roman period in Britain would be a fruitful line of research particularly its use in festivals, ceremonies and the worship of Bacchus. It would also be very interesting to explore the evidence for wine in relation to the advance of Christianity, particularly the distribution of amphorae and the evidence for early Church plate.

However, of primary importance is a more detailed study of the assemblages in Belgic Gaul as described in Roymans (1990) and Haselgrove (1996) in the light of the evidence from southern England. This would enable firmer conclusions to be drawn on the relations between the two regions.

The author has explored the evidence for only 100 years in one country, out of 3,000 years of wine making and drinking throughout the world, but remains struck, not only by its continuing hold in social and religious practice, but by the similarity of the ceremonial objects associated with it during that timespan.

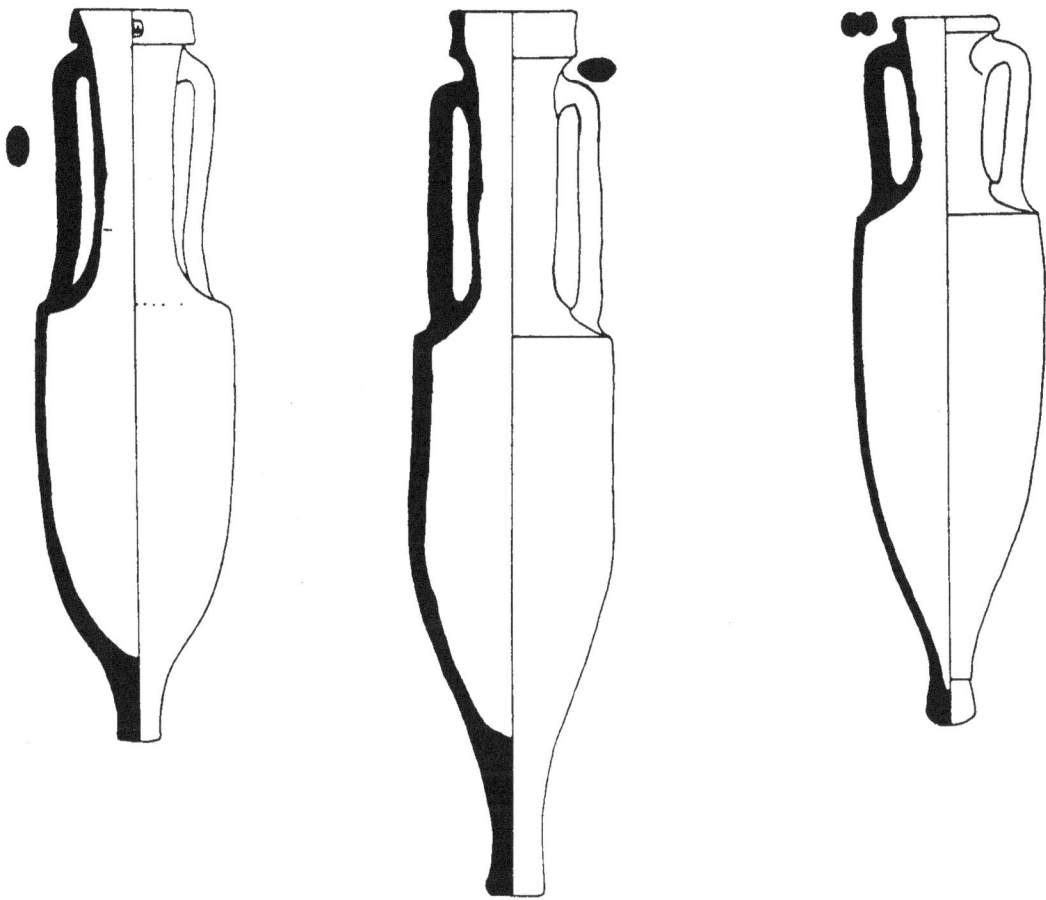

Fig. 1 Amphorae primarily under discussion. Dressel 1A; Dressel 1B; Dressel 2-4 (Peacock & Williams, 1986)

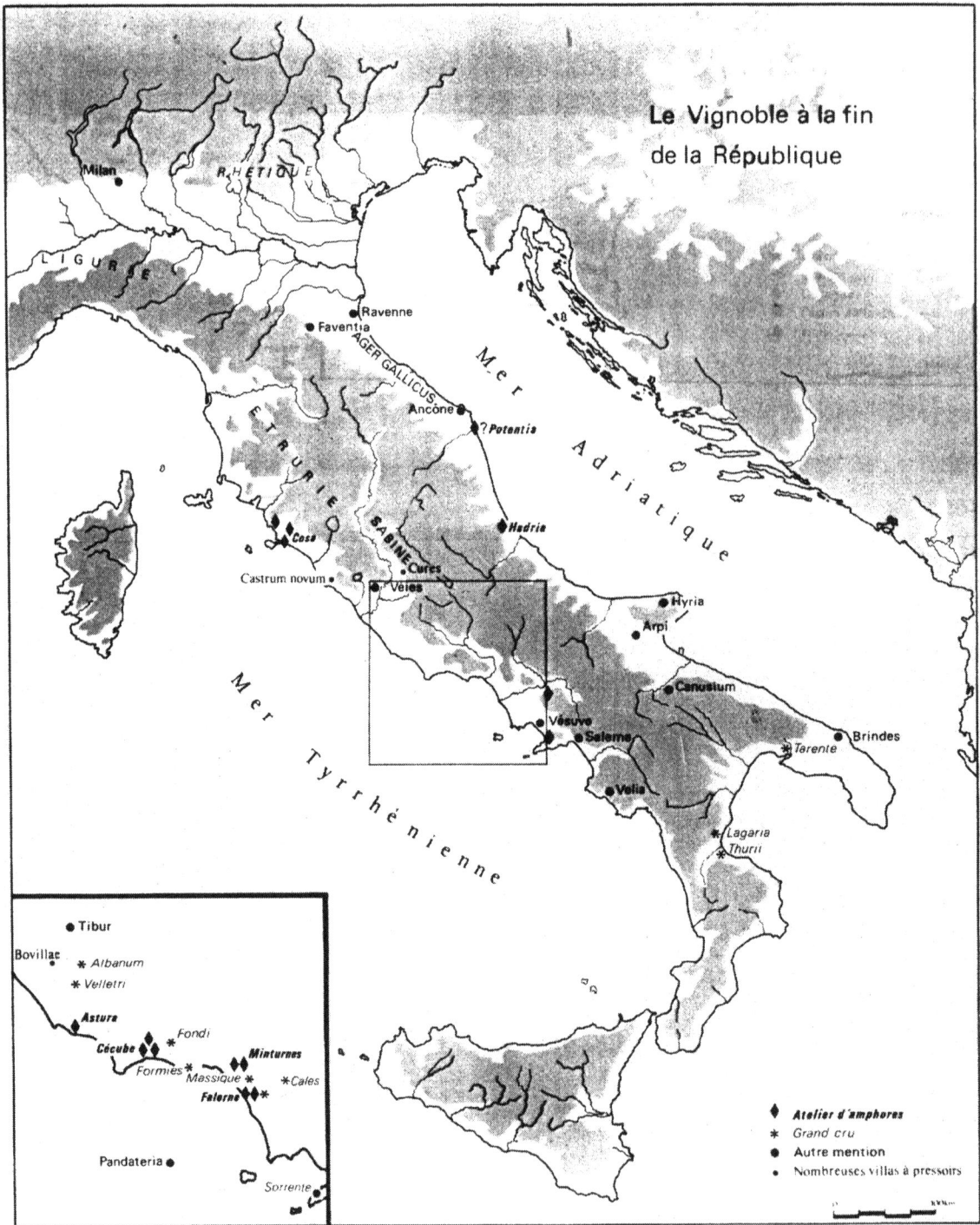

Fig. 2   Vineyards at the end of the Republic (Tchernia, 1986) (*Courtesy of Ecole Française de Rome*)
♦ amphorae production sites ✳ reputed wines ● other vineyards mentioned • several villas with wine presses

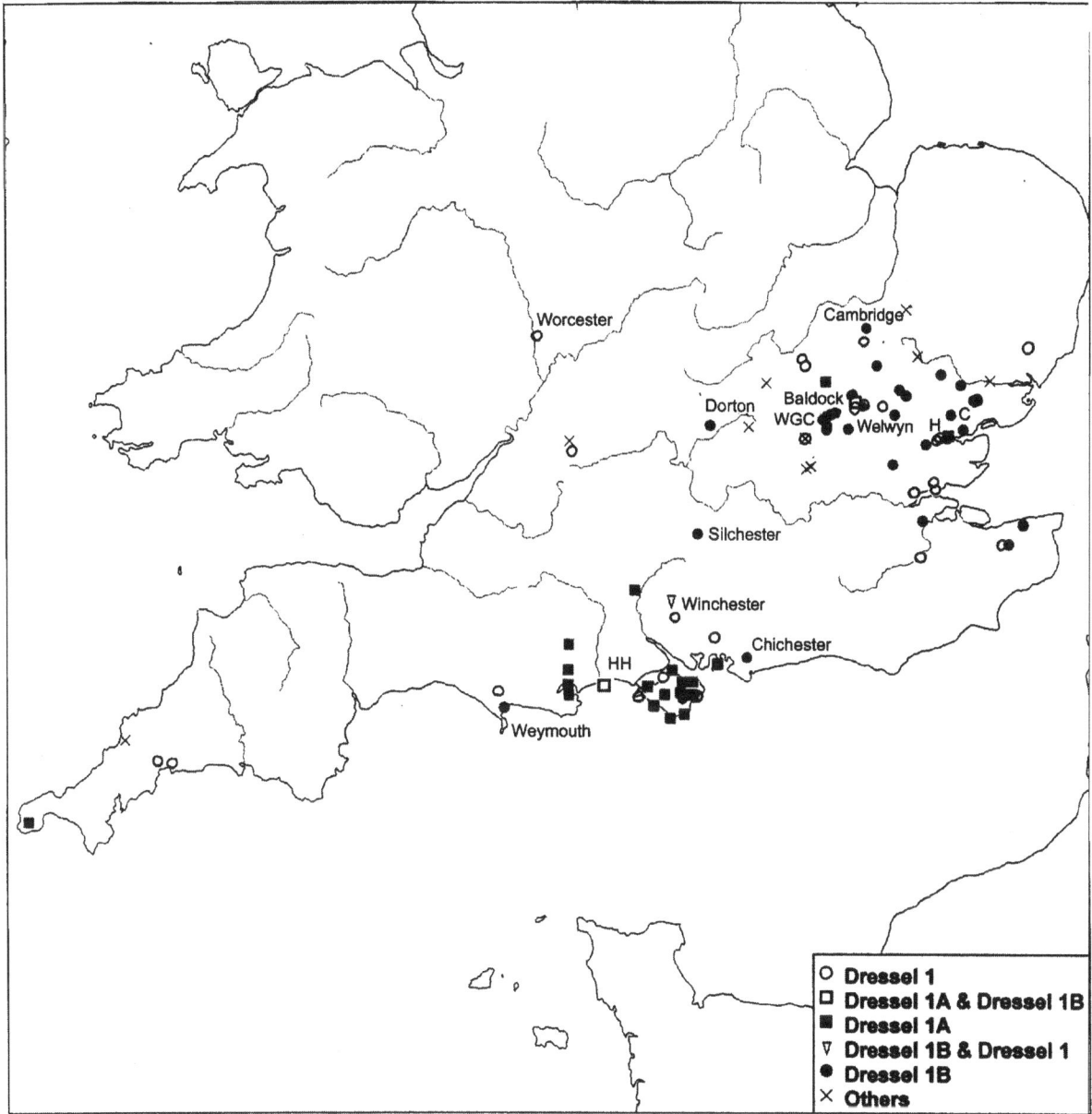

Fig. 3 The distribution of Dressel 1 (1A and 1B where identified) amphorae in southern Britain. (See Appendix 1 for names of sites included on this map.)

Fig. 4 The distribution of Dressel 2-4 amphorae in southern Britain. (See Appendix 1 for names of sites included on this map.)

Fig. 5 Distribution map of amphorae of Dressel Form 1 (Callender, 1965)

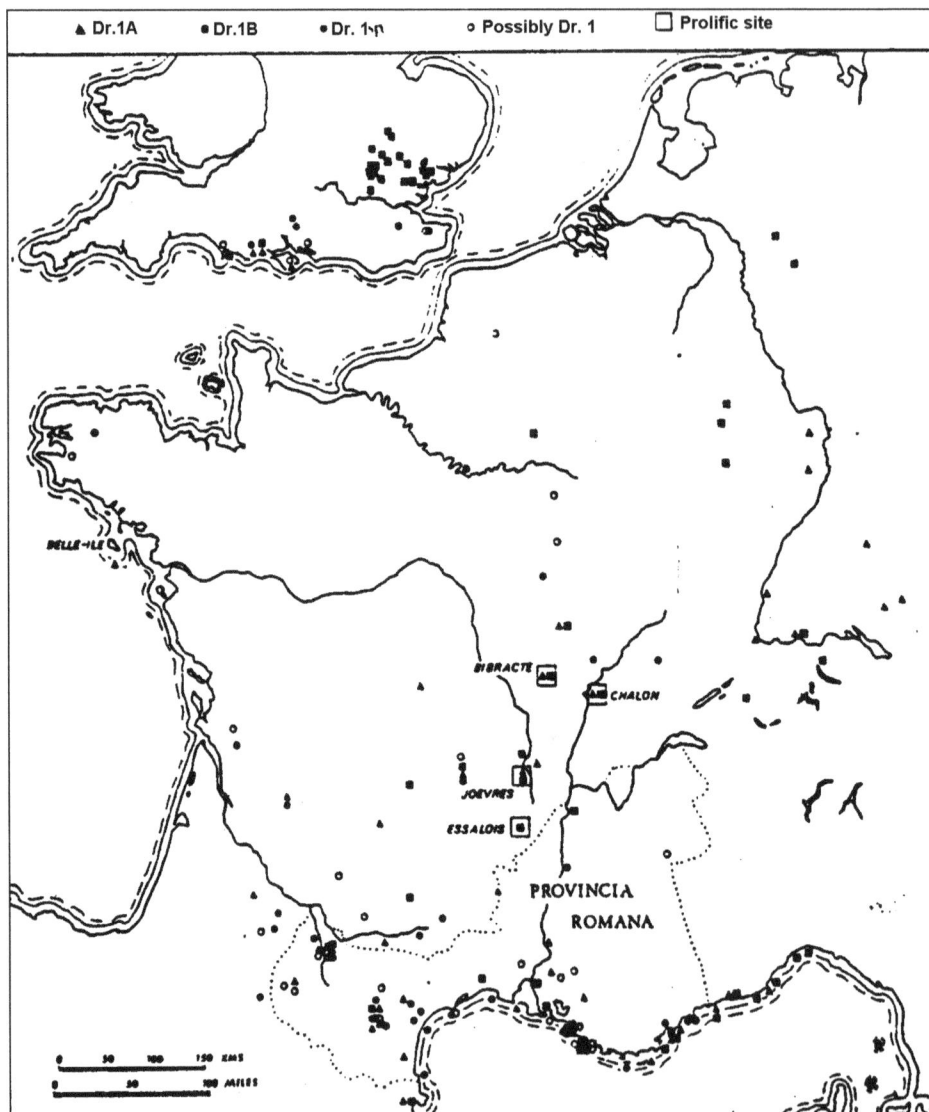

Fig. 6 Distribution map of Dressel 1 amphorae in Gaul and Britain (Peacock, 1971)

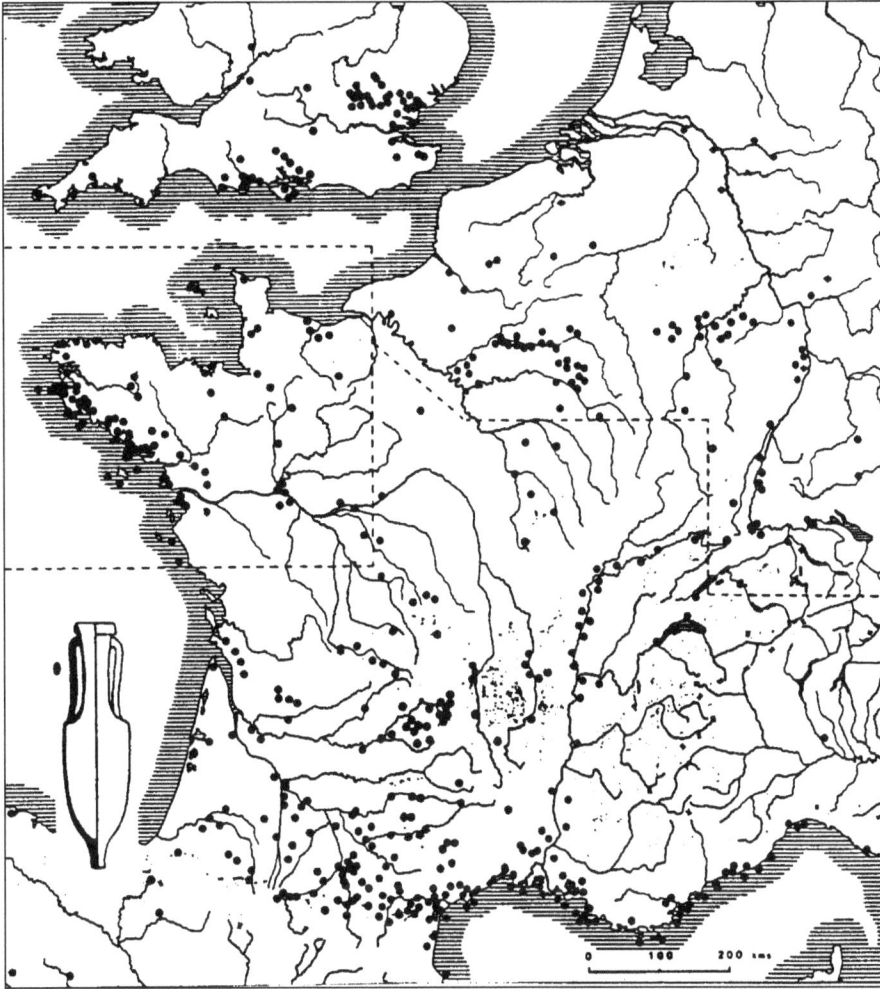

Fig. 7 The distribution of Graeco-Italic and Dressel 1 amphorae in western Europe
● Graeco-Italic amphorae ◆ Dressel 1B on Augustan military sites (Fitzpatrick, 1985)

Fig. 8 The distribution of Dressel 1A, 1B and 1sp. in Britain (Fitzpatrick 1985)

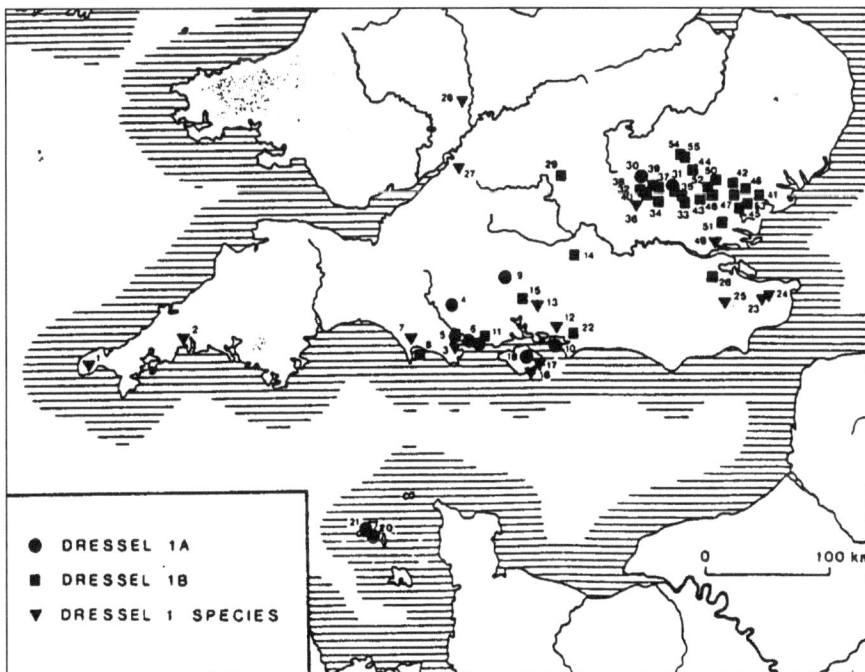

47

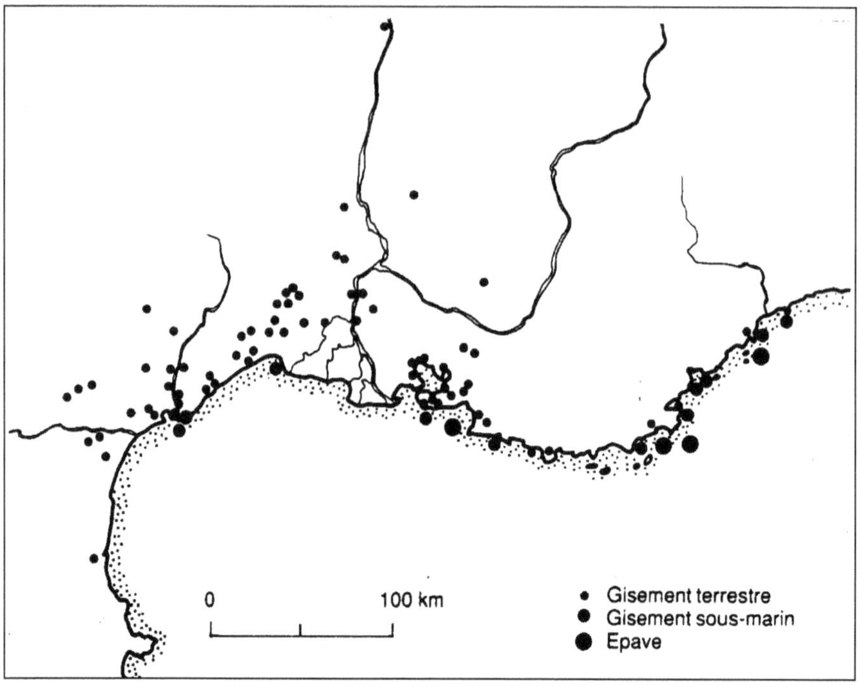

Fig. 9 Distribution of Etruscan amphorae along the south coast of Gaul (after Bouloumié. 1982 in Laubenheimer, 1990: 17) ● dryland sites; ● underwater sites; ● wrecks

Fig. 10 Map of the east of France showing the sites of Hallstatt date where fragments of Massaliote amphorae have been found (Flouest, 1993)

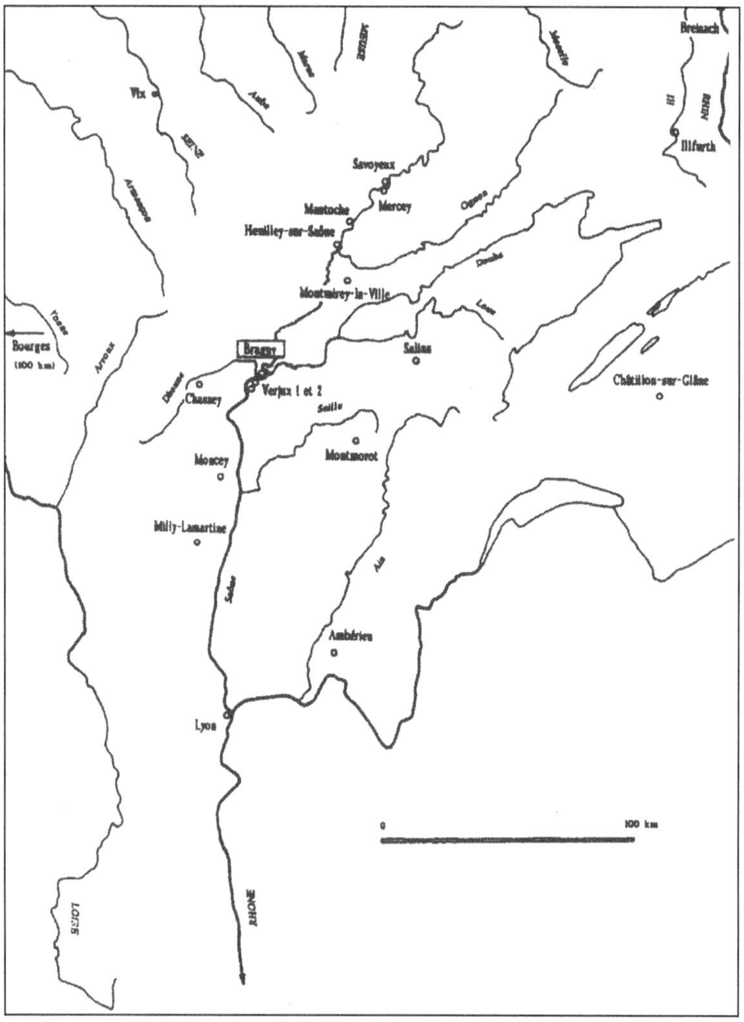

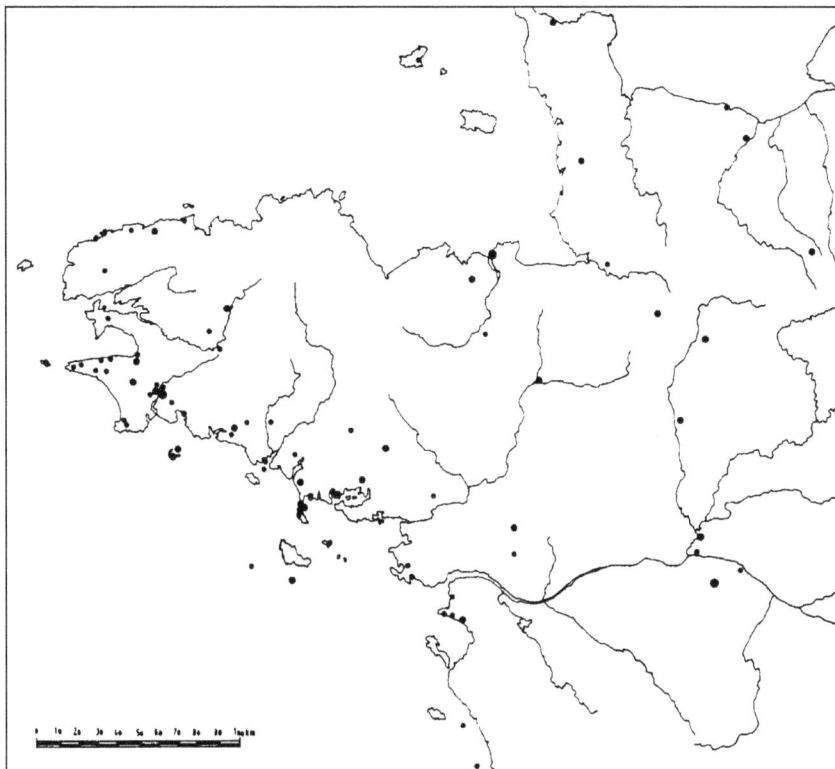

Fig. 11   Distribution of Dressel 1 amphorae in western France: small dots represent single finds, medium-sized dots 2-10 amphorae, large dots over 10 amphorae (Galliou, 1984: 27, fig. 1) (*Courtesy of Society of Antiquaries of London*)

Fig. 12   Findspots of Dressel 1 wine amphorae in Belgic Gaul (Haselgrove, 1990)

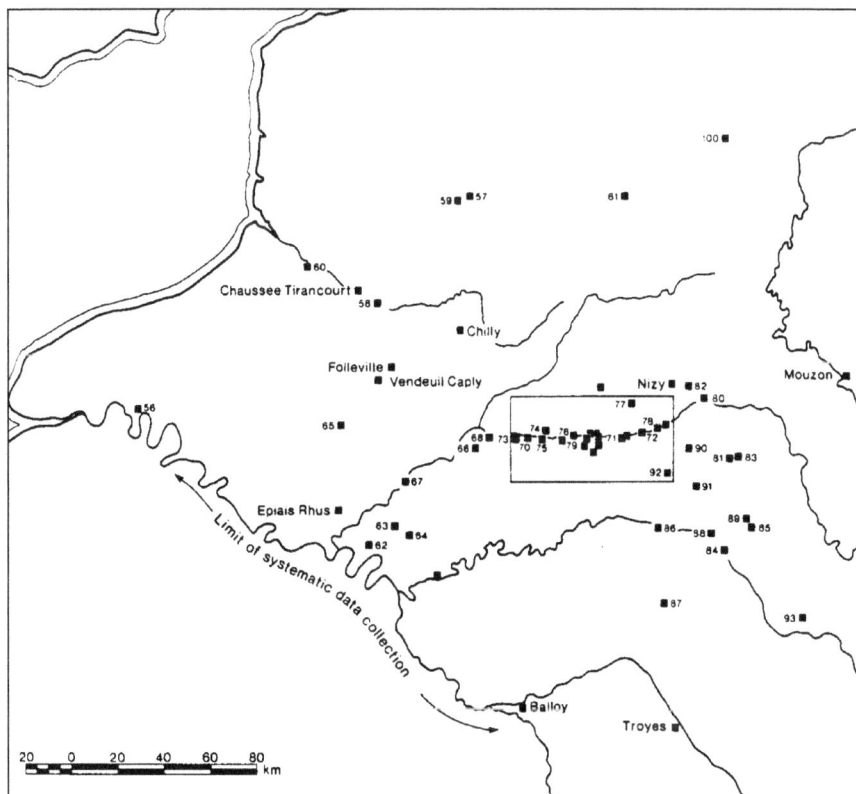

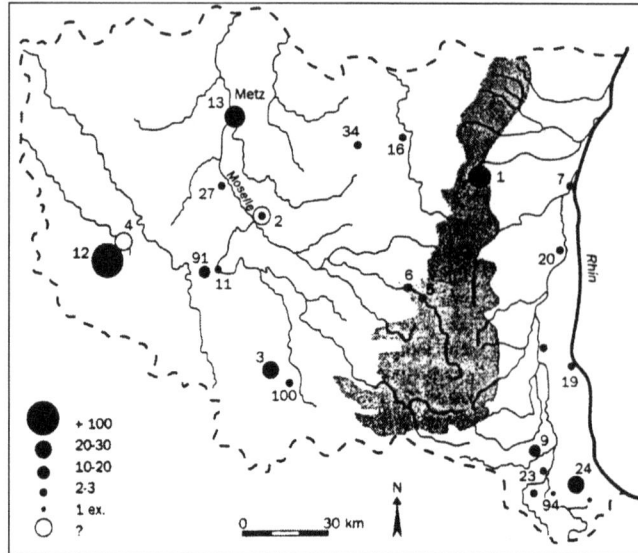

Fig. 13 Map showing distribution of Dressel 1 amphorae in north-east Gaul (Baudoux, 1996)

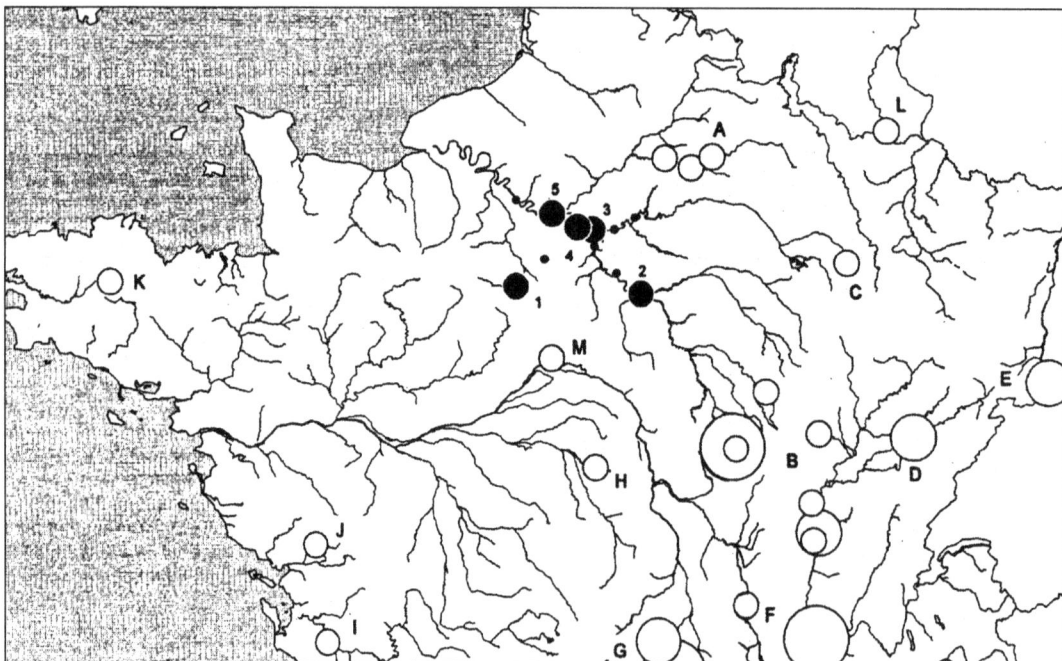

Fig. 14 Main concentrations of Republican wine amphorae in northern Gaul (at 1997) (Poux & Selles, 1998)
  ○ largest diameter = more than 1000 amphorae; smallest diameter = less than 100 amphorae
  A Aisne Valley; **B** Burgundy (Bibracte, Châlon-sur-Saône, Alésia, Tournus); **C** Naix;
  D Besançon; **E** Bâle; **F** Lyon (Lyon, Roanne); **G** Auvergne (Clermont-Ferrand, Corent, Gergovie, Levroux); **H** Levroux; **I** Saintes; **J** Fontenay-le-Comte; **K** Paule-Saint-Symphorien;
  L Luxembourg (Titelberg, Clémency); **M** Orléans
  ● new discoveries in Ile-de-France: largest diameter = more than 100 amphorae; smallest diameter = less than 30 amphorae
  1 Chartes; **2** Varennes-sur-Seine; **3** Paris; **4** Nanterre; **5** Meulan-lea-Mureaux

50

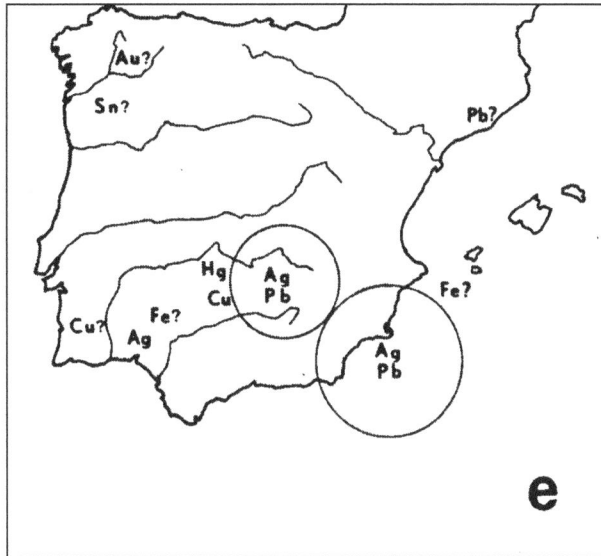

Fig. 15   Map showing the mining regions of the Iberian peninsula at the end of the Roman Republican period
(Domergue, 1990) (*Courtesy of École Française de Rome*)

Fig. 16   Dressel 1 and Lamboglia 2 sherds and an anvil at the mine of Sortijón del Cuzna (Cordoba)
(Domergue, 1990) (*Courtesy of École Française de Rome*)

Fig. 17 Scene depicting workers extracting ore or clay in a mine, with amphora. Painted plaque from Penteskouphia, Corinth (second half of 6th century BC) (F. 871; *Antikensammlung - Staatliche Museen zu Berlin Preußischer Kulturbesitz*)

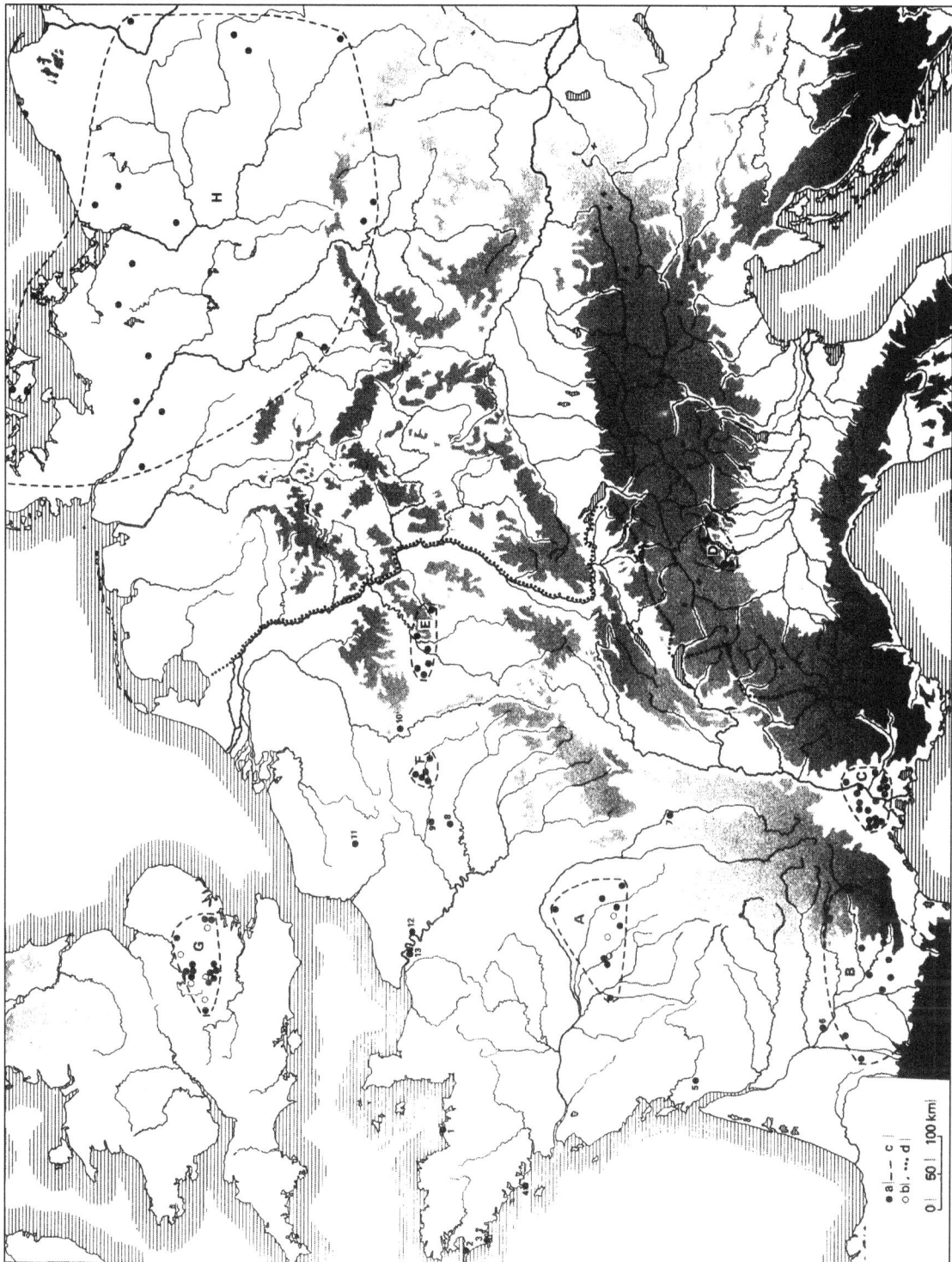

Fig. 18 Map showing location of groups of rich graves comparable with the Fléré-la-Rivière group (Ferdière & Villard, 1993)

KEY: **a** comparable burials; **b** others, possible; **c** limit of the groups; **d** limit of Gaul (under the Empire)

Groups: **A** Fléré-la-Rivière burials; **B** Toulouse funerary shafts; **C** Saint-Laurent-des-Arbres;
D northern Italian burials; **E** Goeblingen-Nospelt burials; **F** Champagne group; **G** Lubsöw group

Other Burials: **1** Saint-Jacut-de-la-Mer (Côtes-d-Amor); **2** Goulien (Finistère); **3** Saint-Jean-Trolimon (Finistère); **4** Quiberon (Morbihan); **5** Tesson (Charente-Maritime); **6** Boé (Lot-et-Garonne); **7** Chassenard (Allier); **8** Armentières (Aisne); **9** Presles-et-Boves (Aisne); **10** Tremblois (Ardennes); **11** Arras (Pas-de Calais); **12** Belbeuf (Seine-Maritime); **13** La Mailleraye-sur-Seine (Seine-Maritime)

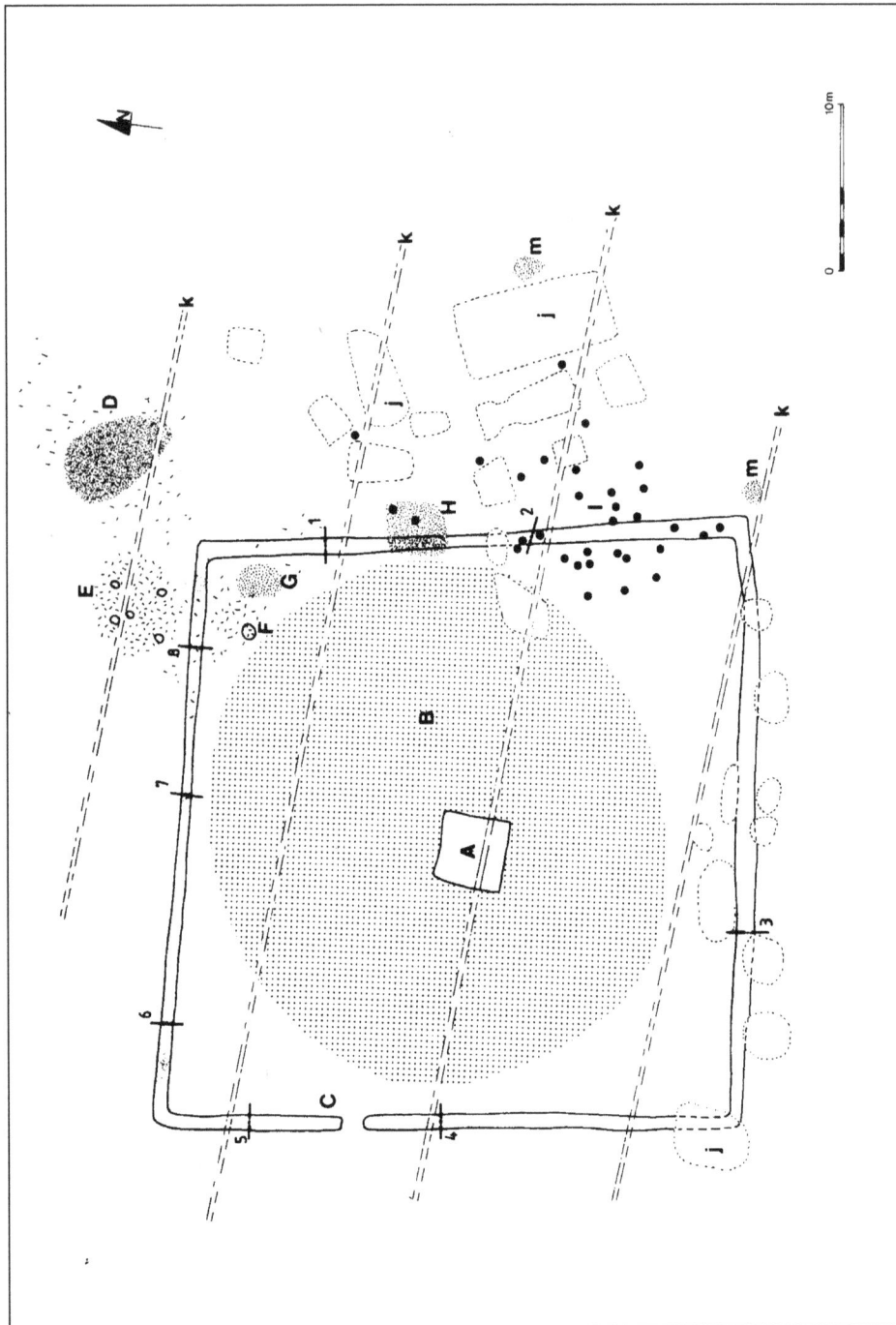

Fig. 19 Plan of the tomb and enclosure at Clemency (Metzler et al. 1991)
A Funerary chamber; B natural mound which served as a base for the site; C enclosure ditch with entrance; D main pyre site; E amphorae 'pavement' and five stakeholes; F ditch; G burnt structure; H additional pyre site; I offering pits; j flax-retting pits; k modern drainage; m burnt structures (modern?)

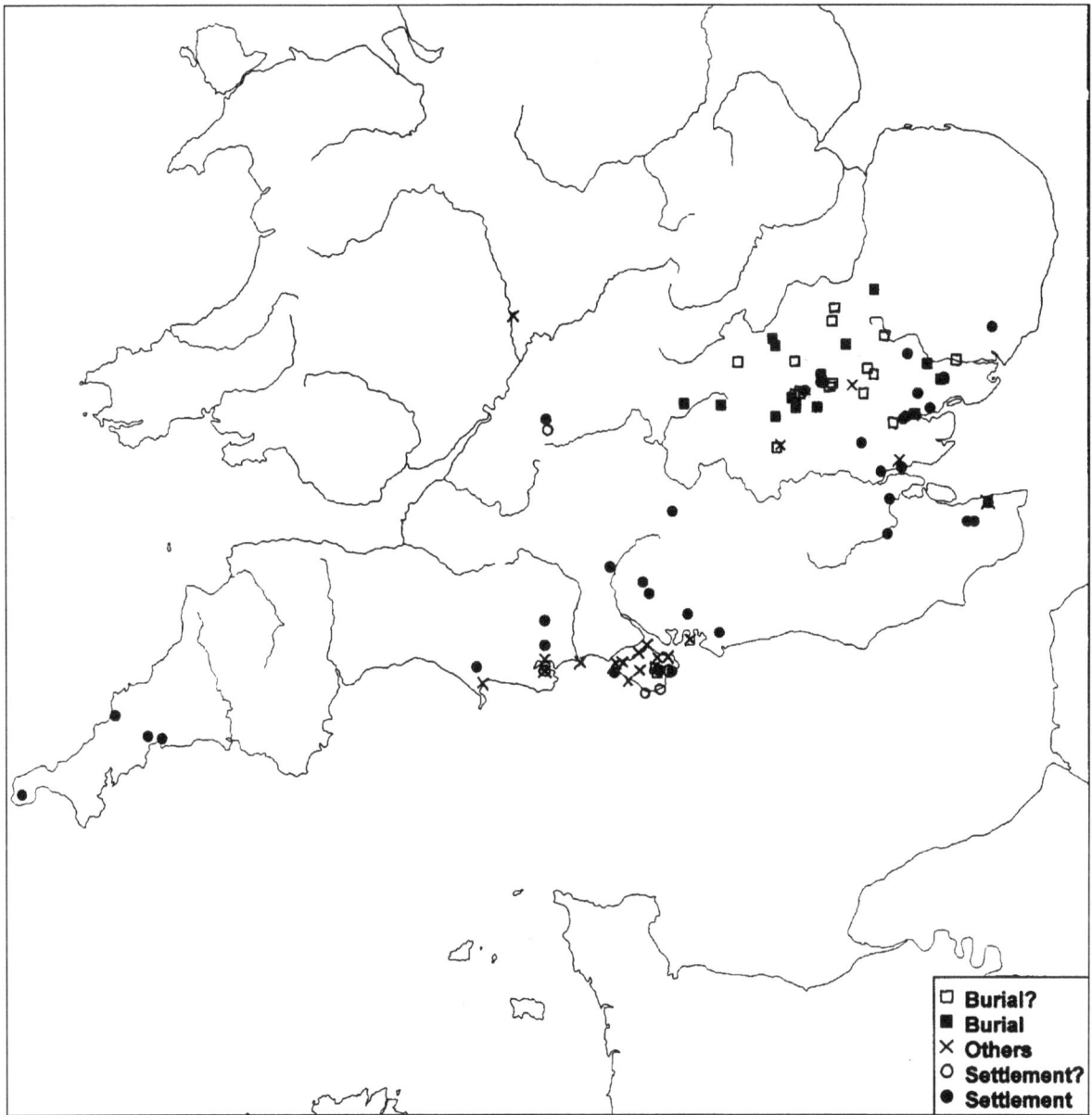

Fig. 20 Map showing the distribution of Dressel 1 and Dressel 2-4 amphorae found on settlement and burial sites in southern Britain. Others = unknown; wreck; temple; industrial; beach

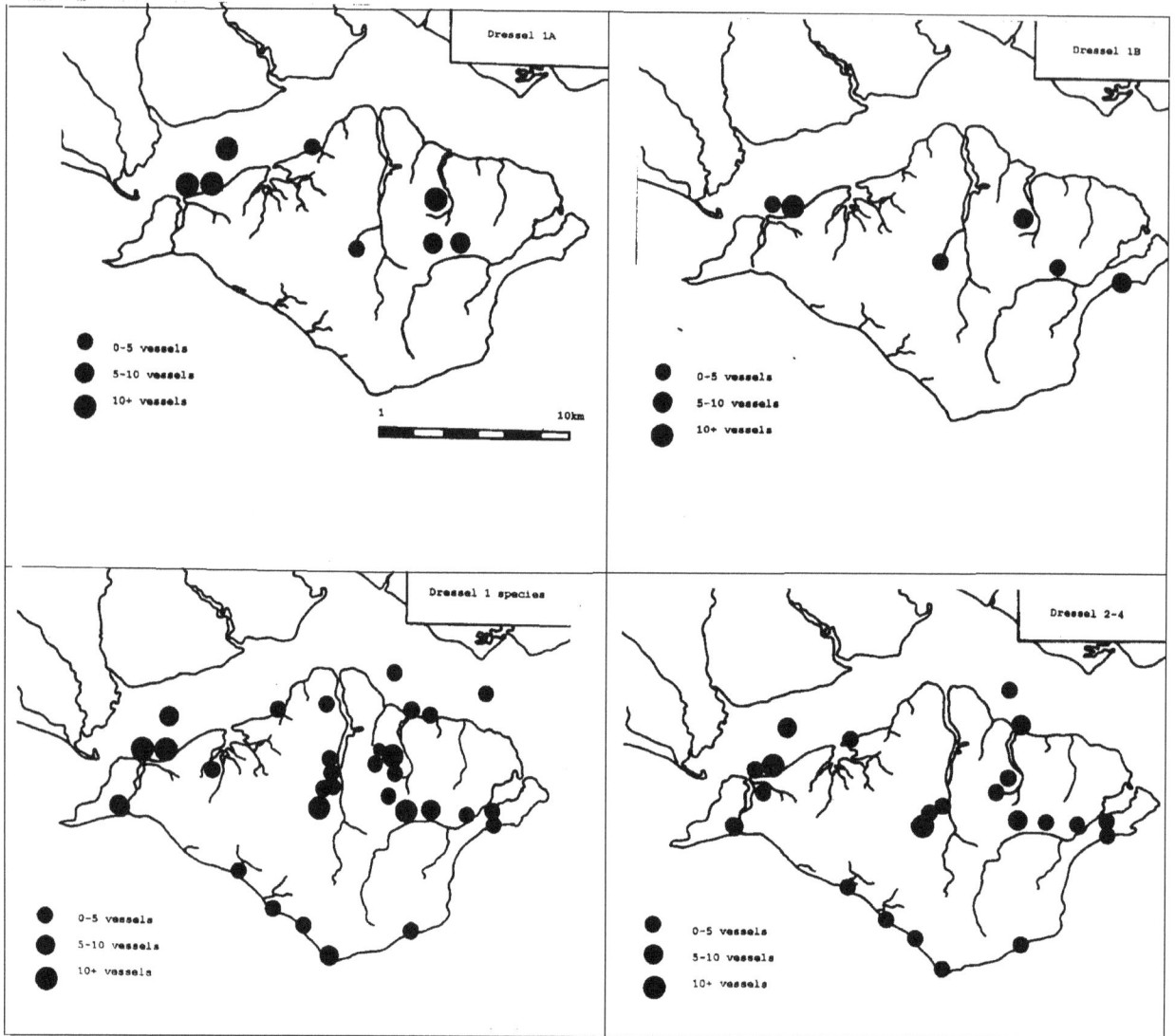

Fig. 21 Maps showing distribution of Dressel 1 and Dressel 2-4 amphorae on the Isle of Wight (Trott, forthcoming)

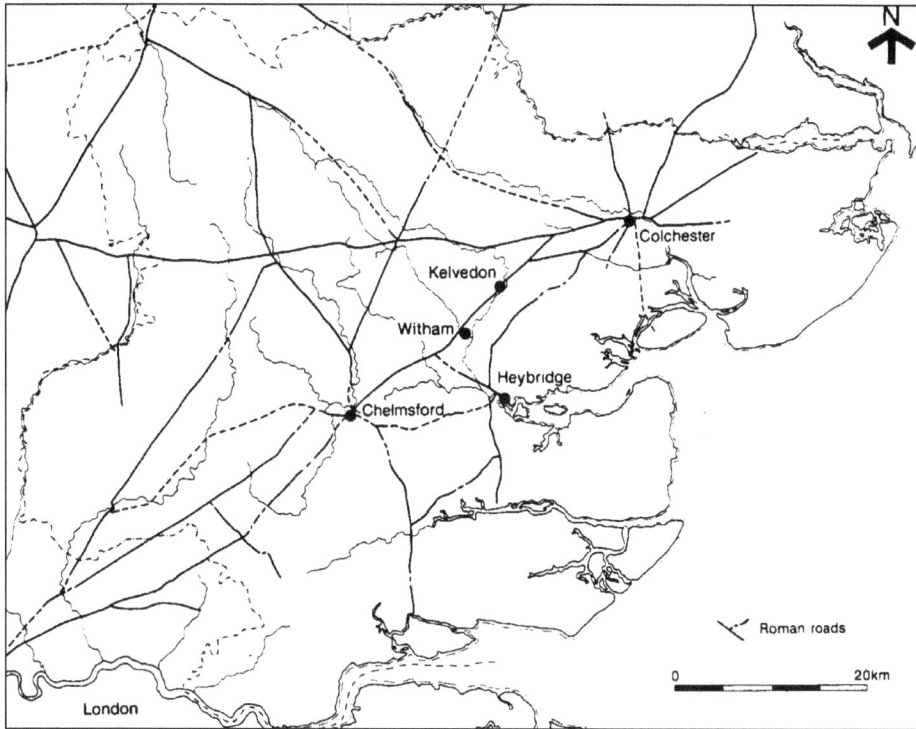

Fig. 22 Map showing location of Heybridge (Atkinson & Preston, 1998)

Fig. 23 Elms Farm, Heybridge: schematic plan showing location of excavation areas (Atkinson & Preston, 1998)

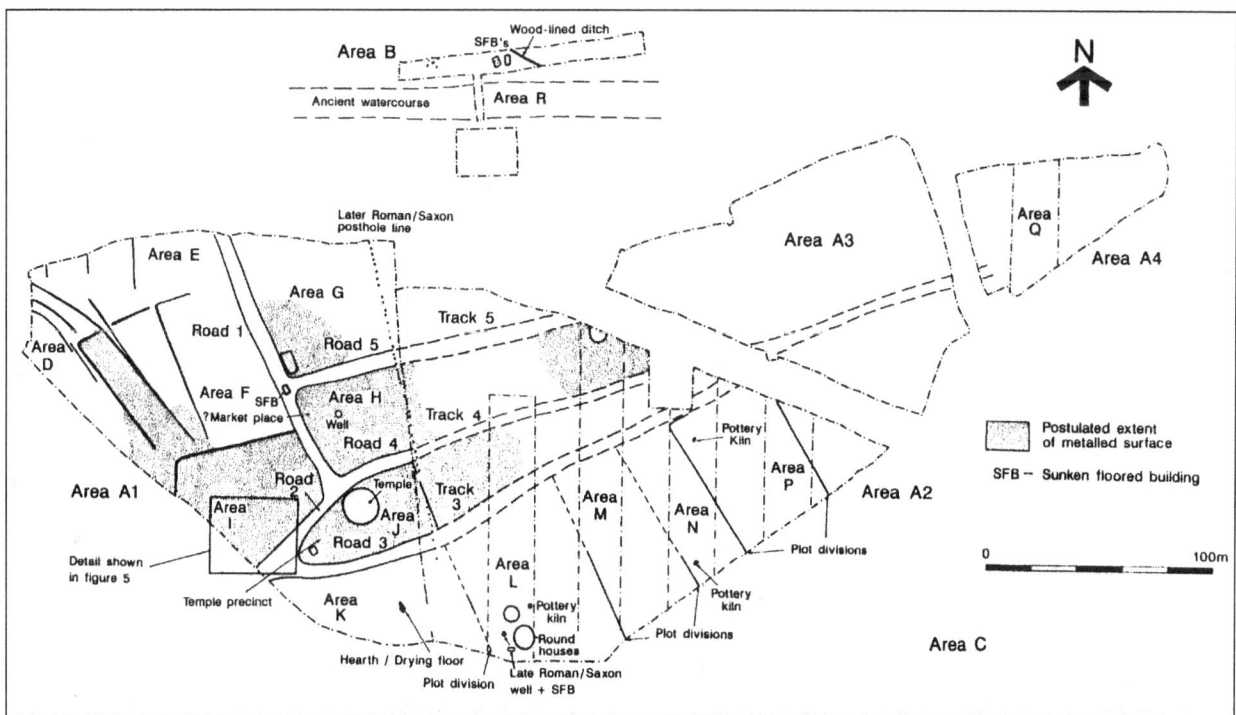

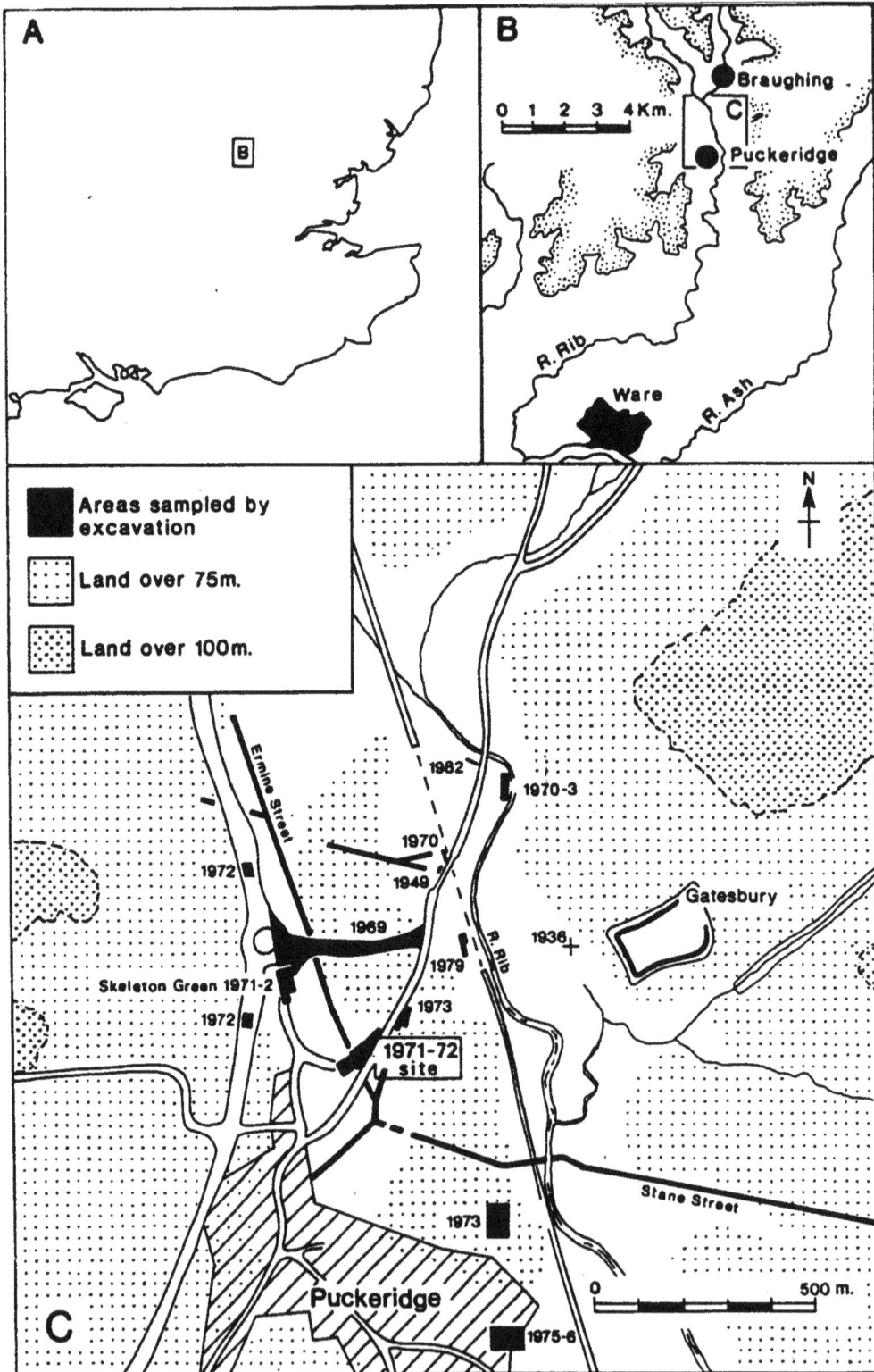

Fig. 24 Location of Ermine Street site and other areas of excavation at Braughing (Potter & Trow, 1988)

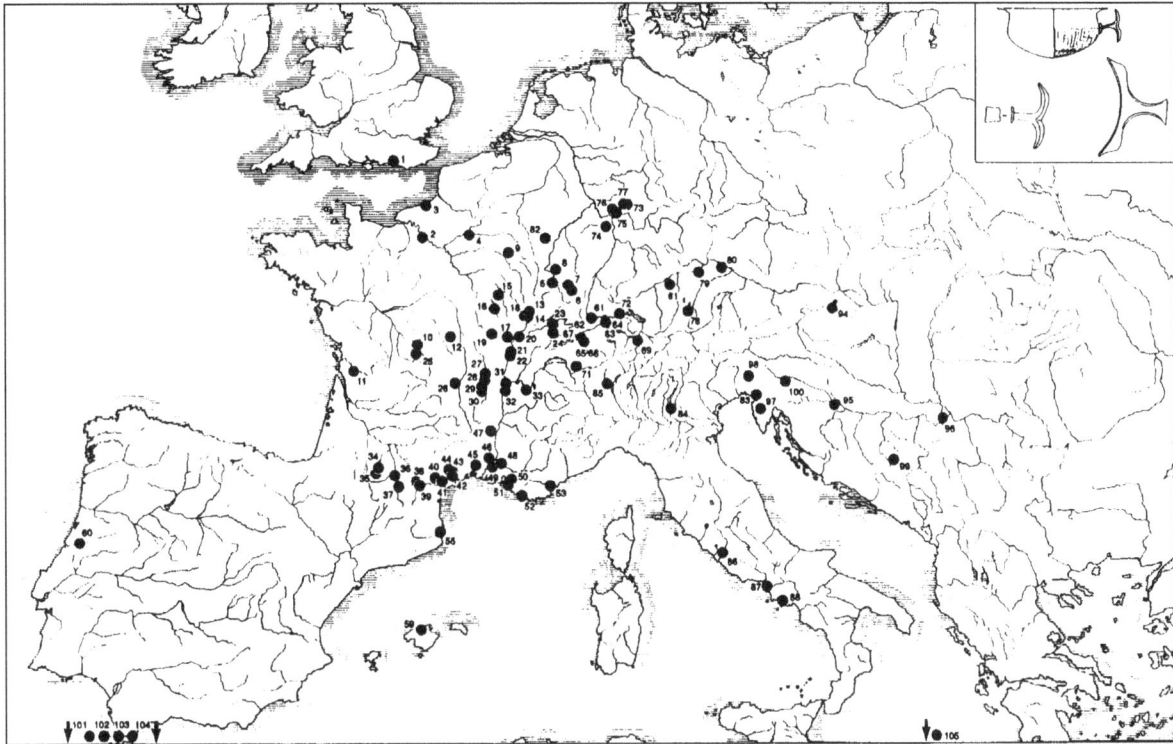

Fig. 25 Map showing the distribution of strainers (Guillaumet, 1991)

Fig. 27 Excavator with copper-alloy ewer from
Elms Farm, Heybridge (1998)

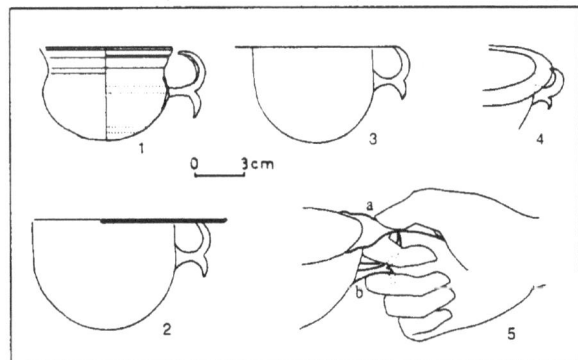

Fig. 26 Reconstruction drawing of strainer (Guillaumet, 1991)

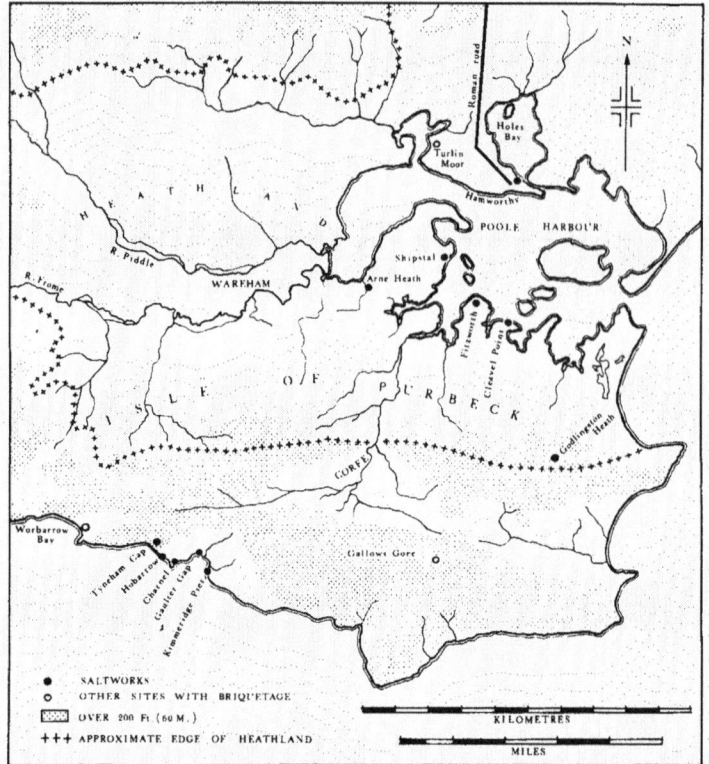

Fig. 28 Prehistoric and Roman saltworks in Purbeck and Poole, Dorset (Farrar, 1975) (*Courtesy of Colchester Archaeological Group*)

Fig. 29 The Salt Industry and its Hinterland (Bradley, 1975) (*Courtesy of Colchester Archaeological Group*)

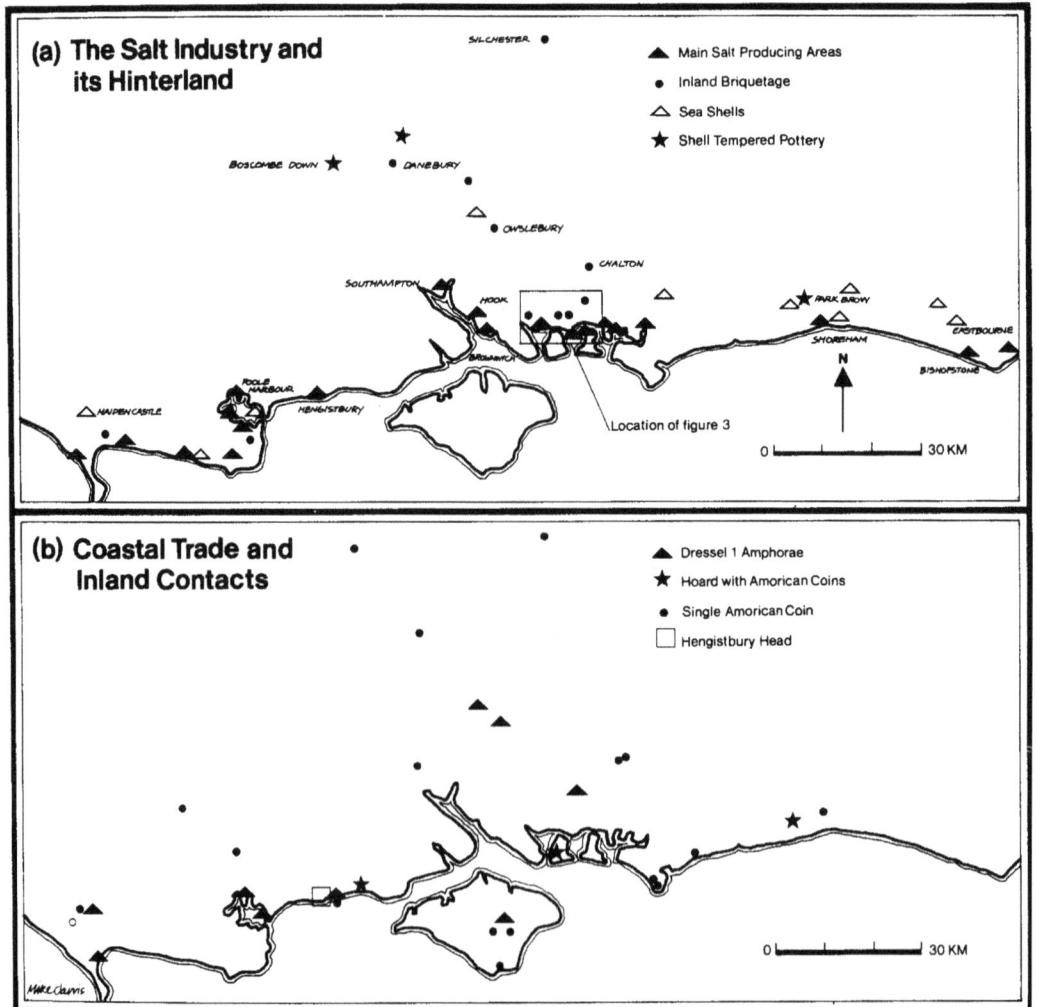

60

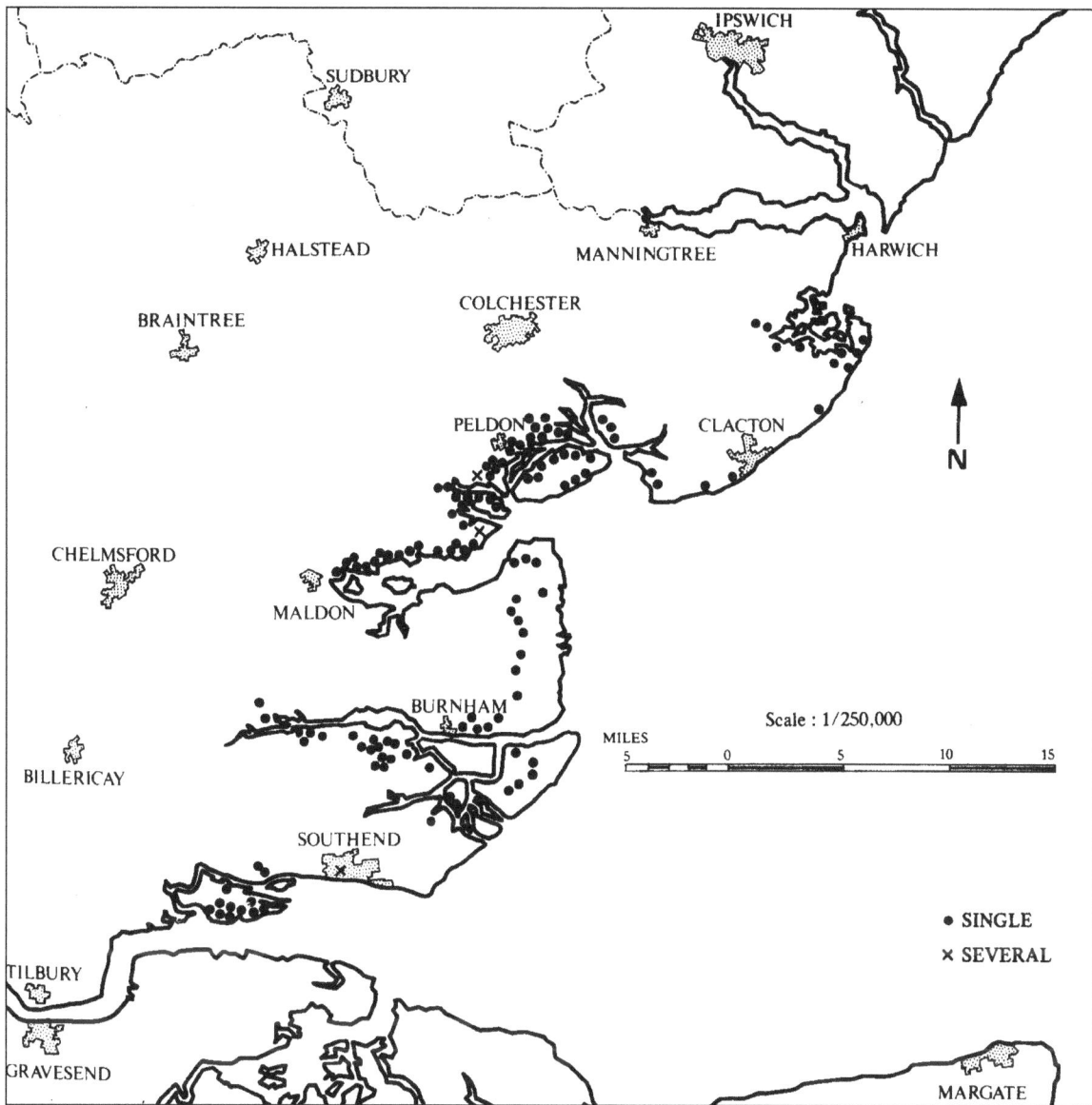

Fig. 30 Map showing the distribution of the Red Hills of Essex as known in 1975 (de Brisay, 1975) (*Courtesy of Colchester Archaeological Group*)

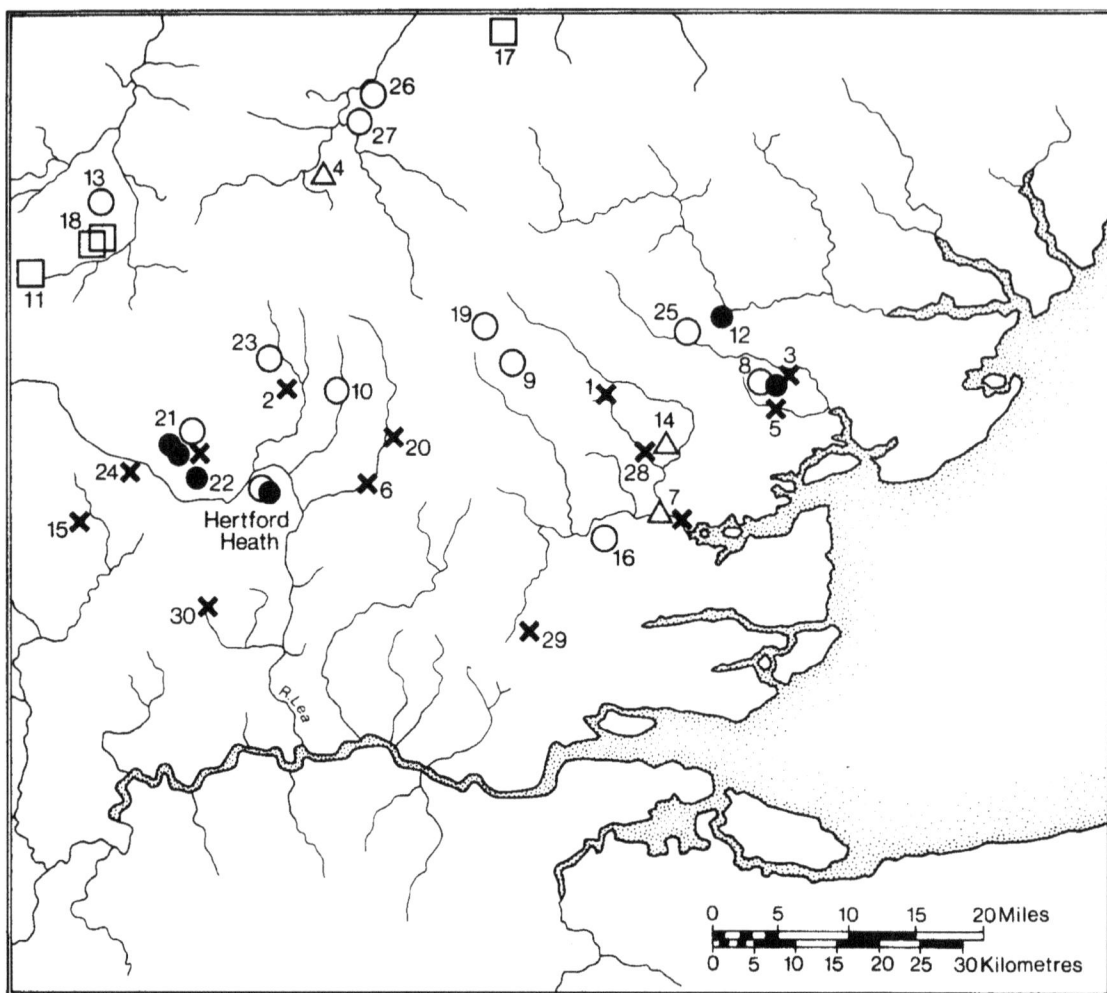

Fig. 31 Map showing the location of some late Iron Age burials and settlements in south-east England (Hüssen, 1983)

● Welwyn-type with Dressel 1B amphorae ○ possible Welwyn-type graves with Dressel 1/1B amphorae □ Welwyn-type graves with other amphorae △ possible Welwyn-type graves with other amphorae ✕ major Late La Tène settlements

1 Braintree; **2** Braughing; **3** Colchester (Camulodunum, Sheepen); **4** Foxton; **5** Gosbecks; **6** Harlow; **7** Heybridge; **8** Lexden; **9** Lindsell; **10** Little Hadham; **11** Maulden Moor; **12** Mount Bures; **13** Old Warden; **14** Rivenhall; **15** St. Albans (Verulamium, Prae Wood); **16** Sandon; **17** Snailwell; **18** Stanfordbury; **19** Thaxted; **20** Wallbury; **21** Welwyn; **22** Welwyn Garden City; **23** Westmill; **24** Wheathampstead; **25** White Colne; **26** Cambridge; **27** Trumpington; **28** Witham; **29** Billericay; **30** Hadley Wood

62

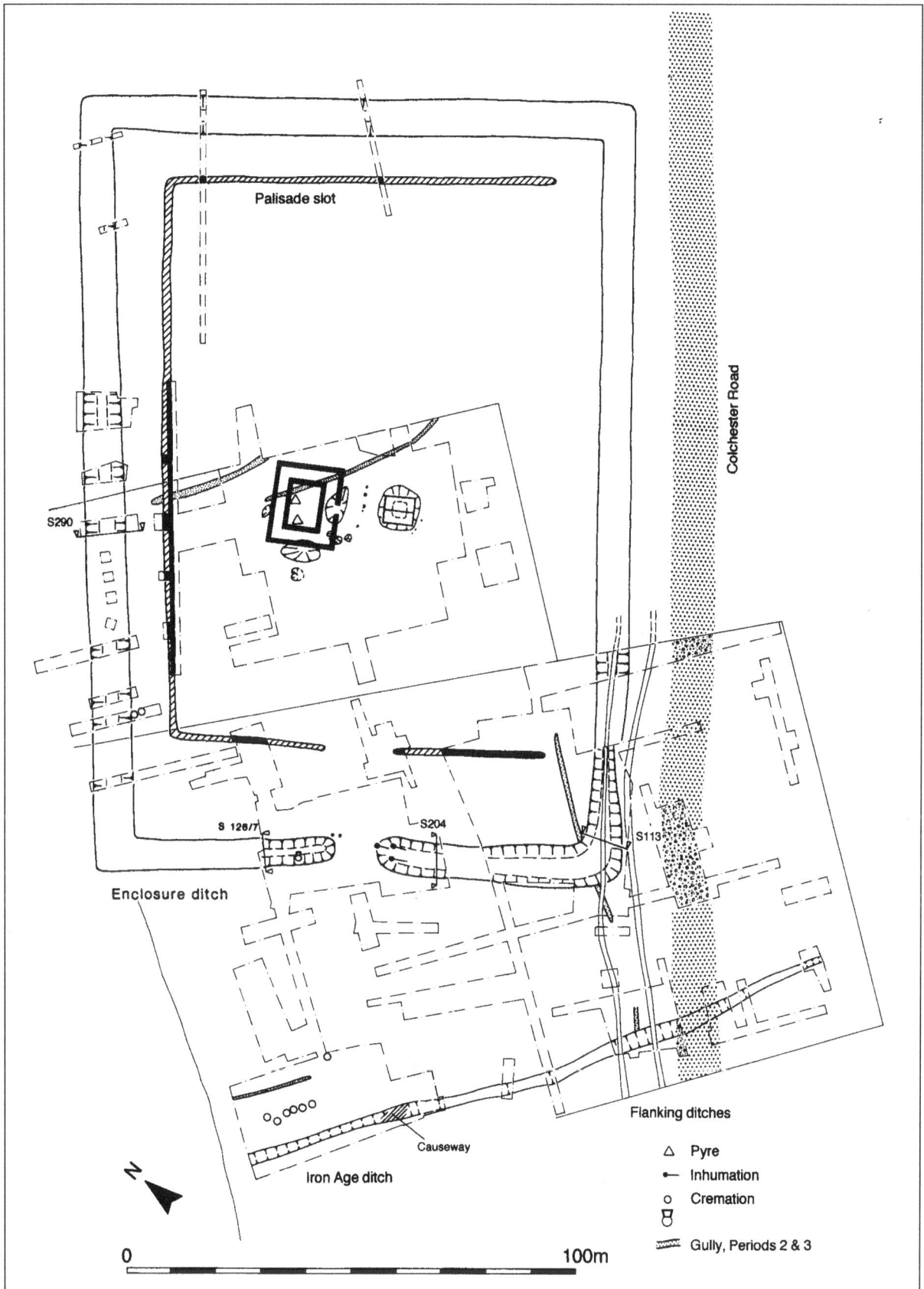

Labels in figure:

Palisade slot

Colchester Road

S290

S 126/7

S204

S113

Enclosure ditch

Flanking ditches

Causeway

Iron Age ditch

N

△ Pyre
•— Inhumation
○ Cremation
⊟ [cremation vessel symbol]
▨ Gully, Periods 2 & 3

0   100m

Fig. 32   The ceremonial enclosure showing the main features and the excavated areas at Folly Lane, St. Albans (Niblett, 1999: 15)

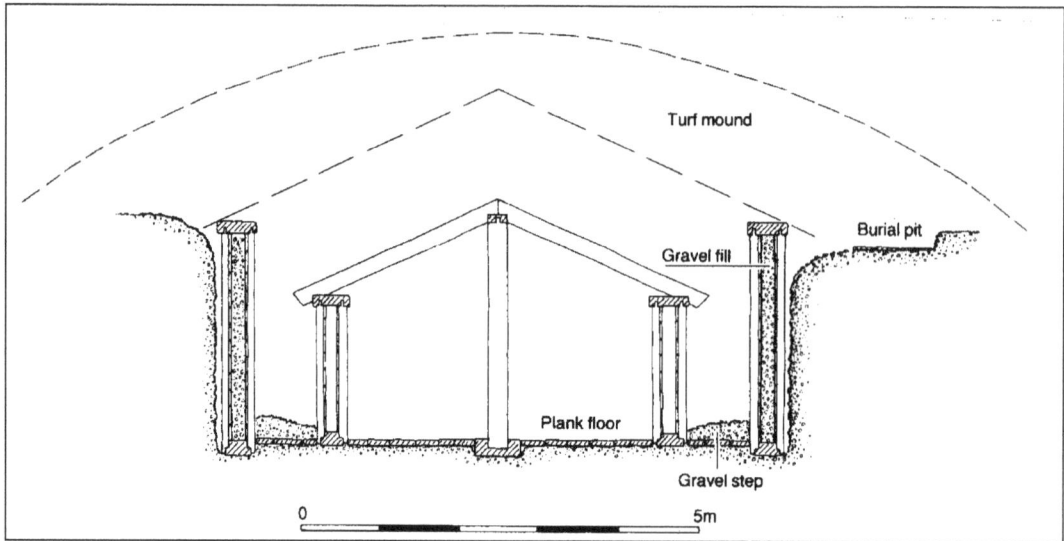

Fig. 33   Diagrammatic section of the funerary shaft, burial pit and turf stack at Folly Lane, St Albans (Niblett, 1999: 44)

Fig. 34   Distribution of amphora burials in Roman Britain (Callender, 1965)

Fig. 35 Graves marked by amphorae at the Isola Sacra necropolis north of Ostia (Photograph: Leonard von Matt, Toynbee, 1971; plate 18)

Fig. 36 Map showing the distribution of burials with wine amphorae, those with bronze vessels and those with both.

△ Bronze Vessel
✕ Others
■ Wine Amphorae & Bronze Vessel
○ Wine Amphorae

65

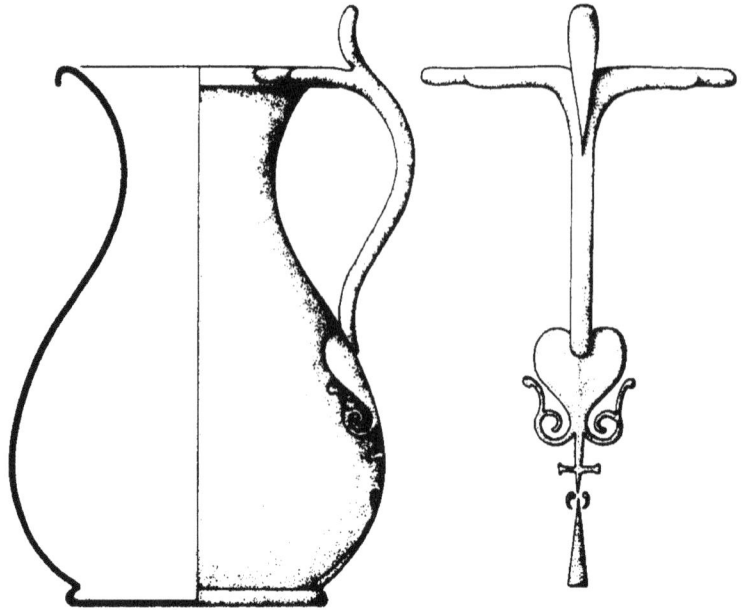

Fig. 37 The bronze vessel from Kjaerumgaard after which this series is named (Eggers 122; Boube, 1991: 39)

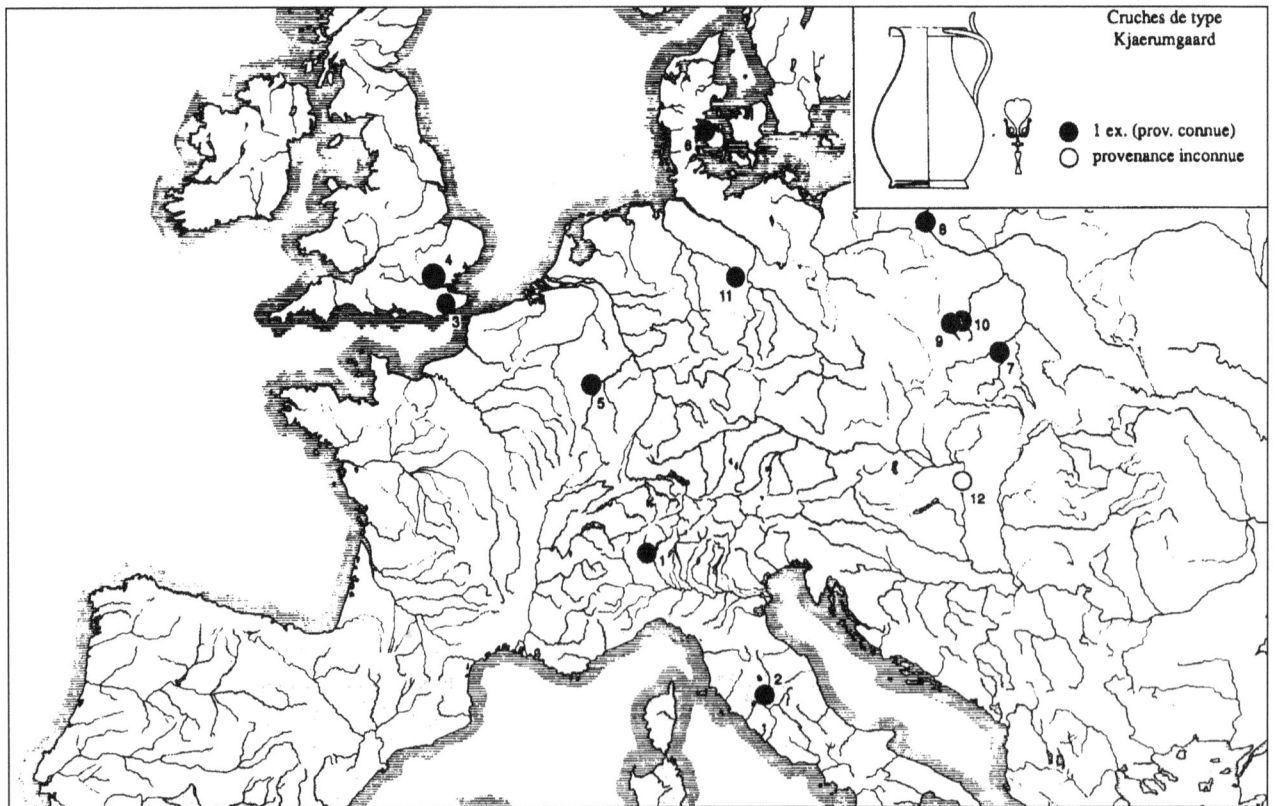

Fig. 38 The distribution of Kjaerumgaard type jugs (Boube, 1991: 37)

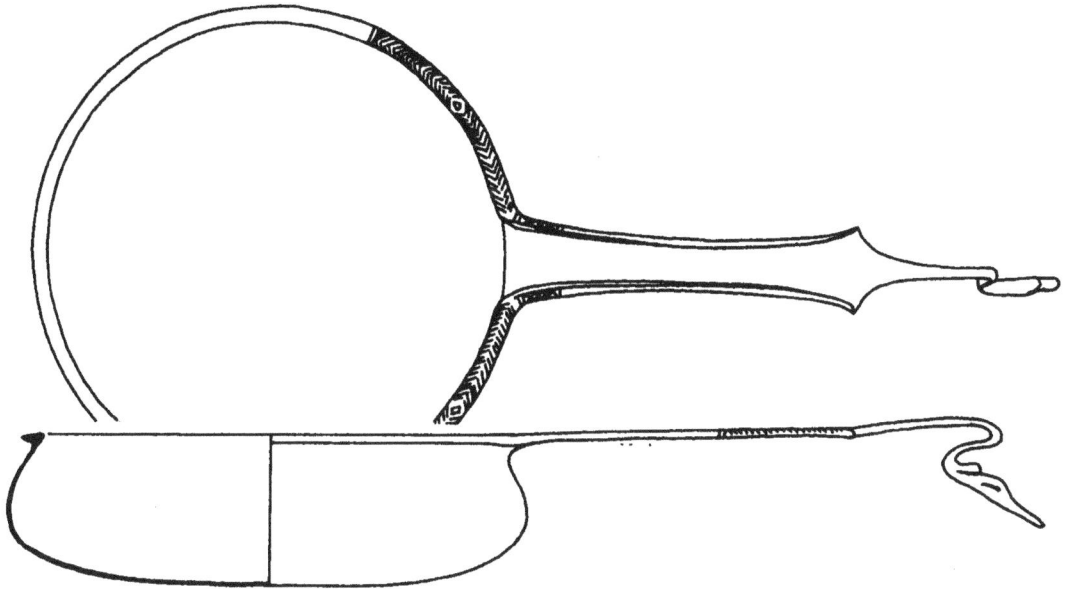

Fig. 39 Aylesford type patera from the cemetery at Ornavasso, S. Bernardo, tomb 161 (Eggers 130; Feugère & de Marinis, 1991: after Graue, 1974)

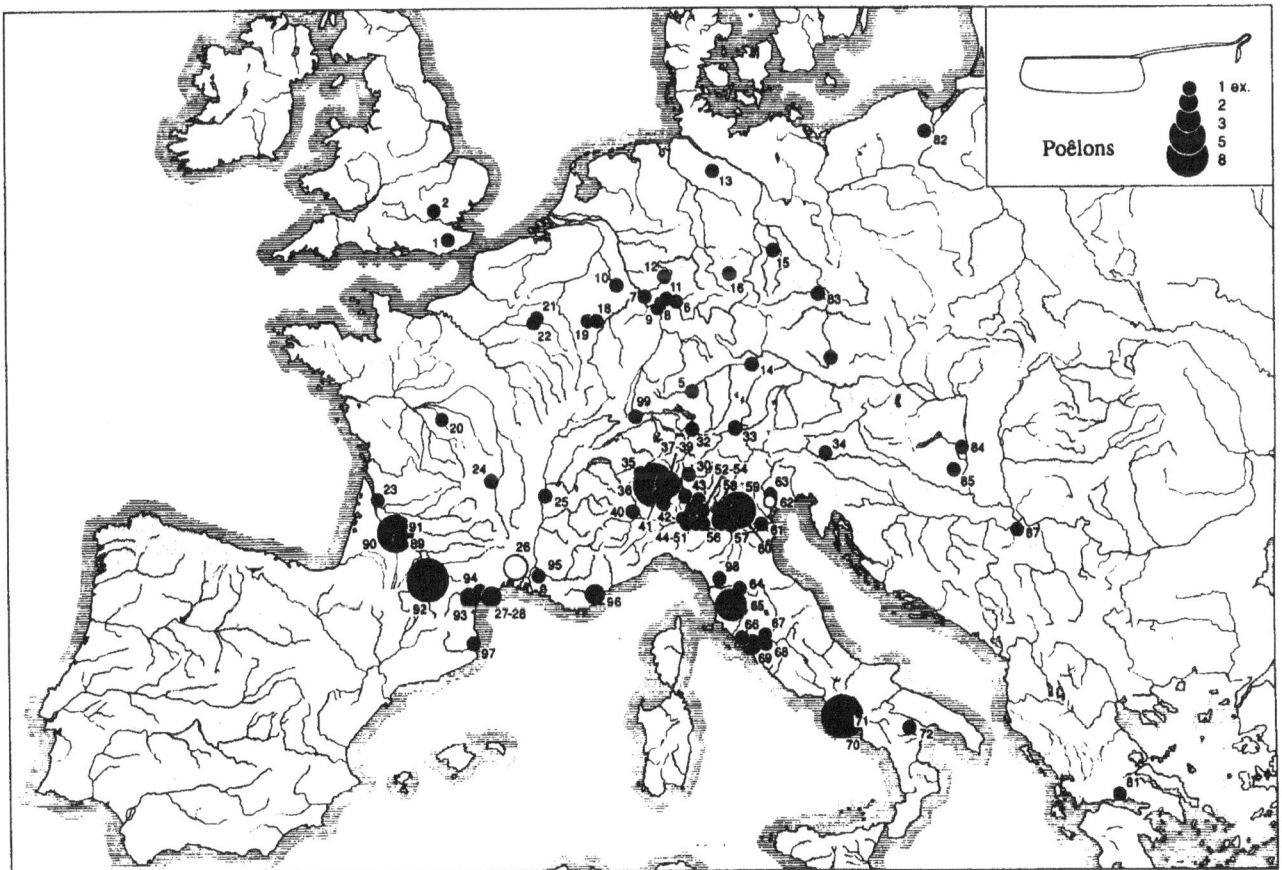

Fig. 40 Map showing distribution of Aylesford type paterae (Feugère & de Marinis, 1991: 105

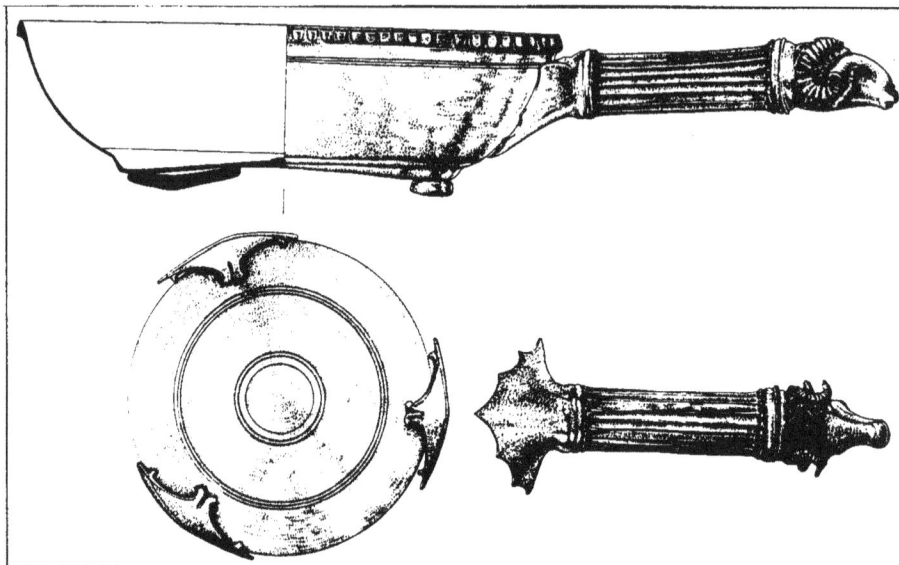

Fig. 41 Patera No.2, with details, from Antran (Eggers 155) (Pautreau, 1999)

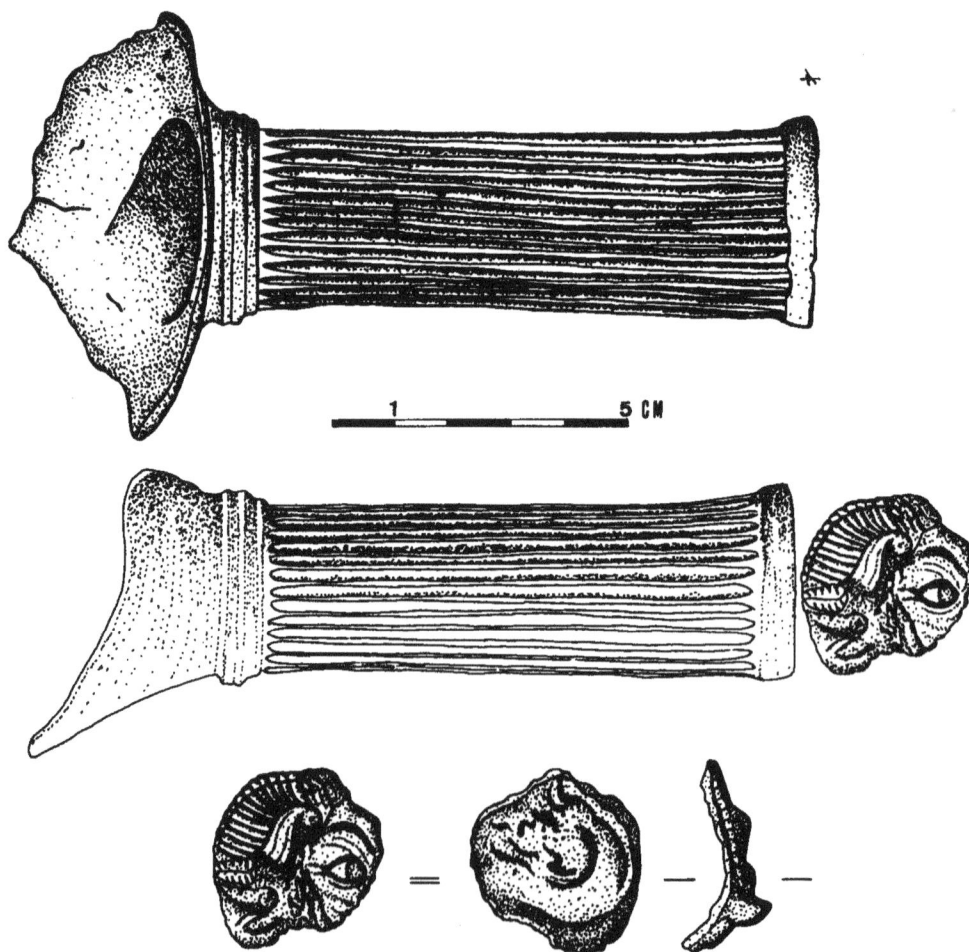

Fig. 42 Handle of Patera No. 56 with details, from Fléré-la-Rivière (Ferdière & Villard, 1993)

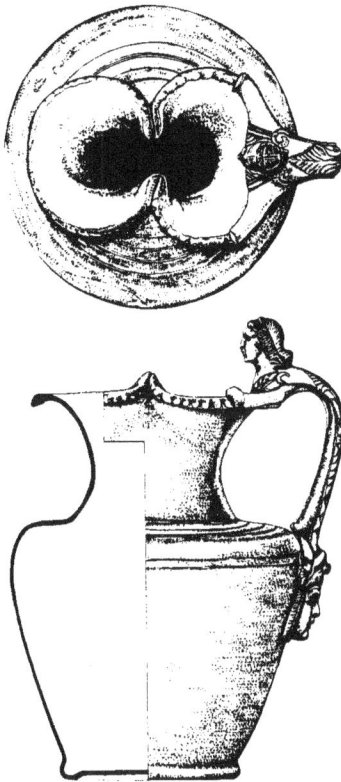

Fig. 43 Bronze oenochoe No. 1, with details, from Antran (Eggers 124) (Pautreau, 1999)

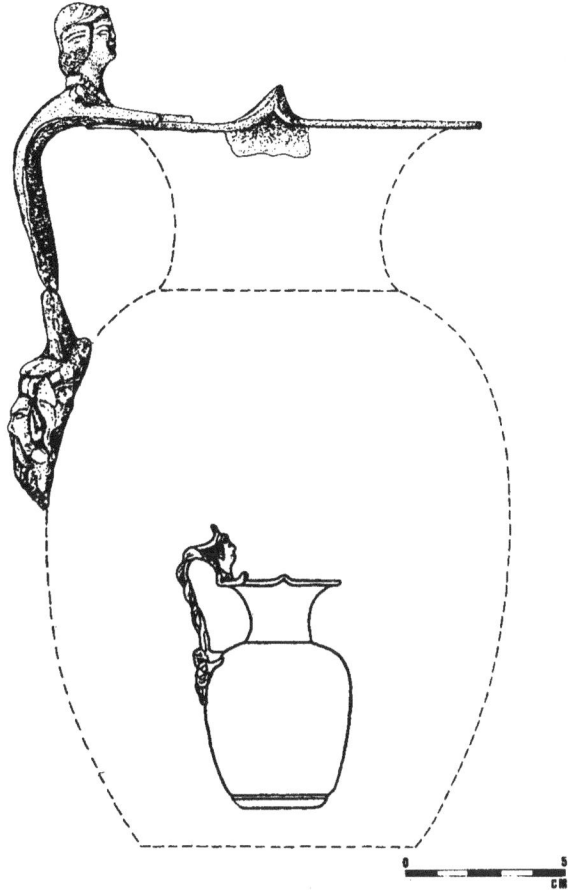

Fig. 44 Bronze oenochoe No. 53 from Fléré-la-Rivière (Ferdière & Villard, 1993)

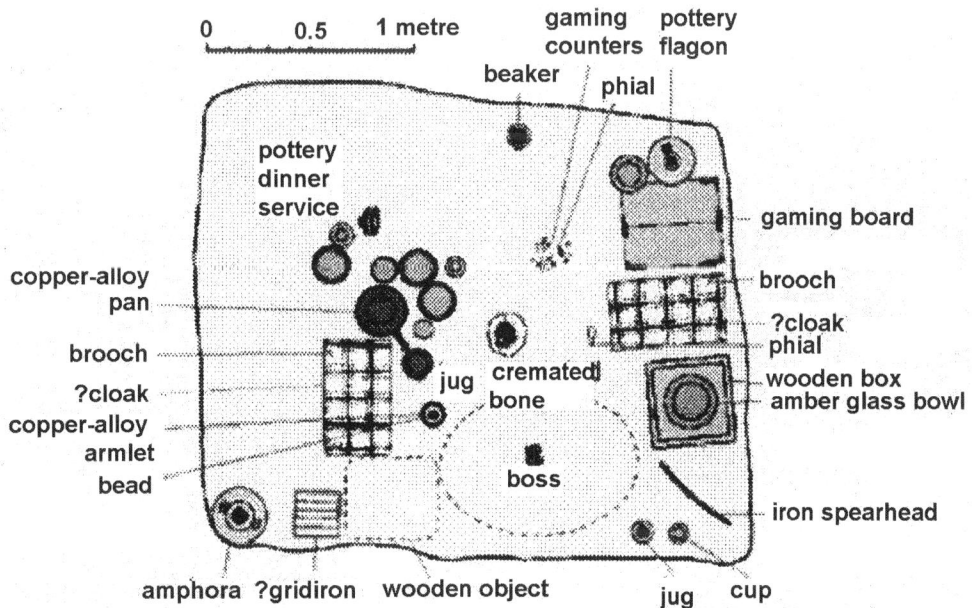

Fig. 45 Plan of the grave goods laid out in the Warrior's Grave, Stanway (CAT Web Site)

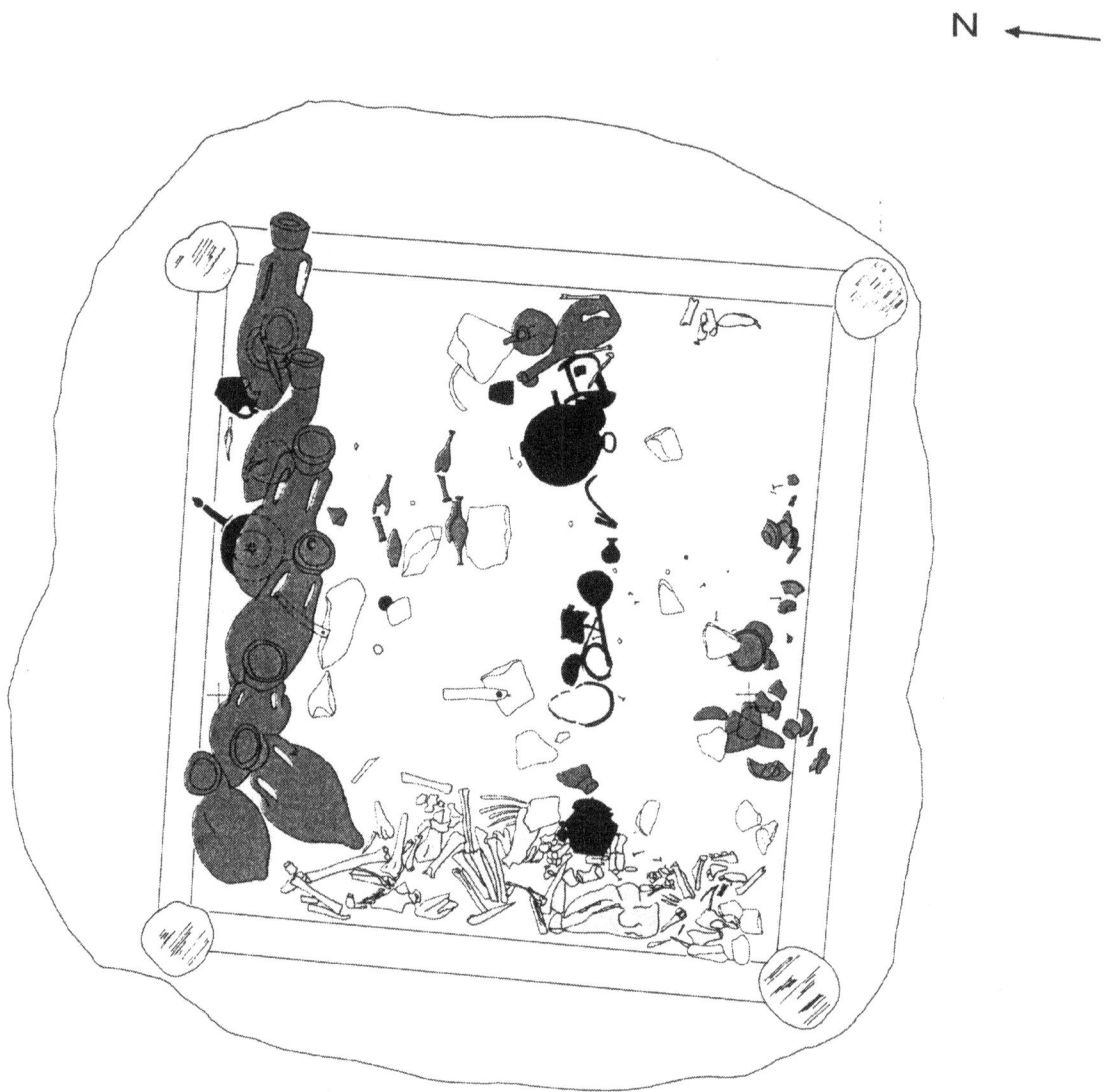

Fig. 46 Plan of the deposition of objects in the grave at Antran (Pautreau, 1999: 27)

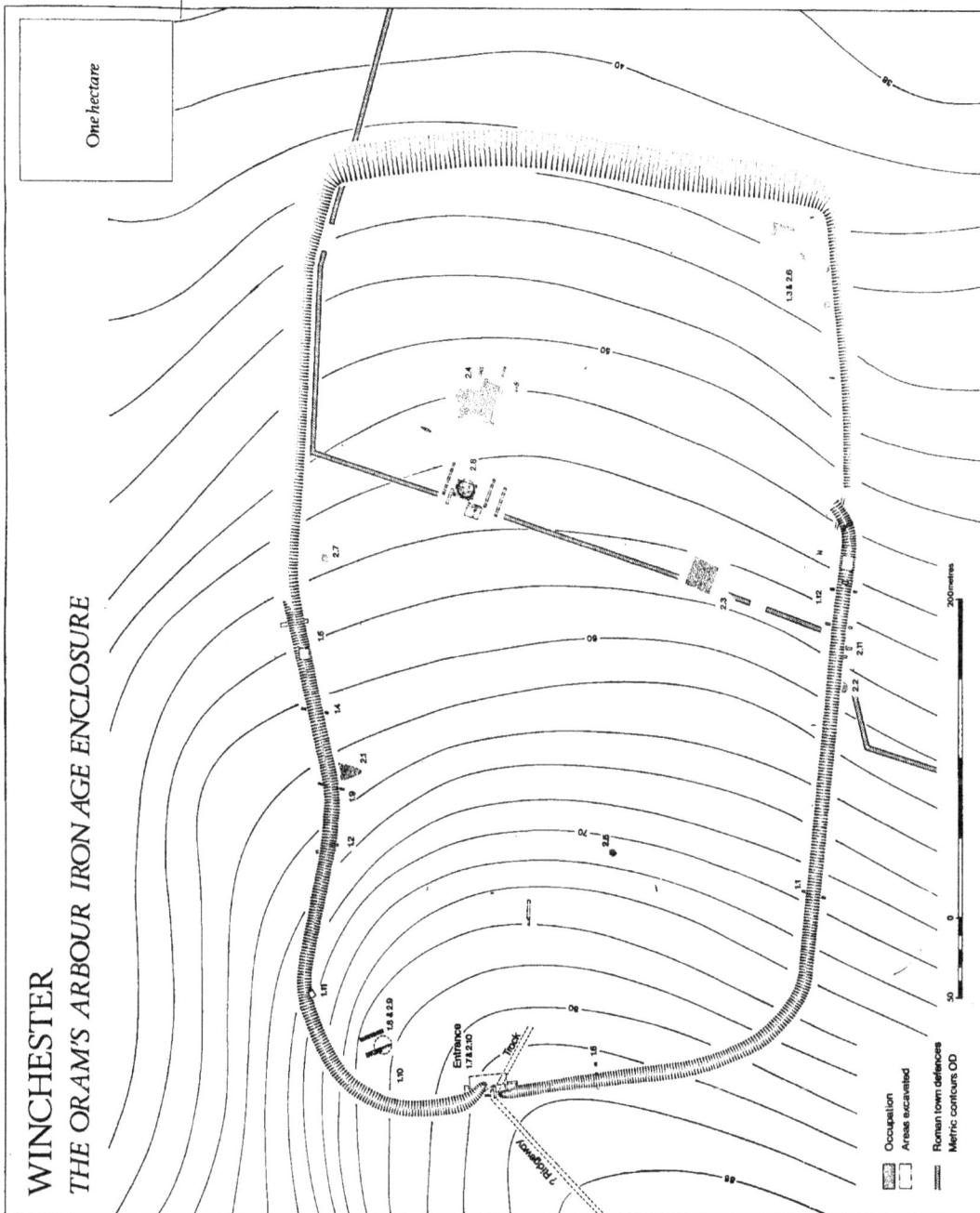

Fig. 47 Pre-Roman Iron Age features at Oram's Arbour, Winchester in 1975 (Biddle, 1975) (*Courtesy of Society of Antiquaries of London*)

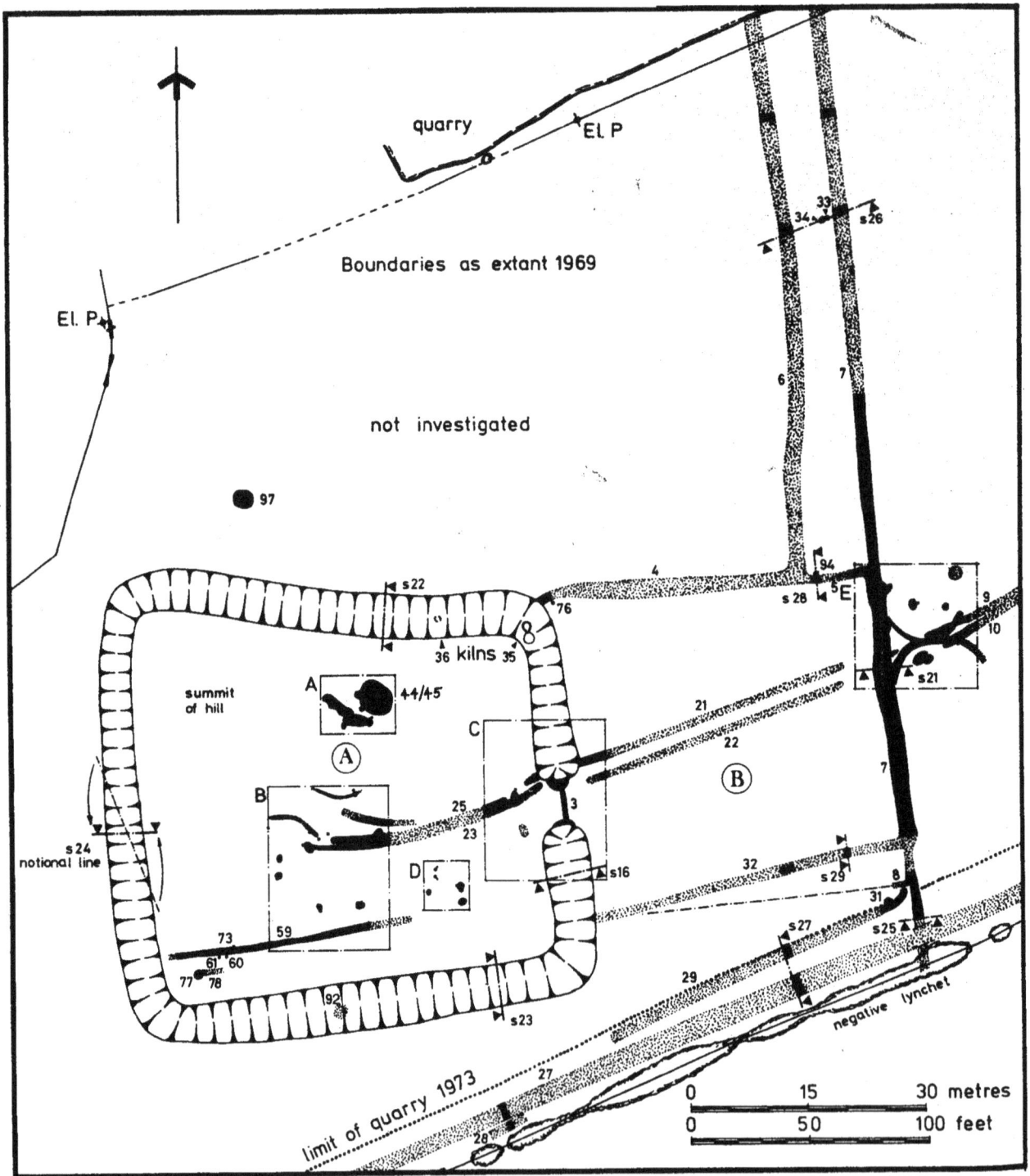

Fig. 48 Site plan of the main area investigated at Gun Hill; the positions of the main sections (S16 and S21-29) and the areas examined in detail (Areas A-E) are marked. Features plotted from crop marks are stippled (Drury & Rodwell, 1973)

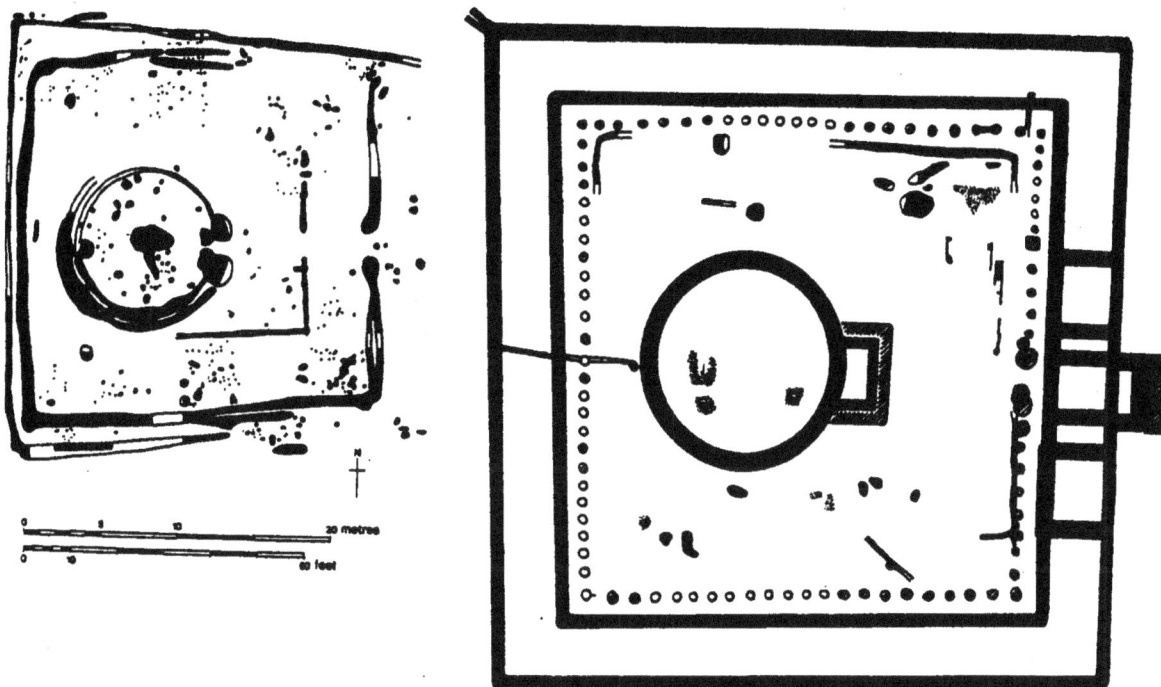

Fig. 49 Plans of the Iron Age (left) and Romano-British temples at Hayling Island (King & Soffe, 1994) (*Courtesy of Hampshire Field Club and Archaeological Society*)

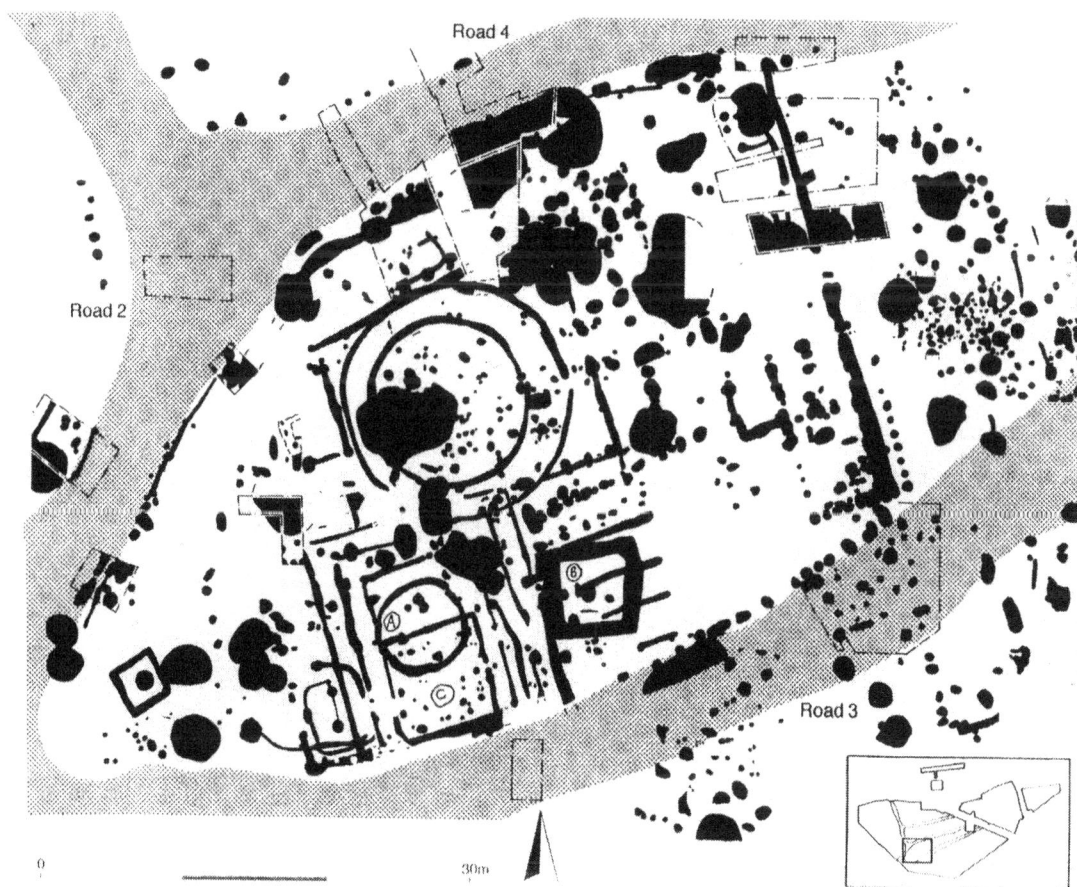

Fig. 50 Plan of the temple precinct remains at Heybridge (Atkinson & Preston, 1998)

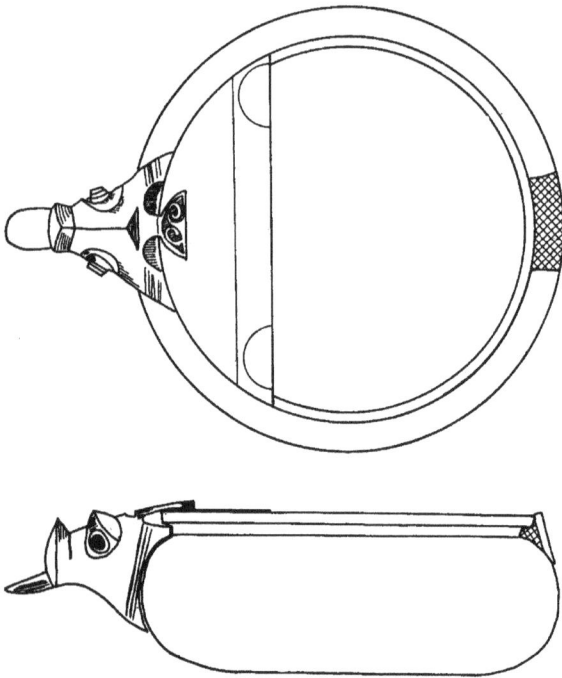

Fig. 51 Reconstruction of the fish-head spout from Felmersham
(Kennett, 1970) (*Courtesy of Society of Antiquaries of London*)

Fig. 52 Wooden pale decorated with metal
sheet (No. 10) from Antran
(Pautreau, 1999)

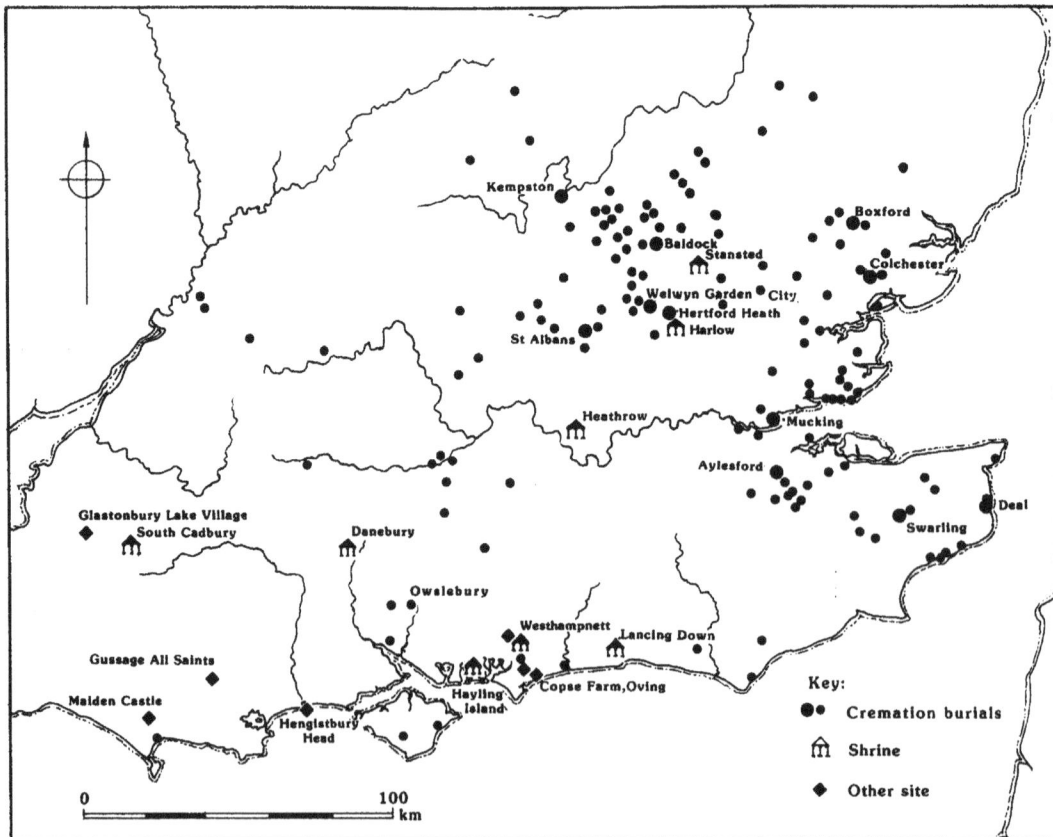

Fig. 53 Distribution of late Iron Age cremation burials and selected shrines and settlements in southern
England (Fitzpatrick, 1997)

74

TABLES

Ariadne - princess of Crete, daughter of Minos and Pasiphae, wife of Bacchus	*felines* - most often panther or leopard, constant companion, also tigers and lions	*Priapus* - ithyphallic and anthropomorphic, adopted into Roman pantheon, sometimes seen with fruit-filled apron, sickle and hunting-dog.
Bacchus - portrayed as a child, young man or earlier (until the 4th century BC) as a bearded man	*Liber* - Italian predecessor and alter ego of Bacchus/Dionysos	*"Risus"* - free-standing bust of male infant (may be hybrid of Celtic and Roman imagery)
cantharus - two-handled drinking cup, stock attribute	*Lycurgus* - king of Thrace or Arabia, mortal enemy of Bacchus/Dionysos	*ram* - particularly severed head, also bull, goat and fawn (or stag) but none of these animals are exclusively Bacchic.
combination - modern term meaning composite figure of two or more human or animal heads or members used in intaglio design	*Maenads* - female devotees of Bacchus/Dionysos	*Satyrs* - Bacchus' half-human, half-beast companions
Cupids and *genii* - distinguished by having at least one Bacchic attribute	*Marsyas* - a double pipe playing Satyr	*Semele* - mother of Bacchus
Dionysos - Greek precursor to Roman Bacchus	*masks* - Bacchus sometimes represented by a mask	*Silenus* - Bacchus' tutor usually depicted as an elderly and bearded Satyr. Sometimes depicted with ram's and goat's horns.
dolphins and *hippocamps* - transported mortal souls to Paradise	*Methe* - female personification of drunkenness	*theatrical masks/motifs* - Bacchus was patron of the theatre
Indian elephant - specifically associated with Bacchus, also a symbol of eternity,	*Pan* - Graeco-Roman god associated with nature and fertility represented as a man with horns, ears and legs of a goat with pipes.	*thyrsus* - slender wooden rod terminating with a pine-cone, the Bacchic wand
Faunus - patron of woods, fields and flocks, particularly cattle	*parrot* - symbol of eternity, also represented Bacchus' travels in India	

Table 2 List of chief Dionysiac subjects found in art from Roman Britain (after Hutchinson, 1986: 123)

NAME: GR	DATE	AMPHORAE	BRONZE DRINKING EQUIPMENT
Flere-la-Riviere (Indre) CL: 507,7x2224,1	20-1 AD	13 Pascual 1 amphorae lined up in 2 rows against the W wall.	Oenochoe handle and mouthpiece, feminine head at top, terminates in image of Silenus. Eggers 124 Patera handle terminates in ram's head Eggers 150. Ladle. Strainer. 2 basins. 2 big bowls, one with ring handles with palmette. Bronze vases. 2 pales with bronze fittings.
Chatillon-sur-Indre, "le Moulin de la Grange" (Indre) CL: 511,600x2222,950?	2nd quarter – middle of 1st century BC	7 amphorae, Dr.1A or Pascual 1.	3 bronze vessels, oenochoe - decorated handle Kelheim type Eggers 122. Patera, swans neck handle (Eggers 130), Flat bronze bowl.
Dun-sur-Auron "Place de la Tournoise" (Cher) CL: 517,875x2209,475	50-20 BC	Not clear from report. Pottery preserved min. 30 vases, mostly broken, 4 in tact.	3 identical colanders. No drawings LTIII 2BC (Tiberius).
Berry-Bouy "Fontillet" (Cher) CL: 598,750x2235,100	20-1 BC	10 amphorae Dr. 1B, upright placed along N side; contained ashes and wood charcoal.	Drinking set placed on coffin. Oenochoe-handle terminates top in female head, base is bearded male cf. Eggers 124 Patera-handle animal at termination, tubular form. Bronze basin, flat with ring handles. Simpulum-strainer/ladle.
Menestreau-en-Villette "Le Cyran" (Loiret) CL: 576,050x2303,925	1st quarter of 1st century AD	1 amphora broken when the superstructure collapse. Contained "un residu graisseux analogue a un depot d'huile". Dr. 1B Fabric Italian production.	Ceramic drinking set placed at the head.
Primelles "Le Grand Malleray" (Cher) CL: 588,725x2213,950	10 BC - AD 10	4 amphorae placed 1 in each corner. 3 Pascual 1; 1 Dressel 20 or Haltern 70. Amphorae contained bird bones.	Ceramic drinking set.
Neuvy-Pailloux "Villesaison" (Indre) CL: 565,850x2212,875	AD 40-50 NB Tomb painted AD 30; grave goods deposited AD 50 cf. Folly Lane	57 amphorae. Pascual 1 - mid 1AD. Empty? Garum stamp; Tarraconaise stamp. Piled up on two levels in E corner of tomb.	Oenochoe - trefoil jug; handle found in different place. Top of handle feminine figure, base broken. cf. Fontillet, Berry-Bouy, Fléré, Eggers 124. Bronze amphora (other egs. Campania, 1st half of 1AD - this type known from Bulgaria/Thrace)

Table 3 Amphorae and bronze drinking equipment found in the graves of the Fléré-la-Rivière Group (after Ferdière & Villard, 1993)

Complete	With neck broken	Fragmented	Container
Snailwell	Dorton	Lexden C	Aston Clinton
Stanfordbury A	Mount Bures	Folly Lane	Foxton
Stanfordbury B		Elms Farm, Heybridge	Lindsell
Welwyn A(?)		Warrior's Grave, Stanway	Lord's Bridge
Welwyn B(?)		(Holborough, Snodland)	
Baldock (?)			
Welwyn Garden City (?)			
Hertford Heath(?)			

Table 4 The treatment of wine amphorae in graves.

<u>NB</u> The chamber at Welwyn Garden City contained five amphorae, of which one was complete, the remaining four may have had their necks broken. The amphorae at Hertford Heath may also represent both conditions - one complete Dressel 1B plus one neck and rim found nearby?

Buckets found in burials			
With wine amphora	**Without wine amphora**	**As cremation vessel**	**Hoard/Isolated Find**
Welwyn Garden City	Welshpool (D)	Grave 13 Petham, Swarling (I)	Santon Downham
Welwyn Grave A	Alkham (D)	Grave Y, Aylesford (D)	Felmersham Bridge (D)
Hertford Heath	Harpenden (D)	Grave X, Aylesford	Harpenden
Baldock, The Tene (D)		Marlborough	
Old Warden, Quints Hill (I)		Hurstbourne Tarrant	
Great Chesterford (?) (D)			

Table 5 Buckets in late Iron Age burials and hoards (D) Elaborately decorated (I) Iron bands/handle

APPENDIX 1 Dressel 1/ Dressel 2-4 findspots

NO.	NAME OF SITE	COUNTY	NGR	AMPHORAE	CONTEXT
1	Bouldner Beach	Isle of Wight	SZ 380 900	Dr.1A	Beach
2	Thorness Beach	Isle of Wight	SZ 460 940	Dr.1	Beach
3	Aston Clinton	Buckinghamshire	SP 874 123	Dr.2-4	Burial
4	Colchester, Lexden C	Essex	TL 975 247	Dr.1B, Dr.2-4	Burial
5	Dorton	Buckinghamshire	SP 684 133	Dr.1B, Dr.2-4	Burial
6	Folly Lane, St. Albans	Hertfordshire	TL 150 070	Dr.2-4	Burial
7	Great Chesterford	Essex	TL 500 420	Dr.1B	Burial
8	Hertford Heath	Hertfordshire	TL 352 113	Dr.1B	Burial
9	Heybridge, Elms Farm	Essex	TL 847 082	Dr.1	Burial
10	Little Amwell, Hertford Heath	Hertfordshire	TL 252 113	Dr.1B	Burial
11	Mount Bures	Essex	TL 907 322	Dr.1B, Dr.2-4	Burial
12	Old Warden, Quints Hill	Bedfordshire	TL 135 446	Dr.1	Burial
13	Stanfordbury	Hertfordshire	TL 148 412	Dr.1	Burial
14	Welwyn	Hertfordshire	TL 232 159	Dr.1B	Burial
15	Welwyn Garden City, Grave 1	Hertfordshire	TL 254 131	Dr.1B	Burial
16	Arreton Down	Isle of Wight	SZ 540 870	Dr.1A	Burial?
17	Baldock, The Tene	Hertfordshire	TL 248 335	Dr.1A	Burial?
18	Cambridge, Jesus Lane	Cambridgeshire	TL 450 588	Dr.1B	Burial?
19	Colchester, Park Field, Lexden	Essex	TL 970 250	Dr.1B	Burial?
20	Colchester, St. Clare Road	Essex	TL 990 250	Dr.1B	Burial?
21	Datchworth	Hertfordshire	TL 265 185	Dr. 1B	Burial?
22	Great Canfield	Essex	TL 590 180	Dr.1B	Burial?
23	Hadham Ford	Hertfordshire	TL 430 220	Dr.1B	Burial?
24	Heybridge	Essex	TL 850 080	Dr.2-4	Burial?
25	Kedington	Suffolk	TL 700 460	Dr.2-4	Burial?
26	Lindsell	Essex	TL 645 270	Dr.1B	Burial?
27	Little Hadham	Hertfordshire	TL 440 227	Dr.1	Burial?
28	Newchurch	Isle of Wight	SZ 550 850	Dr.1	Burial?
29	Newport Goods Yard	Isle of Wight	SZ 490 880	Dr.1?	Burial?
30	Sandon	Essex	TL 740 040	Dr.1B	Burial?
31	Stanmore, Stanmore Park	Middlesex	TQ 153 923	Dr.2-4	Burial?
32	Stratford St. Mary	Essex	TM 050 340	Dr.2-4	Burial?
34	Thaxted	Essex	TL 610 300	Dr.1B	Burial?
35	Trumpington, Dam Hill	Cambridgeshire	TL 440 540	Dr.1	Burial?
36	Welwyn, Mardlebury	Hertfordshire	TL 253 175	Dr.1B	Burial?
37	Westmill	Hertfordshire	TL 380 271	Dr.1	Burial?
38	Woburn	Bedfordshire	SP 960 330	Dr.2-4	Burial?
39	Hengistbury Head	Hampshire	SZ 170 900	Dr.1A, Dr.1B, Dr.2-4	Entrepot
40	Grange Chine	Isle of Wight	SZ 410 810	Dr.1A	Industrial
41	Heybridge, Osea Road	Essex	TL 850 080	Dr.1B	Industrial
42	South Benfleet, Benfleet Creek	Essex	TQ 770 860	Dr.1	Industrial
43	Brockley Hill	Middlesex	TQ 174 939	Dr.2-4	Pottery
44	Fishbourne Beach	Isle of Wight	SZ 550 920	Dr.1A	Quay
45	Yarmouth Roads	Isle of Wight	SZ 350 890	Dr.1A	Quay?
46	Eastern Solent	Isle of Wight	SZ 500 980	Dr.1	Sea floor
47	Ryde Middle Bank	Isle of Wight	SZ 590 920	Dr.1A	Sea floor
48	Western Solent	Isle of Wight	SZ 500 980	Dr.1A	Sea floor
49	Atherfield Point	Isle of Wight	SZ 450 790	Dr.1,Dr.2-4	Settlement
50	Bagendon	Gloucestershire	SP 010 060	Dr.2-4	Settlement
51	Bigberry, near Canterbury	Kent	TR 110 570	Dr.1	Settlement
52	Braughing, Gatesbury Track	Hertfordshire	TL 390 240	Dr.1, Dr.1A, Dr.1B, Dr.2-4	Settlement
53	Braughing, Puckeridge, Station Road	Hertfordshire	TL 380 230	Dr.1, Dr.2-4	Settlement
54	Braughing-Gatesbury	Hertfordshire	TL 390 230	Dr.1	Settlement
55	Briddlesford Lodge	Isle of Wight	SZ 530 390	Dr.1	Settlement
56	Burgh by Woodbridge	Suffolk	TM 230 510	Dr.1	Settlement

APPENDIX 1 Dressel 1/ Dressel 2-4 findspots

57	Canterbury	Kent	TR 140 570	Dr.1, Dr.1B, Dr.2-4	Settlement
58	Canvey Island, Thorney Bay	Essex	TQ 780 830	Dr.1	Settlement
59	Carn Euny	Cornwall	SW 400 280	Dr.1A	Settlement
60	Castle Dore	Cornwall	SX 100 540	Dr.1	Settlement
61	Chichester	Sussex	SU 860 040	Dr.1B	Settlement
62	Colchester, Sheepen	Essex	TL 987 257	Dr.1B, Dr.2-4	Settlement
63	Colchester, St. Mary's Rectory	Essex	TL 990 250	Dr.1B	Settlement
64	Corrals Coal Yard, Newport	Isle of Wight	SZ 490 880	Dr.1	Settlement
65	Cyprus Road, Newport	Isle of Wight	SZ 490 880	Dr.2-4	Settlement
66	Danbury, Twitty Free Camp	Essex	TL 790 060	Dr.1	Settlement
67	Danebury	Hampshire	SU 320 360	Dr.1A	Settlement
68	Doreshill Farm	Isle of Wight	SZ 530 890	Dr.1	Settlement
69	Elmsworth Farm	Isle of Wight	SZ 440 920	Dr.2-4	Settlement
70	Freshwater Bay	Isle of Wight	SZ 340 850	Dr.1	Settlement
71	Gestingthorpe	Essex	TL 810 380	Dr.1B	Settlement
72	Gun Hill, West Tilbury	Essex	TL 800 070	Dr.1	Settlement
73	Gussage All Saints	Dorset	SU 000 100	Dr.1A	Settlement
74	Havenstreet	Isle of Wight	SZ 560 900	Dr.1A, Dr.1B, Dr.2-4	Settlement
75	Heybridge	Essex	TL 850 080	Dr.1; Dr.1B	Settlement
76	Heybridge, Elms Farm	Essex	TL 847 082	Dr.1A, Dr.1B, Dr.2-4	Settlement
77	Horndean	Hampshire	SU 700 130	Dr.1	Settlement
78	Kelvedon	Essex	TL 860 180	Dr.1B	Settlement
79	King Harry Lane, Prae Wood, St. Albans	Hertfordshire	TL 150 070	Dr.1	Settlement
80	Knighton	Isle of Wight	SZ 560 860	Dr.1A	Settlement
81	Lake Farm, Wimborne	Dorset	SY 990 980	Dr.1A	Settlement
82	Maiden Castle	Dorset	SY 660 880	Dr.1, Dr.2-4	Settlement
83	Medina Road, Newport	Isle of Wight	SZ 490 880	Dr.1	Settlement
84	Mount Joy Hill, Newport	Isle of Wight	SZ 490 880	Dr.1A	Settlement
85	Mucking, Linford Quarry	Essex	TQ 680 810	Dr.1	Settlement
86	Owlesbury	Hampshire	SU 510 230	Dr.1	Settlement
87	Puckeridge, Station Road F4 LIA pit	Hertfordshire	TL 380 230	Dr.1	Settlement
88	Quarr Beach	Isle of Wight	SZ 560 920	Dr.1	Settlement
89	Quarry Wood, Loose, near Maidstone	Kent	TQ 710 510	Dr.1	Settlement
90	Redcliff Battery, Sandown	Isle of Wight	SZ 623 854	Dr.1	Settlement
91	Rochester	Kent	TQ 720 680	Dr.1B	Settlement
92	Shalfleet Manor Farm	Isle of Wight	SZ 410 890	Dr.1	Settlement
93	Silchester	Hampshire	SU 620 620	Dr.1, Dr.1B	Settlement
94	South Weald Camp	Essex	TQ 579 946	Dr.1B	Settlement
95	Thorley	Isle of Wight	SZ 370 880	Dr.2-4	Settlement
96	Tolleshunt D'Arcy, Hill Farm	Essex	TL 920 110	Dr.1B	Settlement
97	Trethurgy	Cornwall	SX 030 550	Dr.1	Settlement
98	Undercliff Gardens, Newport	Isle of Wight	SZ 490 880	Dr.2-4	Settlement
99	Watton-at-Stone, Broomhall Farm	Hertfordshire	TL 290 190	Dr.1B	Settlement
100	Whale Chine	Isle of Wight	SZ 460 780	Dr.1	Settlement
101	Winchester	Hampshire	SU 480 290	Dr.1, Dr.1B	Settlement
102	Brading Villa	Isle of Wight	SZ 600 860	Dr.1A	Settlement?
103	Cirencester	Gloucestershire	SP 020 010	Dr.1	Settlement?
104	Gills Cliff, Ventnor	Isle of Wight	SZ 560 770	Dr.1A	Settlement?
105	Green Island, Poole Harbour	Dorset	SZ 000 860	Dr.1	Settlement?
106	Mersley Farm	Isle of Wight	SZ 550 860	Dr.1A	Settlement?
107	St. Catherines Point	Isle of Wight	SZ 490 750	Dr.1A	Settlement?
108	Yaverland	Isle of Wight	SZ 610 850	Dr.1	Settlement?
109	Hayling Island	Hampshire	SU 720 010	Dr.1A	Temple
110	Bowcombe	Isle of Wight	SZ 460 860	Dr.1A	Unknown
111	Combley Farm	Isle of Wight	SZ 540 880	Dr.1	Unknown
112	Green Island, Poole Harbour	Dorset	SZ 000 860	Dr.1A	Unknown

APPENDIX 1 Dressel 1/ Dressel 2-4 findspots

113	Hamworthy, Poole	Dorset	SY 990 910	Dr.1, Dr.1A, Dr.2-4	Unknown
114	Highstead	Kent	TR 210 660	Dr.1B	Unknown
115	Maldon	Essex	TL 840 070	Dr.1B	Unknown
116	Stansted Airport, Catering Site	Essex	TL 530 220	Dr.1	Unknown
117	Worcester	Worcestershire	SO 850 550	Dr.1	Unknown
118	Weymouth Bay	Dorset	SY 690 800	Dr.1B	Wreck?

APPENDIX 2

The adoption of wine in Britain?

What little is written of the British tribes' adoption of wine is more indirect and related to events that took place post-Conquest.

> "Even the barbarians now learned to indulge pleasant vices, and the interruption of civil war afforded a sound excuse for his [Trebellius Maximus, Governor of Britain] inaction". (Tacitus *Agricola* 16)

This passage refers to events post AD 60 in Britain. Tacitus writes again of Agricola's policy after AD 70 when he began to unite the British tribes by "prosecution of sound measures" for example, assisting communities, erecting temples, market places and houses.

> "Moreover he began to train the sons of chieftains in a liberal education, and to give a preference to the native talents of the Briton as against the trained abilities of the Gaul .... and little by little the Britons went astray into alluring vices: to the promenade, the bath, the well-appointed dinner table. The simple natives gave the name of 'culture' to this factor of their slavery." (Tacitus *Agricola* 21)

The "vices" to which Tacitus refers reflect in many ways the pinnacle of what many Romans considered to be the outward signs of a civilised society. In this passage however, the writer may be more concerned with the cynicism of Roman foreign policy.

Cassius Dio writes of Boudica's dramatic speech to her men raising their spirits ready for battle. Amongst other insults she describes the adversary as follows:

> "But these are not the only respects in which they [the Romans] are vastly inferior to us: there is also the fact that they cannot bear up under hunger, thirst, cold, or heat, as we can. They require shade and covering, they require kneaded bread and wine and oil, and if any of these things fail them, they perish; for us, on the other hand, any grass or root serves as bread, the juice of any plant as oil, any water as wine, any tree as a house." (Cassius Dio[1], *Roman History* LXII.5.5)

She goes on to say:

> "... if indeed, we ought to term those people men who bathe in warm water, eat artificial dainties, drink unmixed wine, anoint themselves with myrrh, sleep on soft couches etc." (Cassius Dio, *Roman History* LXII.6.4)

The speech presumably describes Dio's own imagined ideas on how the Romans would have appeared to Boudica and contradicts earlier writers by describing drinking 'unmixed wine' as a Roman failing. However, imagination aside, as with the Suebi and Nervii tribes on the continent, there is absent archaeological evidence to suggest that the Iceni did not adopt wine (see **Fig. 3** and **4** for the distribution of Dressel 1 and Dressel 2-4 which are clearly absent from Icenian territory) (Sealey, 1997:6).

There is no mention of the adoption of wine or specific wine drinking practices either ritual or secular, for example, banquets.

---

[1] Cassius Dio was a Greek historian writing 150 years after the revolt in c. AD 210-30; Tacitus also gives a short account of the Icenian rebellion in *Agricola*, 16.

GAZETTEER 1 Dressel 1 and other wine amphorae findspots (where no bronze vessels present)

NAME OF SITE	COUNTY	NMR	CONTEXT	DATE	LOCATION	AMPHORAE	REFERENCES
Maulden Moor	Bedfordshire	TL 060 380	Burial	LIA (Lexden phase?)		Amphora, "several urns of different forms and sizes containing bones and ashes and fragments of red pottery enriched with figures and other ornaments" (Lysons & Lysons, 1913) All lost.	Whimster, R. (1981); Lysons & Lysons (1913) p.24; Peacock, D.P.S. (1971)
Old Warden (uncertain location)	Bedfordshire	c. TL 11 44 Uncertain location.	Burial?	Lexden phase? Early 1st century AD	Found during cutting of Warden railway tunnel in 1850s.	1, type unknown, now lost.	NMR TL 14 SW 7; Whimster, R. (1981)
Woburn	Bedfordshire	c. SP 96 33	Burial?	1st century AD?		2 amphorae found independently - both Greco-Roman (Koan) type (post-16BC). Now lost. Grounds of Woburn Abbey in 1800 and 1833.	Whimster, R. (1981); Peacock, D.P.S. (1971)
Aspley Heath, Wavendon Heath	Buckinghamshire	c. SP 92 34	Burial?		Found ante-1813 on Wavendon Heath (2 miles to E of Woburn Park)	Southern Spanish amphora Dr. 9-11, with one handle missing, now lost.	Whimster, R. (1981); Peacock, D.P.S. (1971); Lysons & Lysons (1813)
Aston Clinton	Buckinghamshire	c. SP 874 123	Burial	1st century AD?	Found full of ashes and burnt wood at depth of 2' in 1877, close to junction of Lower Icknield and Akeman Ways.	Amphora Dr.2-4 (not Dr.1). Top missing. Found buried on its side about 2' from surface. Filled with burnt wood and earth (poss. from S. Spain).	Smith, R.A. (1911-12); Farley, M. (1983); Whimster, R. (1981)
Dorton	Buckinghamshire	SP 6845 1331 (SP 61 SE 21)	Burial	Early 1st AD? Mirror - heirloom, amphora reused?	Found during gaspipe construction June 1977. RB pottery plus 9 struck flints, scraper etc. found also. No Roman roads recorded in vicinity. 500m to SW Roman potsherds SP61SE18. No satellite burials. Situated in prominent position but no trace of mound.	Parts of 3 amphorae; necks removed from all 3 and in 2 cases deliberately smoothed; Dr. 1B, one unknown; Dr. 2-4. Lay flat on bottom of grave. Resin present. Possible symbolic use of amphorae to represent wine - reused?	Farley, M. (1983); Whimster, R. (1981); Fitzpatrick, A. (1985)
Cambridge, Jesus Lane	Cambridgeshire	c. TL 450 588	Burial?			1 Dr.1B (body only)	Whimster, R. (1981); Fitzpatrick, A. (1985); Fox, C. (1923); Peacock, D.P.S. (1971)
Foxton	Cambridgeshire	TL 41 48	Burial			Amphora (as cremation vessel)	Rodwell, W. (1976); Whimster, R. (1981); Fox, 1923

GAZETTEER 1 Dressel 1 and other wine amphorae findspots (where no bronze vessels present)

Site	County	Grid ref	Context		Description	Amphora (as cremation vessel)	References
Lord's Bridge	Cambridgeshire	TL 395 545	Burial?		1818 discovery amphora covered with stone slab, black terra cotta vase full of human bone, 2 smaller red terra cotta vases with ladles - Birchall's Type III bowl? may be from same deposit.		Clarke, E.D. (1821)in Fox (1923), p.61; Whimster, R. (1981)
Trumpington, Dam Hill	Cambridgeshire	c. TL 44 54	Burial?		Fox also cites 'barrel-urn' from parish, associations unknown.	1 Dr.1 (probably 1B, body only, rim and neck missing)	Whimster, R. (1981); Fitzpatrick, A. (1985); Fox, C. (1923)
Carn Euny	Cornwall	SW 40 28	Settlement		Site of a souterrain and settlement. Amphora found in Courtyard House IV/V - topsoil.	2 Dr. 1A (base fragment [52] and body sherd [765] of a different fabric).	Christie, .M.L. (1978); Fitzpatrick, A. (1985)
Castle Dore	Cornwall	SX 10 54	Hillfort		Hillfort	1+ Dr.1 or Dr.2-4	Fitzpatrick, A. (1985)
St. Mawgan in Pydar	Cornwall		Settlement	early 1st century AD	Huts dating before mid-1st century AD (Hut A) to first half of 2nd century AD.	Camulodunum 185 (Haltern 70), handle	Peacock, D.P.S. (1971)
Trethurgy	Cornwall	SX 03 55	Settlement		Site of rural settlement.	1 Dr.1 sp. (poss. 1A)	Fitzpatrick, A. (1985)
Green Island, Poole Harbour	Dorset	SZ 00 86	Settlement?		Site of rural settlement.	1 Dr.1 sp. (poss. 1A)	Fitzpatrick, A. (1985)
Green Island, Poole Harbour	Dorset	SZ 00 86	Uncertain			Dr.1A, rim sherd and body sherd.	Peacock, D.P.S. (1971)
Gussage All Saints	Dorset	SU 00 10	Settlement		Site of rural settlement.	4+ Dr.1 (of which 2 probably 1A)	Fitzpatrick, A. (1985)
Hamworthy, Poole	Dorset	SY 99 91	Uncertain		Uncertain context.	3+ Dr.1 (one of which probably 1A)	Fitzpatrick, A. (1985)
Hamworthy, Poole	Dorset	SY 99 91	Uncertain		Unstratified assemblage of IA and Roman pottery	Dr.1, 6 handle fragments; Koan type, 3 bases, 1 shoulder, 1 handle fragment; globular amphorae, 4 rim sherds, 5 handles, all unstamped.	Peacock, D.P.S. (1971)
Jordon Hill, Weymouth	Dorset	SY 699 823	Settlement/Temple?	IA	Cemetery 300 yds N and NE of Romano-Celtic temple occupied 1st/2nd centuries AD, poss. pre-Conquest origins. Near burials several floors of white clay, clay-lined hollows containing ashes, animal bones and sherds.	RB settlement (SY78SW1) Pebbled floor observed 1935 with fragment of amphora. Substantial stone building excavated in 1969, 3rd-4th C. pottery sealed beneath rubble and mortar floor.	NMR SY 68 SE 14; Whimster, R. (1981)
Lake Farm, Wimborne	Dorset	SY 99 98	Settlement		Settlement	2 Dr.1A (one rim)	Fitzpatrick, A. (1985); Potter, T.W. & Trow, S.D. (1988) p.119
Maiden Castle	Dorset	SY 66 88	Hillfort		Hillfort.	2+ (probably Dr.1)	Fitzpatrick, A. (1985)

GAZETTEER 1 Dressel 1 and other wine amphorae findspots (where no bronze vessels present)

Site	County	Grid ref	Site type	Date	Context	Amphorae	References
Maiden Castle	Dorset	SY 66 88	Hillfort	50/30 BC-mid 2nd century AD	Hillfort,	Fragments of Dr.1 body (Wheeler's excavations). 5 fragments of Dr.2-4 (minimum 3 vessels), all body sherds except junction between handle and body (5355). 8 fragments of Dr.1/Pascual 1 (minimum 4 vessels).	Peacock, D.P.S. (1971); Sharples, N.M. (1991)
Weymouth Bay	Dorset	SY 69 80	Wreck?		Dredged from mid-channel.	Dr.1B	Smith, R.A. (1911)
Weymouth Bay	Dorset	SY 69 80	Wreck?		Wreck, dredged from sea bed.	Dr.1B (stamped P)	Peacock, D.P.S. (1971); Fitzpatrick, A. (1985)
Canewdon	Essex	TQ 89 94	Burial?		3 tall amphorae found and smashed in gravel digging. Probably part of a grave group.	3 vessels, type unknown.	Rodwell, W. (1976)
Canewdon Wick	Essex	TQ 911 948	Burial?		Gravel quarrying. OS also reports single cremation burial at Canewdon Wick.	3 broken amphorae (probably not Dr.1) broken during gravelling in parish in 1938.	Whimster, R. (1981); Rodwell, W. (1976) p.322
Canvey Island, Thorney Bay	Essex	TQ 78 83	Settlement		Settlement site destroyed by the sea.	1 Dr.1 or Dr.2-4 (at least one sherd)	Rodwell, W. (1976); Fitzpatrick, A. (1985)
Colchester, North Hill	Essex	TL 99 25	Roman colonia	AD 49-60	Insulae 10 and 18 of the colonia of Colchester established AD 49.	Rim and neck of amphora Cam.185B (Haltern 70?, wine vessel). Breaks in the three pieces worn, probably lying as rubbish before incorporated into floors. 2 graffiti - amphora handle 'P' (unstratified); amphora base 'VII' (unstratified).	
Colchester, Park Field, Lexden	Essex	TL 97 25	Burial?		From a grave in the Belgic cemetery? Rodwell, 1976	1 Dr.1B with rim missing.	Smith, R.A. (1911-12); Fitzpatrick, A. (1985); Rodwell, W. (1976); Peacock, D.P.S. (1971)
Colchester, Sheepen	Essex	TL 987 257	Oppidum	Site first occupied first decade AD (first coins Cunobelinus).	Oppidum	Hawkes & Hull - 46 Dr.1B sherds of which 12 survive. 1 Pascual 1. Sealey - Dr.1 min. 5 vessels, 5 Dr.1B (2 rim sherds; 3 handles) analysed lt.; min. 44 Dr.2-4 vessels - Italian origin, Catalan origin (2 body sherds), rim and spike, poss. Baetican origin.	Fitzpatrick, A. (1985); Peacock, D.P.S. (1971); Sealey, P.R. (1985)
Colchester, St. Clare Road	Essex	TL 99 25	Burial?		Burial?	1 Dr.1B (rim only, stamped HI[E])	Rodwell, W. (1976); Fitzpatrick, A. (1985); Peacock, D.P.S. (1971)

GAZETTEER 1 Dressel 1 and other wine amphorae findspots (where no bronze vessels present)

Site	County	Grid ref.	Site type	Date	Context/Description	Amphora	References
Colchester, St. Mary's Rectory	Essex	TL 99 25	Settlement		Insula 25 of the *Colonia* at Colchester. From Boudiccan burnt daub, Phase 2 ie. post-Boudiccan destruction level, AD 60, pre-rebuilding. <u>Not</u> in the Claudian pits found under Insula 25 and Insula 10 (see North Hill).	Rim of amphora, Cal.1. (Dr.1B); rim of amphora Cal.2.	Dunnett, B.R.K. (1971); Fitzpatrick, A. (1985)
Colne Engaine	Essex	TL 85 30	Burial			Dr. 20 (associated with cremation)	Whimster, R. (1981)
Danbury, Twitty Free Camp	Essex	TL 79 06	Settlement		Rural enclosed settlement site.	Dr.1 or Dr.2-4 (single sherd)	Fitzpatrick, A. (1985)
Earl's Colne	Essex	c. TL 86 28	Burial			Dr. 20 (as cremation vessel?)	Whimster, R. (1981)
Gestingthorpe	Essex	TL 81 38	Settlement		Rural settlement	1 Dr.1B	Fitzpatrick, A. (1985)
Great Canfield	Essex	TL 59 18	Burial?		Burial?	1 Dr.1B	Fitzpatrick, A. (1985)
Gun Hill, West Tilbury	Essex	TL 80 07	Settlement?/ ditch /salt production	mid-1st century AD	Rural settlement. Dr.1 sherd unstratified in ditch F1 south, of sub-rectangular enclosure A, dominating summit of hill with single south-east facing entrance. Ditch V-shaped. Ditch partly deliberately refilled. Evidence for gateway formed by 2 posts.	1 Dr.1 or Dr.2-4 (single body sherd c.30cm diameter, wall thickness 2.2cm, Peacock's Fabric 1, likely to be Dr.1)	Rodwell, W.J. & Drury, P.J. (1973); Rodwell, W. (1976); Fitzpatrick, A. (1985)
Heybridge	Essex	c. TL 85 08	Settlement		Probably derived from extensive IA and Roman settlement of Heybridge.	1 Dr.1B (rim)	Rodwell, W. (1976); Fitzpatrick, A. (1985)
Heybridge	Essex	c. TL 85 08	Burial?		TL80NE2 Cremation cemetery? (Spindle amphora and large urn); TL80NE46 Cremation cemetery; TL80NE1 Cremation cemetery; IA/Roman? all beside Roman road RRX107C.	Koan (Dr. 2-4) and southern Spanish amphorae from parish from further burials? Dr.1B (stamped PE)	Peacock, D.P.S. (1971); Rodwell, W. (1976); Whimster, R. (1981)
Heybridge, Elms Farm	Essex	TL 847 082	Burial	LIA/Romano-British	Settlement on R. Chelmber, opposite bank to Maldon.	1 Dr.1 from Area W in burial.	Essex County Council (1999)
Heybridge, Elms Farm	Essex	TL 847 082	Pyre site	LIA/Romano-British	Settlement on R. Chelmer, opposite bank to Maldon.	Pit 15417 (Group M36, Area M) assemblage of broken and burnt amphorae (at least 3 Dr.1B vessels) with frags. of other pottery; remains of pyre, stake holes holding a structure? Whole site 42 Dr.1 amphorae. Dr.1 sherds in under-pyre 'vents'.	Atkinson, M. & Preston, S. (1999)

85

GAZETTEER 1 Dressel 1 and other wine amphorae findspots (where no bronze vessels present)

Site	County	Grid ref	Type	Period	Notes	Vessels	References
Heybridge, Osea Road	Essex	TL 85 08	Salt production site		Salt production site.	1 Dr.1B (rim), unstratified.	De Brisay, K. (1975); Rodwell, W. (1976); Fitzpatrick, A. (1985)
Kelvedon	Essex	TL 86 18	Settlement	LIA/Romano-British	LIA settlement succeeded by small Roman town (*Canonium*). Briquetage recorded here (Rodwell, 1979)	1 Dr.1B (rim) Rodwell, K. 1972: 4-7 Dr.1B Eddy, 1982 including fragments of two handles and a trimmed down spike with a hole drilled vertically through the tip. May have been used as a weight. Contexts of all sherds not stated.	Rodwell, K.A. (1972); Rodwell, W. (1976); Eddy, M.R. (1982); Fitzpatrick, A. (1985)
Lindsell	Essex	c. TL 645 270	Burial		Found 1782 amphora associated with a cremation which may also have contained a Pascual 1.	Dr. 1B (body only); possibly Pascual 1 (spike only) and Dr.20 (handle only) associated?	Rodwell, W. (1976); Whimster, R. (1981); Fitzpatrick, A. (1985); Peacock, D.P.S. (1971)
Lofts Farm, Heybridge	Essex	TL 8508	Settlement	IA	Excavations 2km from Heybridge, Paul N. Brown, unpubl.	Dr.1 body sherd	Sealey, P. in Craven, P. (1998)
Maldon	Essex	TL 84 07				1 Dr.1B rim with traces of pitch (stamped PE)	Peacock, D.P.S. (1971)
Marks Tey	Essex	c. TL 91 23	Burial		Found during construction of flyover for A12.	Group of unidentified amphorae, possibly Dr. 1.	Rodwell, W. Essex Arch. Hist. 8 (1976) p.250-51; Whimster, R. (1981); Fitzpatrick, A. (1985)
Mount Bures	Essex	TL 907 322 (TL 93 SW 6)	Burial	post-10BC, late pre-Claudian conquest or early conquest.	Discovered 1849 near Mount Bures. No trace of excavation now. TL 90753215 cropmarks excavated at Middle Field, 4 IA ditches (pottery 40BC - 60AD).	5 amphorae (1 Dr.1B (possibly Dr.2-4); 4 Dr. 9-11). Supported by iron fire dogs. Varying reports - 6 amphorae? Only body of Dr.1B, neck and handles removed.	Smith, R.A. (1911-12); Whimster, R. (1981); Fitzpatrick, A. (1985); Peacock, D.P.S. (1971)
Mucking, Linford Quarry	Essex	TQ 68 81	Settlement; salt production site		Rural settlement; briquetage recorded at Mucking (Rodwell, 1979).	1 Dr.1 sp. (burnt handle fragment)	Rodwell, W. (1976); Fitzpatrick, A. (1985); Antiquaries Journal, 57
Rivenhall, Rivenhall End	Essex	c. TL 83 16	Burial?		Found standing upright 1936 - other Aylesford burials reported in vicinity in 19th century	Spanish amphora	Rodwell, W. (1976); Whimster, R. (1981)
Sampford	Essex		Burial		Burial	1 Dr.1B (with rim missing)	Fitzpatrick, A. (1985); Peacock, D.P.S. (1971); Fox, C. (1923)
Sandon	Essex	c. TL 74 04	Burial?		Pair of Dr.1B found in gravel digging.	2 Dr.1B	Rodwell, W. (1976); Whimster, R. (1981); Fitzpatrick, A. (1985)

GAZETTEER 1 Dressel 1 and other wine amphorae findspots (where no bronze vessels present)

Site	County	Grid ref	Site type	Phase	Circumstances	Amphora	Reference
South Benfleet, Benfleet Creek	Essex	TQ 77 86	Salt production site		Salt production site	1 Dr.1 or Dr.2-4 (single sherd)	Rodwell, W. (1976); Fitzpatrick, A. (1985)
South Weald Camp	Essex	TQ 579 946	Hillfort		Sub-circular univallate small hill fort (ditch 3.5m across, 1.5m deep). Dr.1B rim sherd found in Trench B in SW quadrant across rampart. Found in top soil (Context 202) but LIA pottery also found. Poss. assoc. with reinforcement (revetment) later burnt.	Dr.1B rim sherd.	Medleycott, M., Bedwin, O. & Godbold, S. (1995)
Southend, Root's Hall	Essex	TQ 874 868	Burial?		OS records cemetery site.	Southern Spanish amphora from burial within the town? (Rodwell)	Whimster, R. (1981); Rodwell, W. (1976)
Southend-on-Sea, Southbourne Grove	Essex	TQ 87 86	Burial		Burial	Spanish amphora	Rodwell, W. (1976)
Southminster	Essex	TQ 95 99	Burial?		Circumstances of discovery unrecorded.	narrow mouthed globular jar'(?)	Whimster, R. (1981)
Stansted Airport, Catering Site	Essex	TL 53 22				Dr.1	Essex County Council (1999)
Stratford St. Mary	Essex	c. TM 05 34	Burial?			Complete Koan type (Cam. 183C/Dr.2-4)	Rodwell, W. (1976); Whimster, R. (1981); Peacock, D.P.S. (1971)
Thaxted	Essex	c. TL 61 30	Burial?		Not closely provenanced. Referred to as White Colne (Whimster). Found 19th century?	1 Dr.1B (complete), probably found with a Pascual 1	Whimster, R. (1981); Rodwell, W. (1976)
Tolleshunt D'Arcy, Hill Farm	Essex	TL 92 11	Settlement		Rural settlement	1+ Dr.1B	Fitzpatrick, A. (1985)
Wickford	Essex	c. TQ 74 93	Settlement/burial?	Lexden phase?	Minor settlement. Single burial from square pit. Disturbed by a later Roman well. Briquetage recorded at Wickford (Rodwell,1979)	Sherds of Dr.20 in pre-Roman contexts.	Rodwell, W. (1976)
Bagendon	Gloucestershire	SP 01 06	Settlement	c.AD 20-50	Site yielded rich collection of pottery including a few amphorae sherds.	A few amphorae sherds - some unidentified, 2 S. Spanish vessels represented; 1 Italian (Dr.2-4?)	Peacock, D.P.S. (1971)
Cirencester	Gloucestershire	SP 02 01	Settlement?			Dr.1	Fitzpatrick, A. (1985)
Saint Peter Port, Kings Road	Guernsey		Settlement			Dr.1 (possibly 1A)	Fitzpatrick, A. (1985)
Danebury	Hampshire	SU 32 36	Hillfort			6 Dr.1 (3 of which probably 1A)	Fitzpatrick, A. (1985)

GAZETTEER 1 Dressel 1 and other wine amphorae findspots (where no bronze vessels present)

Location	County	Grid ref	Site type	Notes	Amphorae	References
Horndean	Hampshire	SU 70 13	Settlement	Rural settlement	1 Dr.1 sp. shoulder fragment	Fitzpatrick, A. (1985)
Owlesbury	Hampshire	SU 51 23	Settlement	Rural settlement	1 Dr.1 sp. handle fragment	Fitzpatrick, A. (1985); Peacock, D.P.S. (1971)
Silchester	Hampshire	SU 62 62	Oppidum?	Major settlement	Dr.1, Dr.1B	Peacock, D.P.S. (1971); Fitzpatrick, A. (1985)
Winchester	Hampshire	SU 48 29	Settlement?/ ditch /salt production	Oram's Arbour IA sub-rectangular enclosure, over 400m in length. Southern ditch (excavated, where amphorae found) partly deliberately refilled. Entrance W.	1 Dr.1 sp. handle stub from lower filling of ditch (Assize Courts North) + Dr.1B rim amongst 'a few sherds and flakes of Dressel Type 1 amphorae...in Phases III and IV' (of southern ditch of IA enclosure).	Biddle, M. (1975); Fitzpatrick, A. (1985); Peacock, D.P.S. (1971)
Braughing	Hertfordshire	TL 3924	Settlement	Surface finds found east of the Rib.	2 Dr.1	Fitzpatrick, A. (1985)
Braughing	Hertfordshire	c. TL 390 250	Settlement; burial?	Within defended enclosure discovery made in 1799	3 amphorae with pointed ends and "containing ashes"	Whimster, R. (1981)
Braughing-Gatesbury	Hertfordshire	TL 39 23	Settlement	Settlement, near Gatesbury Wood, on east side of Wickham Hill.	1+ Dr.1 (59.97% of 26,096 grams); Dr. 30 (2.27% of 26,096 grams).	Partridge, C. (1981)
Braughing-Skeleton Green	Hertfordshire	TL 39 24	Settlement	Settlement W side of Wickham Hill. Settlement covered 100ha or more.	Dr.1 G40(7); Dr.1/2-4 G7F.5; G22 F.52 (lower fill below (5)); Dr.2-4 several contexts 24.4% of assemblage (mostly fragmented), Dr.1 0.7%, Dr.1/2-4 3% Dr.1 likely to be residual as found in c.25-40 context.	Partridge, C. (1981); Fitzpatrick, A. (1985)
Braughing-Wickham Kennels	Hertfordshire	TL 39 24	Settlement	Settlement	Dr.1 sp.	Fitzpatrick, A. (1985)
Crookhams	Hertfordshire		Settlement; ditch	Rural settlement; amphorae found in a gully during a rescue excavation.	2+ Dr.1 (probably 1B, found in a gully)	Fitzpatrick, A. (1985); Peacock, D.P.S. (1971)
Datchworth	Hertfordshire	c. TL 265 185	Burial?		Dr. 1B	Whimster, R. (1981)
Hadham Ford	Hertfordshire	TL 43 22	Burial?	This find is in the same parish as Little Hadham but is not the same find (Fitzpatrick, 1985).	Dr.1B	Whimster, R. (1981)
King Harry Lane - Prae Wood, St. Albans	Hertfordshire	TL 15 07	Settlement	Found in excavation of KHL adjacent to the Prae Wood oppidum. Not associated with a grave (I.M. Stead)	1 Dr.1 (body only)	Rodwell, W. (1976); Fitzpatrick, A. (1985)
Little Amwell, Hertford Heath	Hertfordshire	TL 252 113	Burial	Isolated.	Dr.1B amphora	Whimster, R. (1981)

88

GAZETTEER 1 Dressel 1 and other wine amphorae findspots (where no bronze vessels present)

Little Hadham	Hertfordshire	c. TL 440 227	Burial?	Found 1886, now lost.	1 Dr. 1 (probably 1B)	Rodwell, W. (1976); Whimster, R. (1981); Fitzpatrick, A. (1985); Peacock, D.P.S. (1971)
Puckeridge, Station Road F4 LIA pit.	Hertfordshire	TL 38 23	Settlement	Part of large LIA settlement at Wickham Hill. F4 = shallow sub-rectangular pit. Bottom layer, fragments of charcoal, 'coarse pottery' (Dr.1?, report does not specify) and sherds of terra rubra butt beaker.	1 handle of Dr. 1	Partridge, C. (1980); Fitzpatrick, A. (1985)
Watton-at-Stone, Broomhall Farm	Hertfordshire	TL 29 19	Settlement	Settlement	1 Dr.1B (stamped VAMP)	Fitzpatrick, A. (1985)
Welwyn Church, 150 yds N of	Hertfordshire	TL 22 16	Burial?	From the cemetery. Indications of fire recorded with finds.	Handle of a large amphora.	Smith 1911-12
Welwyn, Mardlebury	Hertfordshire	TL 253 175	Burial?	Discovered before 1905 in pit measuring 1.8-2.1m x 2.4 x 2.7m.	1+ Dr.1B (?) (body)	Fitzpatrick, A. (1985); Peacock, D.P.S. (1971)
Westmill	Hertfordshire	c. TL 380 271	Burial?	Found in 1729.	3, possibly Dr.1 (B?), now lost.	Whimster, R. (1981); Fitzpatrick, A. (1985); Peacock, D.P.S. (1971)
Atherfield Point	Isle of Wight		Settlement		2 Dr.1	Trott, K. (in preparation, C)
Arreton Down	Isle of Wight	SZ 54 87	Burial?	Fill of an inhumation burial. No 100% sure of context - could be residual (Trott, K. pers.comm.)	Dr.1A	Trott, K. (unpubl.)
Bouldner Beach	Isle of Wight	SZ 38 90	Beach	Washed up on a gravel bank, associated with Gallo-Belgic fine wares.	70+ Dr.1; Dr.1A, single top section	Trott, K. (unpubl.)
Bowcombe Manor Farm	Isle of Wight	SZ 46 86	Settlement?	Bowcombe Roman complex - 1940s excavations - ditch with cremation urns and frags. of Dr.1A sherds. Recent fieldwork - 10+ Dr.1A assoc. with Gallo-Belgic pottery (Trott, pers.comm.)	10+ Dr.1A(?); Dr.1B	Trott, K. (unpubl.)
Brading Villa	Isle of Wight	SZ 60 86	Settlement?	Sherds found in pre-villa layers.	Dr.1A +	Trott, K. (1999)
Briddlesford Lodge	Isle of Wight	SZ 54 88	Settlement		Dr.1	Trott, K. (unpubl.)
Combley Farm	Isle of Wight	SZ 54 88	Settlement?	Buried soil in drainage ditch.	Dr.1 single sherd.	Tomalin, D.J. (forthcoming, A)

GAZETTEER 1 Dressel 1 and other wine amphorae findspots (where no bronze vessels present)

Corrals Coal Yard	Isle of Wight		Settlement?	Within wall matrix of medieval priory.	Dr.1A large body sherd	Whitehead (1996)
Cyprus Road	Isle of Wight		Settlement		2 Dr.2-4	Sherwin (1926)
Doreshill Farm	Isle of Wight		Settlement?		Dr.1	Connell & Trott (forthcoming)
Eastern Solent	Isle of Wight	SZ 50 98	Sea floor		Dr.1 fragments (recovered during fishing?)	Trott, K. (unpubl.)
Elmsworth Farm	Isle of Wight		Settlement		Dr. 2-4	Trott, K. (unpubl.)
Fishbourne Beach	Isle of Wight	SZ 55 92	LIA/Roman quay	Quay (Trott)	Dr.1A handle	Tomalin, D.J. (forthcoming, A)
Freshwater Bay	Isle of Wight	SZ 34 85	Settlement/field scatter?	Several Dr.1A sherds collected from a field scatter. Field overlooking bay on west coast of Isle of Wight.	Dr.1 +	Trott, K. (unpubl.)
Gills Cliff, Ventnor	Isle of Wight	SZ 56 77	Settlement?	Rural settlement? IA roundhouse and associated midden pit.	4 examples of Dr.1A	Fitzpatrick, A. (1985); Benson, G.C. (1954)
Grange Chine	Isle of Wight	SZ 41 81	Salt production	Recovered from 2 LIA coastal salt working floors.	2+ Dr.1A	Trott, K. (in preparation, B)
Havenstreet	Isle of Wight		Settlement		7 Dr.1A; 6 Dr. 1B; 4 Dr. 1/Pa.1; Dr. 1sp.	Connell & Trott (forthcoming)
Knighton	Isle of Wight	SZ 56 86	Settlement/ditch?	Rural settlement, enclosure ditch. Half a mile from Mersley Farm.	4+ Dr.1A (4 rims, 2 handle fragments and many body sherds) (min.8? Trott)	Fitzpatrick, A. (1985); Peacock, D.P.S. (1971)
Medina Road	Isle of Wight		Settlement?	Dr.1 sherd with pottery discovered during drainage works in 1930s.	Dr.1	Tomalin, D.J. (1992)
Mersley Farm	Isle of Wight	SZ 55 86	Settlement/ditch	Large IA enclosure ditch containing Dr.1A. Further enclosure 400 yards downhill, burial site, enclosure ditch, Dr.1A.	Dr.1A	Trott, K. (in preparation, A)
Mount Joy Hill, Newport	Isle of Wight		Settlement?	Dr.1A with IA sherds found during construction of a modern cemetery.	Dr.1A	Tomalin, D.J. (1992)
Newchurch	Isle of Wight	SZ 55 85	Burial?	Single Dressel 1 type species was recovered from the plough-soil during an amateur investigation of an IA grave with associated Gallo-Belgic wares' (Trott, *pers. comm.*)	Dr.1	Tomalin (1998: 97-102)

GAZETTEER 1 Dressel 1 and other wine amphorae findspots (where no bronze vessels present)

Site	Region	Grid ref.	Type	Description	Amphora	Reference
Newport Goods Yard	Isle of Wight	SZ 49 88	Burial?	Reported in 1869 during railway construction - early Roman amphorae and cremation urns with associated ditches and bone (human?) filled pits observed.		Trott, K. (unpubl.)
Quarr Beach	Isle of Wight		Settlement?		Dr.1	Tomalin (forthcoming, A)
Redcliff Battery, Sandown	Isle of Wight	SZ 623 854	Settlement?/salt production	Rural settlement? U-shaped gulley 8m along the site contained rich deposit of Belgic wares associated with suspected salt-processing containers and 1st century Samian and frags. of Dr.1. Feature poss. assoc. with timber building on the edge of cliff.	Dr.1 sp.; Dr. 1B	Tomalin, D.J. (1979; 1990: 91-120)
Ryde Middle Bank	Isle of Wight	SZ 59 92	Sea floor	Possibly anchorage debris (Trott)	2+ Dr.1A trawled during fishing.	Trott, K. (forthcoming, A)
St. Catherines Point	Isle of Wight	SZ 49 75	Settlement/ditch	Possible example of Dr.1A from middle fill of a MIA coastal defensive ditch.	Dr.1A	Trott, K. (in preparation, D)
Shalfleet Manor Farm	Isle of Wight		Settlement		Dr.1	Trott, K. (unpubl.)
Somerton	Isle of Wight		Settlement		Dr.1	Connell & Trott (forthcoming)
Thorley	Isle of Wight		Settlement?		Dr.2-4	Connell & Trott (forthcoming)
Thorness Beach	Isle of Wight	SZ 46 94	Beach		Dr.1	Trott, K. (unpubl.)
Undercliff Gardens	Isle of Wight		Settlement		Dr.2-4	Trott, K. (unpubl.)
Western Solent	Isle of Wight	SZ 50 98	Sea floor	Possibly from Yarmouth? (Trott)	7+ Dr.1A collected during fishing.	Tomalin, D.J. (forthcoming, A)
Whale Chine	Isle of Wight		Settlement		2 Dr.1	Trott, K. (unpubl.)
Yarmouth Roads	Isle of Wight	SZ 35 89	Anchorage/quay	Wreck? (Peacock, 1984); anchorage? (Trott, pers. com.)	21 Dr. 1A (and 18-20 Dr.20) dredged up	Fitzpatrick, A. (1985)
Yaverland	Isle of Wight	SZ 61 85	Ditch/pit	IA site, settlement. Ditch/pit produced Dr.1	Dr.1	Connell & Trott (forthcoming)
Tranquesous, St. Saviour's	Jersey		Settlement	Settlement	1+ Dr.1A	Fitzpatrick, A. (1985)

GAZETTEER 1 Dressel 1 and other wine amphorae findspots (where no bronze vessels present)

Location	County	Grid ref	Site type	Date	Context	Finds	References
Bigberry, near Canterbury	Kent	TR 11 57	Hillfort	2nd century BC-1st century BC (late)	Hillfort poss. built in 2nd century BC by people from Gaul. 'Customarily regarded as the first obstacle encountered by Caesar after his second landing in Britain in 54 BC' (Thompson). Settlers moved down to Stour valley 2nd half of the 1st century BC.	1 Dr.1 sp. (handle) = No.105 recovered from the spoil heap (as was No.104).	Thompson, F.H. (1983); Fitzpatrick, A. (1985)
Boughton Monchelsea, Kent	Kent	c. TQ 76 51	Burial?		Close to Quarry Wood Camp, Loose.	2 vessels.	Rodwell, W. (1976)
Canterbury	Kent	TR 14 57	Settlement		Roman town rescue excavations: Dr.1B - Mint Yard (near town wall), Cakebread Robey I (edge of temple precinct/theatre), Marlowe (I,II,III,IV centre of town), St. Radigund's (Roman town wall). Dr.2-4 Rosemary Lane (SW of town); Marlow I (centre of town).	45 sherds of which 9 definitely Dr.1B sherds; 2 Dr.2-4 sherds. Likely that remainder Dr.1B. No sherds in pre-Conquest context. All residual? (2.5% of assemblage by weight)	Arthur, P. (1986)
Canterbury, Bridge Hill	Kent	TR 14 57	Settlement		Settlement (oppidum?)	1 Dr.1 sp. (handle and 2 body sherds)	Rodwell, W. (1976); Fitzpatrick, A. (1985); Peacock, D.P.S. (1971); Arthur, P. (1986)
Canterbury, Rose Lane	Kent	TR 14 57	Settlement		Settlement (oppidum?)	3+ Dr.1 (probably 1B)	Rodwell, W. (1976); Fitzpatrick, A. (1985); Peacock, D.P.S. (1971)
Highstead	Kent	TR 21 66				1 Dr.1B or Pascual 1type	Arthur, P. (1986)
Holborough, Snodland	Kent		Burial	c.AD 200-225	Roman barrow, pyre site off barrow site, secondary burial. Latest known of this type of burial.	5 amphorae (imported), smashed. One of west Mediterranean type, the others smaller Greek type. Vessels smashed - wine used as libation.	Jessop, R.F. (1959); Fowler, P. (1959)
Quarry Wood, Loose, near Maidstone	Kent	TQ 71 51	Hillfort?		Hillfort?	1 Dr.1 (single body sherd with handle stamped EB)	Rodwell, W. (1976); Fitzpatrick, A. (1985); Arthur, P. (1986)
Rochester	Kent	TQ 72 68	Settlement		Settlement	1 Dr.1B	Fitzpatrick, A. (1985)

GAZETTEER 1 Dressel 1 and other wine amphorae findspots (where no bronze vessels present)

Brockley Hill	Middlesex	TQ 174 939	late 1st-2nd C AD	Brockley Hill possible site of *Sulloniacae* mentioned in 2nd Antonine Itinerary, 12miles Londinium; 9 miles Verulamium. Evidence of flourishing coarse pottery industry. Deposit (dump?) close to Watling Street - may represent infill of roadside ditch.	25-30 amphorae represented by fragments (1.5cwt). Callender Form 2 (Dr.3-4, Castle; surely Dr.2-4?) copies made locally (granular fabric typical of Brockley Hill and Verulamium region potteries) probably by known potter DARES (stamp on neck A21 DARESFE).	Castle, S.A. (1978)
London	Middlesex	TQ 32 80			Complete southern Spanish amphorae (in Guildhall Museum) of uncertain provenance.	Rodwell, R. (1976)
Stanmore, Stanmore Park	Middlesex	TQ 153 923	Burial?		Koan (Dr.2-4) amphorae (complete, stamped MAR OF on spike) - no supporting evidence.	Whimster, R. (1981); Peacock, D.P.S. (1971); Castle, S.A. (1978); Sealey, P.R. & Davies, G.M.R. (1984)
Burgh by Woodbridge	Suffolk	TM 23 51	Settlement	Rural settlement	2 Dr.1 or Dr.2-4	Fitzpatrick, A. (1985)
Kedington	Suffolk	c. TL 70 46	Burial?	Calcined bone not specifically mentioned.	Upright Koan amphora.	Whimster, R. (1981); Rodwell, W. (1976)
Chichester	Sussex	SU 86 04	Settlement	Settlement	1 Dr.1B (stamped AVALER)	Fitzpatrick, A. (1985)
Worcester	Worcestershire	SO 85 55	Unknown/sal t?		Dr.1	Fitzpatrick, A. (1985)

GAZETTEER 2 Bronze Vessels (findspots)

NAME OF SITE	COUNTY	NMR	CONTEXT	DATE	LOCATION	BRONZE OR SILVER DRINKING EQUIPMENT	REFERENCES
Biggleswade	Bedfordshire	TL 19 44	Isolated find.		No exact findspot - found on builder's dump.	Roman bronze patera , no trace of gilding; handle separately made - terminates in ram's head.	Kennett, *Bedfordshire Archaeological Journal* 4 (1969)
Felmersham Bridge, Sharnbrook	Bedfordshire	SP 990 579 *SP 95 NE 7*	Burial?	1st century AD	All finds lost.	Bronze bucket handle and escutcheons in the shape of cows heads, possible presence of bronze cauldron, now lost. Fish-headed spout, bowl and miscellaneous bronze fragments - suggested by Kennett to be a strainer.	Watson, W. (1949); Whimster, R. (1981); Kennet, D.H. (1970); Kuhlicke, F.W. (1969)
Woodlands, Knob's Crook	Dorset	SU 052 073	Burial	Samian ware c. AD70-85 Early Flavian (earliest Roman barrow in Britain)	Small round barrow covering 3 pits containing cremated bone and burnt clay. cf. Riseholme (AD80-100) and Holborough (AD200-25). Largest pit cremation burial and samian ware. Pits 2 & 3 also filled with contents of pyre.	Fragmentary bronze objects, probably vessels (vessel base found), broken and burnt.	Fowler, P. (1959)
Colchester, Lexden A, St. Clare Road	Essex	TL 975 250	Burial		Found 1922	Bucket fragments	Whimster, R. (1981)
Colchester, Lexden B, Lexden Grange	Essex	c. TL 975 250	Burial		Found 1904.	Bronze and coral cup.	Whimster, R. (1981)
Colchester, Stanway (Inkpot Grave)	Essex	TL 95 24	Burial		Assoc. with Camulodunum cropmark site, 5 enclosures, 3 chambers examined and 3 secondary burials. This grave Enclosure 3, subsidiary burial (high ranking aide?).	Possible bucket/box	Crummy, P. (1995)
Rivenhall	Essex	TL 82 17	Burial?		Ploughed up just to E of villa in 1839. Found in barrow field. Villa - 2 large building - Flavian built over IA and earlier Roman site. Briquetage recorded at Rivenhall (Rodwell, 1979)	Patera and ewer.	Rodwell, W. (1976?) Studies in the Romano-British Villa - Reece (ed.)

GAZETTEER 2 Bronze Vessels (findspots)

Site	County	Grid ref	Type	Date	Description	Reference
Cowley, Birdlip	Gloucestershire	SO 931 153	Burial	IA 50BC - AD47 (Green); c.AD10 (Fox)	Chance discovery in 1879 of group of cist graves, poss. located beneath stone cairns. RB/Roman pottery in vicinity. 600m SE of site possible RB enclosures (SO91NW33). SO91NW28 site of Roman building c. 400m SW of (?). Roman villa 1.75km N of.	Grave 1: Bronze handle? Grave 1: Bronze bucket plates and a sheet-bronze ring not inc. by Bellows (1881) may have come from fourth interment. Grave 2: Bronze rim and side plates of a bucket - buried bottom up over face?	NMR SO 91 NW 11; Whimster, R. (1981)
Grange Road II, Winchester	Hampshire	SU 48 29	Burial	Flavian (AD 70-95)	1 of 2 graves found as a result of a rescue excavation. Rectangular pit. Meal laid out on shale trencher - platter and cup with pig's skull, leg bones and bird bone, spoon, knives. To one side drinking vessels, game. Samian platters and cups, iron styli.	Bronze jug, trefoil (similar to Stanfordbury and Antran), spun on a lathe. Top of handle, female head and bust with arms outstretched, base escutcheon, female mask. Made in Campania, poss. 1st half of 1st C. AD.	Biddle, M. (1967)
Hurstbourne Tarrant, Blagdon Coppice	Hampshire	SU 363 523	Burial	pre-Claudian	Barrow excavated 1905. 8.1m length x 1m high. Central interment.	Stave built wooden bucket with hoops containing calcined bone.	Whimster, R. (1981)
Harpenden	Hertfordshire	c. TL 144 150	Burial?		Discovered in 1867 during railway construction; 4' from surface.	Wooden bucket with rim handles and ram-headed mounts. Sheathed in bronze, mounts coral in nostrils.	Notes, Antiquaries Journal, 8 (1928); Whimster, R. (1981)
Stanfordbury	Hertfordshire	TL 14 41	Unknown	1st century AD	Recorded as being from Stanfordbury in Sir Henry Dryden's account of antiquities from Shefford (1845)	Bronze patera with reeded handle terminating in ram's head. Unusually has a second handle.	Smith, R.A. (1911-12)
Alkham	Kent	TR 25 42	Burial	end 1st century BC- early 2nd century AD	Cremation cemetery, chalk hillside. Group of four large cremation burials.	2 decorated bronze bound wooden buckets cf. Aylesford.	Nurse, K. (1991); Hill, J.D. (pers.comm.)
Grave X, Aylesford	Kent	TQ 731 593 (TQ 75 NW 21)	Burial		Excavation of small flat-grave cremation cemetery 1886-90. Graves X, Y and Z rich, surrounded by 6 simpler graves (Graves A-F).	Large wooden bucket with iron bands and handle, apparently containing cremated remains and 5 pottery vessels.	Whimster, R. (1981)

GAZETTEER 2 Bronze Vessels (findspots)

Site	County	Grid ref	Type	Date	Context	Vessel description	References
Grave Y, Aylesford	Kent	TQ 731 593	Burial		Cremation cemetery. Circular pit coated with chalk. RB burial urns (TQ75NW28)5-600m SW of IA burial ground; rectilinear enclosure to NW c. 500m (TQ75NW82) (APs). RB flagon findspot TQ75NW43 - Larkfield.	Bronze jug of Kjaerumgaard type (25 BC - AD 25). Patera of Aylesford type (pre-20 BC), decorated rim, repousse, simple handle, no decorative termination, broken off?, long flat channeled in the middle. Both found outside bucket with pottery.	Whimster, R. (1981); Feugere, M. & de Marinis, R. (1991); Boube, C. (1991)Rivetted bronze-bound wooden bucket (situla) containing calcined bones, repousse work, handle attachments terminate in figure with headdress.?
Grave Z, Aylesford	Kent	TQ 731 593	Burial		Cremation cemetery. Central deposit - bronze plated wooden tankard probably contained cremated remains.	Bronze plated wooden tankard (container for cremation). Built of staves of wood, bound by bronze plates, handles (ornamental bosses now gone), similar to Elvedon.	Whimster, R. (1981)
Petham, Swarling, Grave 13	Kent	TR 127 526 (TR 15 SW 10)	Burial	1C. BC	Small cemetery excavated in 1925 by Bushe-Fox (19 graves of which 17 contained calcined bone and material objects). Grave 13 - circular grave pit 1.05m diameter; 0.9m deep.	Wooden bucket with iron hoops/handles - container for cremation.	Whimster, R. (1981)
Welshpool	Montgomeryshire	SJ 22 07	Burial	AD150-200? but objects 1st century AD	Found during development.	Ewer, patera (with umbo), patera with fluted handle repaired in antiquity. Ewer decorated with young boy with serpents round leg on handle (Hercules or Dionysius?) 3 pateras in all one with ram's head terminal on handle, one with Dionysiac motif. 1AD	Boon, G.C. (1961)Portion of spun cauldron in which metalwork patched; bucket escutcheon, a bucranium with portion of handle attached and frag. of bucket made of yew.
Crownthorpe	Norfolk	TG 08 03	Hoard	1st C. AD	Hoard, unpublished. Now in Norwich Castle Museum.	Copper alloy bowl comparable to Ermine Street, Braughing but twice the size. Patera with handle terminating in ram's head. Animal-spouted strainer bowl.	Potter, T.W. & Trow, S.D. (1988)
Elvedon	Suffolk	c. TL 82 79	Burial?	Mid-1st C AD	Only cremation in district of inhumations (NW Suffolk)? Fox. Calcined bone not specifically recorded.	2 handled bronze tankard found at centre of a triangle of inverted globular urns (now lost).	Fox, 1923; Whimster, R. (1981)

GAZETTEER 2 Bronze Vessels (findspots)

Mildenhall	Suffolk	TL 71 74	Burial	1st century AD	Likely that this object from a 1st century bronze vessel from an early Roman burial. Object later re-buried with Anglo-Saxon material. Little known about grave or associated objects except Anglo-Saxon cruciform brooches.	Bronze vessel mount - protome of a winged horse with head, neck and front legs.	Henig, M. (1982)
Santon Downham	Suffolk	TL 81 87	Hoard	Found 1897		Fine bronze jug with trefoil spout, bronze handle of a patera with animal head terminal (mid-1st AD) Large bronze cauldron. Frags. from 2 buckets or tankards.	Fox (1923)
Marlborough, St. Margaret's Mead	Wiltshire	SU 194 689	Burial		Found in 1807. Bucket found with calcined bones.	Bronze-plated wooden bucket with iron bands and handles.	Whimster, R. (1981)

97

GAZETTEER 3 Dressel 1 and other wine amphorae findspots (with bronze vessels present)

NAME OF SITE	COUNTY	NMR	CONTEXT	DATE	LOCATION	AMPHORAE	BRONZE OR SILVER DRINKING EQUIPMENT	REFERENCES
Old Warden, Quints Hill	Bedfordshire	TL 135 446	Burial	LIA (Welwyn type?)	One or more Welwyn type burials found during 19th C. IA cremation burials TL14SW3 beside RR222 (Biggleswade - Old Warden). Possible enclosure (APs) noted at Warden Little Wood (TL 1089 4421). "U" enclosure TL14SW32 by AP.	2 Dr.1 or Greco-Italic (all lost)	2 iron? bucket hoops	NMR TL 14 SW 3; Rodwell, W. (1976); Whimster, ,R. (1981)
Snailwell	Cambridgeshire	TL 645 675 (TL 66 NW 21)	Burial	c.AD 43, late pre-Conquest (excavator 'within a year or two of the Claudian conquest')	Excavated 1953. Excavator suggests 'isolated' position, no barrow(?), near house of deceased? On LIN123 Roman road.TL66NW14 poss. Roman house with hypocast and painted wall plaster found nearby (TL 635 684). Pottery mainly 3rd C. c.1km NW of burial.	3 southern Spanish amphorae: Camulodunum Forms 186B(2) and 185A (Haltern 70), standing up, complete.	Bronze bowl, handle had once been fastened to it, no longer there just one iron rivet.Base of the bowl , pelta shaped object. Inside base decorated. Very simple, probably provincial Roman. More curved than patera?	Whimster, R. (1981); Lethbridge, T.C. (1953)
Colchester, Lexden C	Essex	TL 975 247 (TL 92 SE 13)	Burial	17BC-43AD?	Round low barrow surmounting oval pit 9 x 5.4 x 2.1m. TL92SE68 IA/Roman cemetery 200m N of site. Roman road (TL92SE9) runs between the two sites. Lay just outside Roman town of Colchester. Wooden remains within pit - oak.	4 Dr. 16 amphorae, 10 Koan amphorae, 1 Rhodian amphora. None complete, Dr. 1B sherds (6); 11 Dr.2-4	Bronze jug handle - object broken before burial? 2 vine leaf escutcheons from flagons?	Laver (1924); Foster (1986); Whimster, R. (1981)
Colchester, Stanway (Doctor's grave)	Essex	TL 95 24	Burial	AD 50s	Assoc. with Camulodunum cropmark site, 5 enclosures, 3 chambers examined and 3 secondary burials. Enclosure 5, chamber, sub-enclosure and 3 other burials i) 2 pots ii) 3 pots, small glass pot, glass bead, 6 brooches iii) Doctor's grave.	1 Spanish Dr.7-11 (Cam. 186a) with rim broken off and handles missing although most of neck intact, standing upright in corner of pit. Usually assoc. with garum although there are examples containing wine.	Crushed copper alloy strainer containing organic deposit identified as wormwood (artemesia) (Sealey, pers.comm.). Probably british made. Patera, maker's name stamped on handle - imported from Italy. Vessel had been tinned. Intact.	Crummy, P. (1995); Jackson, R. (1998); Sealey, P.R. (1998, pers. comm.); http://peipa.essex.ac. uk/CAT
Colchester, Stanway (Warrior's grave)	Essex	TL 95 24	Burial	AD 50s	Assoc. with Camulodunum cropmark site, 5 enclosures, 3 chambers examined and 3 secondary burials. This grave Enclosure 3, subsidiary grave (high ranking aide?), very rich.	Amphora from Pompeii region. (Dr.2-4?)	Patera with handle terminating in ram's head. Intact. Copper-alloy trefoil jug; handle terminates in lion's head at top, paw at the base.	Crummy, P. (1995); Crummy, P. (1997); http://peipa.essex.ac. uk/CAT

GAZETTEER 3 Dressel 1 and other wine amphorae findspots (with bronze vessels present)

Site	County	Grid ref	Burial/hoard?	Date	Briquetage recorded at Great Chesterford (Rodwell,1979)	Amphorae	Bronze vessels	References
Great Chesterford	Essex	TL 50 42		Mid 3rd of 1st AD(?)	Briquetage recorded at Great Chesterford (Rodwell,1979)	[1 Dr.1B, now in Audley End House, possibly associated with bucket]	Bronze mounts of a wooden bucket with embossed decoration, boar's head terminals on handles.	Fox, 1923; Fitzpatrick, A. (1985)
Heybridge	Essex	c. TL 85 08	Burial		?	Amphorae	Patella and a bronze jug.	Callender, M.H. (1965)
Heybridge, Elms Farm	Essex	TL 847 082	Settlement	LIA/Romano-British	Settlement on R. Chelmer, opposite bank to Maldon. Settlement contained 2 LIA shrines and cemetery containing at least 13 burials each with cinerary urn, one with 9 brooches; cf. King Harry Lane	200 contexts with amphora (usually a single sherd); 120 contexts Italian; 90 contexts late 1st C. BC - mid-1st C. AD. Dr.1 outnumbers Dr.2-4. 1 Dr.1A rim (unstrat.); 25 (poss. 50) Dr.1B. Re-used in cobbled surface in Area M.	Copper-alloy ewer, top soil Area A2 (not dissimilar to Kjaerumgaard type but await full report)	Atkinson, M. & Preston, S.J. (1998); Sealey, P. in Craven, P. (1998); Essex County Council (1998?)
Hayling Island	Hampshire	SU 72 01	Temple		Temple	1+ Dr 1A	2 bronze tankard handles, one joined rings, the other pair of loops.	Fitzpatrick, A. (1985); King, A. & Soffe, G. (1998); Downey, R., King, A. & Soffe, G. (1980); King, A. & Soffe, G. (1994)
Hengistbury Head	Hampshire	SZ 17 90	Entrepot		Market site? little evidence for settlement. No complete amphorae recovered.	33 Dr.1A rim frags (61 sherds total) 30 vessels min.; 6 Dr.1B frags.; 809 Dr.1 sp. fragments, 56 handle frags., 11 bases; Pascual 1, 40 frags.; Dr.2-4, 15 sherds. 35+ vessels.	Strainer of a type in use from the end of the 2nd C. BC to Tiberius	Fitzpatrick, A. (1985); Peacock, D.P.S (1971); Cunliffe, B. (1987);

GAZETTEER 3 Dressel 1 and other wine amphorae findspots (with bronze vessels present)

Site	County	Grid ref	Type	Date	Description	Amphorae	Bronze vessels	References
Baldock, The Tene	Hertfordshire	TL 248 335	Burial?		Circular grave pit 1.5m x 0.6m found 1968 during road construction. Within IA material found at Walls Field (TL249339) TL23SW48 - settlement established by 1C.BC continued uninterrupted to Roman period. Settlements within 300m of RR22, 100-400m of RR168a.	Dr. 1A amphora (not Dr.1B) (Whimster corrected in Hussen (1983))	Bronze cauldron with iron ring handles containing calcined bone (surrounded by other grave goods), 2 wooden buckets with bronze bands and mounts - human face (stylised), rectangular plaques, swing handles, similar to Aylesford. Yew. Imported.	Stead, I. (1971 and 1968); Whimster, R. (1981); Peacock, D.P.S. (1971)
Braughing, Gatesbury Track	Hertfordshire	TL 39 24	Settlement		Oppidum' or large native settlement, Wickham Hill. F7 = v-shaped ditch running E-W. F41 definite LIA u-shaped ditch running N-S in the SW corner of the site (poss. turning to W at N end of site-poss. NE of enclosure?) Only imported material Dr.1B.	198 amphorae sherds. Dr.1(63.4%); Dr.2-4 (0.7%); Dr.6 (1.7%); Cam.185A (1.7%); Dr.20 (30.1%); unknown (2.4%). Dr.1A and Dr.1B rims present. Dr.1A in F7(3), early level in ditch. Dr.1B appears in several contexts including F7 (all levels) and F41.	SF No.3 (F30) frag. bronze vessel, simple turned over rim.	Partridge, C. (1980); Fitzpatrick, A. (1985)
Braughing, Puckeridge, Station Road, F1 LIA ditch.	Hertfordshire	TL 38 23	Settlement; v-shaped ditch		Oppidum' or large native settlement, Wickham Hill; Station Road on south-west side of Wickham Hill. F1=LIA ditch (layers 1-8, Group 1 (1,2,9), Group 2 (3/4,5,6) Group 3 (7,8), 75m traced between houses.	48 sherds.F1(1) 1 Dr.1. handle; 3 Dr.1/2-4 body; 2 unid. F1(2) 1 Dr.1 spike, 2 handles; 1 Dr.2-4 rim; 6 Dr.1/2-4 body. F1(9) 2 Dr.1/2-4 body. Pre-Conquest F. (3) 1 Dr.1 rim; 11 Dr.1/2-4 body; 2 S. Spanish body. F1(5) 1 Dr.1 handle; 9 Dr.1/2-4 body; 1 unid.	SF No.70 (F1(5)) waste from manufacture/repair of bronze vessel. SF No.91 (F1(2)) frag. of rim of bronze vessel, tinned.	Partridge, C. (1980); Fitzpatrick, A. (1985)
Folly Lane, St. Albans	Hertfordshire	TL 15 07	Burial	AD50	On line of Roman road from Verulamium to Colchester - mortuary chamber lay at centre of huge rectilinear enclosure 500m outside NE gate of Verulamium and within area of pre-Roman oppidum.	Dr.2-4 in funerary shaft and in chamber pit - at least 4 Italian wine amphorae (Dr.2-4) - none complete - all broken.	Frag. of bronze and silver.	Niblett, R. (1993); Niblett, R. (pers.comm.); Niblett, R. (1999)

100

GAZETTEER 3 Dressel 1 and other wine amphorae findspots (with bronze vessels present)

Hertford Heath	Hertfordshire	TL 352 113	Burial	30-15BC	Discovered 1956 through new development. Rectangular grave with turf layer on floor.	1 Dr.1B standing against wall near NW corner. Complete. (Another rim and neck found nearby)	Bronze covered iron ring - bracelet or handle of bucket/cauldron/ horse bit? Poss. wooden tub or wooden structure - iron bands. Poss. lid - "wheel complex" - lot of these things broken. Wine barrel?	Holmes & Frend (1959); Rodwell, W. (1976); Hussen, C.-M. (1983); Fitzpatrick, A. (1985); Peacock, D.P.S. (1971)
Puckeridge-Braughing, Ermine Street	Hertfordshire	TL 37 27	Settlement		Part of large LIA/early Roman settlement. Amphorae sherds found in LPRIA domestic rubbish pits C5, C36, B50 with Gallo-Belgic wares, coins, glass, Arretine - pits in use from early Augustan period. Coin moulds at site.	LPRIA Dr.1B handle APW (Pit C5); 5 body sherds of Dr.1 Pit C5 and ABX (Site A); Dr.2-4 rim and part handle Pit B50 AKA; early Roman - Pelichet 47 flat base with foot-rim from Layer A146 ABX. Dr.1 1%; Dr.2-4 1%;Dr.1/2-4 52.4% (42sh; Pelichet 1% (+Cam.185/6)	Copper-alloy small bowl, cast, finished on a lathe; Crownthorpe best //. Part of burial (D45) in side of well which cut through earlier pit; with 3 samian dishes, casket; part of series of burials. Period III (c.AD 55-100)	Potter, T.W. & Trow, S.D. (1988)
St. Albans, King Harry Lane	Hertfordshire	TL 133 065	Burial	c. 15-10 BC to c. AD43	Cemetery outside the Silchester gate of Verulamium. 445 burials excavated in all, majority in pottery vessels, some (particularly the richer burials) unurned.	6 amphora discovered, one Dr. 2-4 on analysis contained olive oil (Graves 241; 206; 117; 447; 272)	Rim of vessel (37AS/BJ); strainer fragment (325)	Whimster, R. (1981)
Stanfordbury, Grave A	Hertfordshire	TL 148 412	Burial	c. AD43 +	2 massive burial vaults 4.5 x 3.6 x 1.5m, paved with tiling. (A) found 1832 and (B) found in 1934. (Claudian although some of the material may be from nearby cemetery at Shefford. At TL147404 rectangular features (APs) situated above Stanfordbury.)	6 amphorae (5 lost, 1 Spanish, Dr.14?), standing against the wall of vault. One measured at least 2'8"; one contained ball of pitch at the bottom of it.	Bronze jug with trefoil lip, patera and shallow bronze bowl	Smith, R.A. (1911-12); NMR TL 14 SW 1; Whimster, R. (1981); Peacock, D.P.S. (1971)

GAZETTEER 3 Dressel 1 and other wine amphorae findspots (with bronze vessels present)

Site	County	Grid reference	Type	Date	Description	Vessels	Bronze vessels	References
Stanfordbury, Grave B	Hertfordshire	TL 148 412 (TL 14 SW 1)	Burial	c. AD43 + (Claudian/Nero?) although some of the material may be from nearby cemetery at Shefford. At TL147404 rectangular features (APs) situated above Stanfordbury	2 massive burial vaults 4.5 x 3.6 x 1.5m - 2 amphorae, standing against the wall of the vault (now lost).		Bronze handle and box fittings	Smith, R.A. (1911-12); NMR TL 14 SW 1; Whimster, R. (1981)
Welwyn Garden City, Grave 1	Hertfordshire	TL 254 131 (TL 21 SE 4)	Burial	51 BC - 10 BC	Rich burial excavated 1965, rectangular pit 3.15m x 2.1m surrounded by 6 subsidiary satellite graves. TL21SE11 IA site 200m from site with RB kiln. TL21SE13 -IA ditch; TL21SE12 IA sherds in pit or ditch 400m from site.	5 Dr.1B (one stamped HIE or HIB), standing up complete.2 wooden vessels with bronze fittings, wooden vessel with iron bands and ring handles.	Silver cup, bronze strainer - decorated, separate lid, similar to Santon Downham hoard lid converted to strainer original bowl, Roman import. Bronze dish - 2 small pots inside one placed on block of wood of ash? (Stead) - [incense]	Stead, I. (1967); Whimster, R. (1981); Fitzpatrick, A. (1985); Peacock, D.P.S. (1971); Rigby, V. (1995)
Welwyn, Grave A	Hertfordshire	TL 232 159 (TL 21 NW 8)	Burial	50/30-10BC	4 burials, 2 of them "Welwyn type", excavated 1906. Within Welwyn Roman settlement (TL21NW3) (RR21c runs through). TL21NW10 other IA/RB burials in central Welwyn "two urns containing bones and a bronze fibula". 600m SW of Roman villa - poss. IA underneath.	1 Dr.1B (stamped SOS)	2 bronze handles, handle of bronze jug of Kjaerumgaard type (25 BC - AD 25)	Smith (1911-12); Whimster, R. (1981); Fitzpatrick, A. (1985); Boube, C. (1991)

GAZETTEER 3 Dressel 1 and other wine amphorae findspots (with bronze vessels present)

Welwyn, Grave B	Hertfordshire	Burial	50/30-10BC	5 Dr.1B (one stamped AA)	Iron-handled patera of Aylesford type (in use to last quarter of 1st C. BC, oenochoe handle of Kjaerumgaard typ (25 BC - AD 25), tankard with bronze handle. Pair of silver kylix handles, pair of silver vases.	Smith (1911-12); Whimster, R. (1981); Fitzpatrick, A. (1985); Feugere, M. & de Marinis, R. (1991); Boube, C. (1991)
	TL 232 159 (TL 21 NW 8)			Grave pit, unknown dimensions. No specific mention of calcined bone.	

103

BIBLIOGRAPHY

Alexander, J.A. (1975) 'The salt industries of Africa: their significance for European prehistory' in de Brisay & Evans (eds.)

Allen, D.F. (1944) 'The Belgic dynasties of Britain and their coins' *Archaeologia*, 90

Arthur, P. (1986) 'Roman Amphorae from Canterbury' *Britannia*, Vol.17

Athenaeus (1928) *Deipnosophistae* The Loeb Classical Library

Atkinson, M. & Preston, S.J. (1998a) 'The late Iron Age and Roman settlement at Elms Farm, Heybridge, Essex, Excavations 1993-95: An Interim Report *Britannia*, XXIX

Atkinson, M. & Preston, S.J. (1998b) *Hidden Heybridge The Elms Farm Excavation* Essex County Council

Atkinson, M. (1999a) 'Growth and decay of an Essex village' *British Archaeology*, 47

Atkinson, M. & Preston, S. (1999b) *Elms Farm, Heybridge* Finds Groups and Assessment Reports (unpublished extracts, Autumn 1999)

Baker, F.T. (1975) 'Salt Making Sites on the Lincolnshire coast before the Romans' in de Brisay & Evans (eds.)

Bats, M. (1993) 'Amphores massaliètes' in Py (ed.)

Baudoux, J. (1996) *Les amphores du nord-est de la Gaule Contribution à l'histoire de l'économie provinciale sous l'Empire romain* Documents d'Archéologie Française No. 52, Paris

Bestwick, J.D. (1975) 'Romano-British inland salting at Middlewich (*Salinae*), Cheshire' in de Brisay & Evans (eds.)

Bevan, B. (1999) *Northern Exposure: interpretative devolution and the Iron Ages in Britain* Leicester Archaeology Monographs No.4

Biddle, M. (1967) 'Two Flavian Burials from Grange Road, Winchester' *Antiquaries Journal*, 47

Biddle, M. (1975) 'Excavations at Winchester, 1971: 10th and Final Interim Reports: Part 1' *Antiquaries Journal*, 55

Birley, R. (1999) *Roman Records from Vindolanda on Hadrian's Wall* Roman Army Museum Publications

Blagg, T. & Millett, M. (1990) *The Early Roman Empire in the West* Oxbow Books

Boon, G.C. (1961) 'Roman Antiquities at Welshpool' *Antiquaries Journal*, 41: 12-31

Boon, G.C. (1975) 'Segontium Fifty Years On:1 A Roman Stave of Larch-Wood and other Unpublished Finds mainly of Organic Materials, together with a Note on Late Barracks' *Archaeologia Cambrensis*, 124

Boube, C. (1991) 'Les cruches' in Feugère & Rolley (eds.)

Bouloumié, B. (1988) 'Le symposion gréco-étrusque et l'aristocratie celtique' in Mohen, Duval & Eluère (eds.)

Bowie, E.L. (1995) 'Wine in Old Comedy' in Murray & Tecusan (eds.)

Bowman, A.K. (1974) 'Roman Military Records from Vindolanda' *Britannia*, 5

Bradley, R. (1975) 'Salt and Settlement in the Hampshire Sussex Borderland' in de Brisay & Evans (eds.)

Brailsford, J.W. (1962) *Hod Hill Volume I Antiquities from Hod Hill in the Durden Collection* The Trustees of the British Museum: London

Brun, P. (1987) *Princes et Princesses de la Celtique: Le Premier Age du Fer 850-450 av.J.C.*

Brunaux, J.-L. (1996) *Les Religions Gauloises Rituels Celtiques de la Gaule Indépendante* Paris: Editions Errance

Brunaux, J.-L., Meniel, P. & Poplin, F. (1985) *Gournay I: Les fouilles sur le sanctuaire et l'oppidum (1975-84)* Supplement to *Revue Archaeologique de Picardie*

Burnham, B.C. & Johnson, H.B. (1979) *Invasion and Response: the Case of Roman Britain* British Archaeological Reports 73

Caesar (1917) *The Gallic War* (H.J. Edwards, trans.) Loeb Classical Library, London: Harvard University Press

Callender, M.H. (1965) *Roman Amphorae* (with an index of stamps)

Carandini, A. (1979) *Schiavi e padroni nell' Eturia romana: la Villa di Settefinestre dallo scavo alla mostra* Bari: De Donato

Castle, S.A. (1978) 'Amphorae from Brockley Hill, 1975' *Britannia*, Vol.9

Champion, T.C. & Megaw (1985) *Settlement and Society* Leicester University Press

Champion, T.C. (1985) "Written sources and the study of the European Iron Age" in Champion & Megaw (eds.)

Christie, P.M.L. (1978) 'The excavation of an Iron Age Souterrain and Settlement at Carn Euny, Sancreed, Cornwall' *Proceedings of the Prehistoric Society*, 44

Colchester Archaeological Trust Website *http://peipa.essex.ac.uk/CAT*

Collis, J. (1977) "Pre-Roman burial rites in north-western Europe" in Reece, R. (ed.)

Collis, J. (1994) 'An Iron Age and Roman Cemetery at Owlesbury, Hampshire' in Fitzpatrick & Morris (eds.)

Connell, M. & Trott, K. (forthcoming) 'Excavations on the Southern Water Seaclean Wight Pipelines'

Corcoran, J. X.W.P. (1952) 'Tankards and tankard handles of the British Early Iron Age' *Proceedings of the Prehistoric Society* 6

Craven, P. (1998) *The background to Dressel 1 amphora burials in Iron Age Britain: Celtic Thirst or Roman Ritual?* Undergraduate Dissertation, Birmingham University, March 1998 (unpubl.)

Crummy, P. (1995) 'Late Iron Age Burials at Stanway, Colchester' in Swaddling, Walker & Roberts (eds.)

Crummy, P. (1997) *City of Victory The story of Colchester - Britain's first Roman town* Colchester Archaeological Trust

Cunliffe, B. & Rowley, T. (1976) *Oppida: the beginnings of urbanisation in barbarian Europe* British Archaeological Reports

Cunliffe, B. (1984) "Relations between Britain and Gaul in the 1st century BC and early 1st century AD" in Macready & Thompson (eds.)

Cunliffe, B. (1987) *Hengistbury Head, Dorset Vol. 1 The Prehistoric and Roman Settlement 3500 BC - AD 500* Oxford: Oxford University Committee for Archaeology

Cunliffe, B. (1991) *Iron Age Communities in Britain* 3rd edition, London: Routledge

Cunnington, B.H. (1932) 'Was there a second Belgic invasion (represented by bead rim pottery)" *Antiquaries Journal*, 12: 27

d'Arms, John H. (1995) 'Heavy drinking and drunkenness in the Roman World: Four questions for historians' in Murray & Tecusan (eds.)

Dannell, G.B. (1979) 'Eating and drinking in pre-conquest Britain: the evidence of amphora and samian trading with the effect of the invasion of Claudius' in Burnham & Johnson (eds.)

Daubigney, A. (1993) *Fonctionnement Social de l'Âge du Fer: Opérateurs et Hypothèses pour la France* Lons-le Saunier

Davies, R.W. (1971) 'The Roman Military Diet' *Britannia* 2

de Brisay, K.W. & Evans, K.A. (eds.) (1975) *Salt The Study of an Ancient Industry* Report on the Salt Weekend, 20-22 September 1974, Colchester Archaeological Group

de Brisay, K.W. (1975) 'The Red Hills of Essex' in de Brisay & Evans (eds.)

Dietler, M. (1990) 'Driven by drink: the role of drinking in the political economy and the case of early Iron Age France' *Journal of Anthropological Archaeology*, 9

Dietler, M. (1995) 'Early Celtic Socio-political relations: ideological representation and social competition in dynamic comparative perspective' in *Celtic Chiefdom, Celtic State* Cambridge University Press

Dillon, M & Chadwick, N.K. (1967) *The Celtic Realms* London: Weidenfeld & Nicolson

Diodorus Siculus (1939) Book 5, Loeb Classical Library, Volume III

Dodds, E.R. (ed.) (1960) *Euripides The Bacchae* Oxford: Clarendon Press

Domergue, C. (1987) *Catalogue des mines et des fonderies antiques de la péninsule Ibérique* Vols. I and II, Madrid: Diffusion de Boccard

Domergue, C. (1990) *Les mines de la péninsule Ibérique dans l'antiquité Romaine* Collection de l'école Française de Rome - 127

Domergue, C. (1991) 'Les amphores dans les mines antiques du Sud de la Gaule et de la Péninsule Ibérique' *Festschrift für Wilhelm Schulezum 60,*

Geburtstag. Veroflentlichung des Vorgeschichtlichen Seminars Marburg, Sonderband 6. Internationale Archäologie 1: 99-125

Dowden, K. (1992) *Religion and the Romans* London: Bristol Classical Press

Downey, R., King, A. & Soffe, G. (1980) 'The Hayling Island Temple and Religious Connections across the Channel' in Rodwell (ed.)Temples, Churches and Religion in *Roman Britain* Rodwell, W. (ed.) British Archaeological Reports 77(i)

Dressel, H. (1879) 'Di un grande deposito di anfore rinvenuto nel nuovo quartiere del Castro Pretorio' in *BCAR*, VII: 36-112 and 143-196 (republished in *Saggi sull'instrumentum romano*, Pérouse, 1978: 258-387)

Drury, P.J. & Rodwell, W.J. (1973) 'Excavations at Gun Hill, West Tilbury' *Essex Archaeology and History The Transactions of the Essex Archaeological Society* Vol.5 3rd series

Dunbabin, K.M.D. (1995: 252-265) "Scenes from the Roman *Convivium: Frigida non derit, non derit calda petenti* (Martial xiv.105)" in Murray & Tecusan (eds.)

Dunbabin, K.M.D. (1993) 'Wine and water at the Roman *convivium*' *Journal of Roman Archaeology* 6: 116-41

Dunnett, B.R.K. (1966) 'Excavations on North Hill, Colchester' *Archaeological Journal*, 123

Dunnett, B.R.K. (1971) 'Excavations on the site of the former St. Mary's Rectory, 1967' *Trans. Essex Archaeological Society*, Vol.3 (3rd series)

Earwood, C. (1993) *Domestic wooden artefacts in Britain and Ireland from Neolithic to Viking Times* Exeter: Exeter University Press

Eddy, M.R. & Turner, C. (1982) *Kelvedon The Origins and Development of a small Roman Town* Essex County Council Occasional Paper No.3

Edgeworth Reade, J. (1995) 'The Symposion in Ancient Mesopotamia: Archaeological Evidence' in Murray & Tecusan (eds.)

Eggers, H.J. (1951) *Der römische Import im freien Germanien* (Atlas der urgeschichte 1), Hamburg

Ellison, A. & Henig, M. (1978) "Objects from a Romano-British temple on West Hill, Uley, Gloucestershire" *Antiquaries Journal*, 58: 368-370

Farley, M. (1983) 'A Mirror Burial at Dorton, Buckinghamshire' *Proceedings of the Prehistoric Society*, 49

Farrar, R.A.H. (1975) 'Prehistoric and Roman Saltworks in Dorset' in de Brisay & Evans (eds.)

Ferdière, A. & Villard. A. (1993) *La Tombe augusténne de Fléré-la-Rivière (Indre) et les sépultures aristocratiques de la cité des Bituriges* Mémoire 2 du Musée d'Argentomagus, Saint Marcel

Feugère, M. & Rolley, C. (1991) *La vaiselle tardo-républicaine en bronze* Université de Bourgogne, Centre de recherches sur les techniques gréco-romaines No.13, Dijon

Feugère, M. & de Marinis, R. (1991) 'Les poêlons' in Feugère & Rolley (eds.)

Fitzpatrick, A.P. (1985) 'The distribution of Dressel 1 amphorae in North-West Europe' *Oxford Journal of Archaeology*, 4(3)

Fitzpatrick, A.P. (1987) 'The Structure of a Distribution Map: Problems of Sample Bias and Quantitative Studies' *Rei Cretariæ Romanæ Favtorum* Acta 25/26

Fitzpatrick, A.P. (1989) "The Uses of Roman Imperialism by the Celtic Barbarians in the later Republic" in *Barbarians and Romans in North West Europe*, Barrett, J., Fitzpatrick, A.P. and Macinnes, L. (eds.)

Fitzpatrick, A.P. (1991) 'Death in a Material World: The Late Iron Age and Early Romano-British Cemetery at King Harry Lane, St. Albans, Hertfordshire' (Review of Stead & Rigby) *Britannia*, Vol. 22

Fitzpatrick, A.P. (1993) 'Ethnicity and Exchange: Germans, Celts and Romans in the late Iron Age' in *Trade and Exchange in Prehistoric Europe*, Scarre & Healy (eds.)

Fitzpatrick, A.P. (1989) 'The Submission of the Orkney Islands to Claudius: New Evidence?' *Scottish Archaeological Review* 6

Fitzpatrick, A.P. (1994) 'The Late Iron Age Cremation Cemetery at Westhampnett, West Sussex' in Fitzpatrick & Morris (eds.)

Fitzpatrick, A.P. & Morris, E.L. (1994) *The Iron Age in Wessex: Recent Work* Association Française d'Etude de l'Age du Fer

Fitzpatrick, A.P. (1997) *Archaeological excavations on the route of the A27 Westhampnett bypass, West Sussex 1992 Vol.2 The Late Iron Age, Romano-British and Anglo Saxon cemeteries* Wessex Archaeology Report No.12

Fitzpatrick, A.P. (forthcoming) 'Cross-Channel Exchange. Hengistbury Head and the end of hillforts' Association Française d'Etude de l'Age du Fer conference, Winchester

Flouest, J.-L. (1993) 'Activité métallurgiques et commerce avec le monde méditerranéen au Ve siècle av. J.-C. à Bragny-sur-Saône (Saône-et-Loire)' in Daubigney (ed.)

Flouest, J.-L. & Stead, I.M. (1981) *Iron Age Cemeteries in Champagne The Third Interim Report on the Excavations carried out between 1971 and 1978* British Museum Occasional Paper No. 6

Forcey, C. (1998) 'Whatever happened to the heroes? Ancestral cults and the enigma of Romano-Celtic temples' in Forcey, Hawthorne & Witcher (eds.)

Forcey, C., Hawthorne, J. & Witcher, R. (1998) *Proceedings of the 7th Annual Theoretical Roman Archaeology Conference (April 1997)* Oxbow

Formenti, F. & Duthel, J.M. (1996) 'The analysis of wine and other organics inside amphoras of the Roman period' in McGovern, Fleming & Katz (eds.)

Foster, J. (1986) *The Lexden Tumulus of a re-appraisal of an Iron Age burial from Colchester, Essex*, British Archaeological Reports 156

Foster, J. (1999) 'The Metal Finds' in Niblett p.133

Fowler, P.J. (1965) 'A Roman Barrow at Knob's Crook, Woodlands, Dorset' *Antiquaries Journal*, 45

Fox, C. (1923) *The Archaeology of the Cambridge Region*, Cambridge University Press

Galliou, P. (1984) 'Days of Wine and Roses? Early Armorica and the Atlantic Wine Trade' in Macready & Thompson (eds.)

Garnsey, P., Hopkins, K. & Whittaker, C.R. (1983) *Trade in the Ancient Economy* London: Chatto & Windus

Gomez de Soto, J. (1993) 'Cooking for the Elite: Feasting Equipment in the late Bronze Age' in Scarre & Healy (eds.)

Goudineau, C. & Peyre, C. (1993) *Bibracte et les Eduens* Editions Errance

Graue, J. (1974) *Die Gräberfelder von Ornavasso* (Hamburger Beiträge zur Arch., Beih. 1), Hamburg

Green, C. (1961) 'East Anglian coast-line levels since Roman times' *Antiquity*, XXXV

Green, M.J. (ed.) (1995) *The Celtic World* London: Routledge

Green, M.J. (1995) 'The gods and the supernatural' in M.J. Green (ed.)

Griffin, J. (1995) 'Regalis inter mensas laticemque Lyaeum: Wine in Virgil and Others' in Murray & Tecusan (eds.)

Grottanelli, C. (1995) 'Wine and Death - East and West' in Murray & Tecusan (eds.)

Guillaumet, J.-P. (1977) 'Les passoires de la fin de la Tène en Gaule et dans le mond Celtique' *Gallia*, 35

Guillaumet, J.-P. (1991) 'Les passoires' in Feugère & Rolley (eds.)

Gwilt, A. & Haselgrove, C. (1997) *Reconstructing Iron Age Societies* Oxbow Monograph 71

Haselgrove, C. (1982) 'Wealth, prestige and power: the dynamics of late Iron Age political centralisation in south-east England' in Renfew & Shennan (eds.)

Haselgrove, C. (1988) 'Iron Age coins' in Potter & Trow (eds.)

Haselgrove, C. (1990) 'The Romanisation of Belgic Gaul: some archaeological perspectives' in Blagg & Millett (eds.)

Haselgrove, C. (1996) 'Roman impact on rural settlement and society in southern Picardy' in *From the Sword to the Plough: Three Studies on the earliest Romanisation of Northern Gaul* Roymans, N. (ed.) Amsterdam University Press

Haselgrove, C. (forthcoming) 'Mediterranean influence on southern Belgic Gaul between the fifth and the first centuries BC'

Hawkes, C.F.C. & Dunning, G.C. (1930) 'The Belgae of Gaul and Britain' *Archaeological Journal*, Vol. 87

Hawkes, C.F.C. & Hull, M.R. (1947) *Camulodunum* (Reports of the Research Committee of the Society of the Society of Antiquaries of London, No.14) London

Hawkes, C.F.C. (1982) "Colchester before the Romans or who were our Belgae? A Lecture of 1950 reappraised by Christopher Hawkes" *Essex Archaeology and History*, Vol. 14

Hearne, C.M. & Cox, P.W. (1994) 'The Development of Settlement, Industry and Trade on the Purbeck

Heath and Southern Shores of Poole Harbour, Dorset' in Fitzpatrick & Morris (eds.)

Hedeager, L. (1978) "A quantitative analysis of Roman imports in Europe north of the Limes (0-400 AD) and the question of Roman-Germanic exchange" in Kristiansen & Paluden-Müller (eds.)

Hedeager, L. (1992) *Iron-Age Societies* Oxford: Blackwell

Henig, M. (1982) 'A Roman bronze vessel-mount from Mildenhall, Suffolk' in Exhibits at Ballots *Antiquaries Journal*, 62

Henig, M. (1982) 'Seasonal feasts in Roman Britain' *Oxford Journal of Archaeology*, 1(2)

Henig, M. (1984) *Religion in Roman Britain* Batsford

Herodotus, Book 3

Hill, D. & Jesson, M. (1971) *The Iron Age and its Hillforts* University of Southampton Monograph Series No. 1

Horne, P.D. & King, A.C. (1980) 'Romano-Celtic Temples in Continental Europe: A Gazeteer of those with known plans' in Rodwell (ed.)

Hüssen, C-M. (1983) *A Rich Late La Tène Burial at Hertford Heath, Hertfordshire* British Museum Occasional Paper No.44

Hutchinson, V.J. (1986) *Bacchus in Roman Britain: The Evidence for His Cult* British Archaeological Reports 151

Jackson, R. (1990) *Camerton: The Late Iron Age and Early Roman Metalwork* British Museum Publications: London

Jackson, R. (1998) 'Early surgical kit from Stanway' *The Colchester Archaeologist*, 11

Jessup, R.F. (1959) 'Barrows and Walled Cemeteries in Roman Britain' *Journal of British Archaeological Association*, 22

Kennett, D.H. (1969) 'A Roman Patera from Biggleswade' *Bedfordshire Archaeological Journal*, 4

Kennett, D.H. (1970) 'The Felmersham Fish-head Spout: a suggested reconstruction' in Notes, *Antiquaries Journal*, Vol.50

King, A. & Soffe, G. (1994) 'The Iron Age and Roman Temple on Hayling Island' in *The Iron Age in Wessex: recent work* A.P. Fitzpatrick & Elaine L. Morris (eds.)

King, A. & Soffe, G. (1998) 'Internal Organisation and Deposition at the Iron Age Temple on Hayling Island' *Proceedings of the Hampshire Field Club Archaeological Society* Vol. 53p.35-47 (Hampshire Studies, 1998)

Kristiansen, K. & Paluden-Müller, C. (1978) *New Directions in Scandinavian Archaeology* Lyngby: The National Museum of Denmark

Kuhlicke, F.W. (1969) 'Postscript on the Iron Age finds from Felmersham Bridge' *Bedfordshire Archaeological Journal*, 4, p.81-2

Laubenheimer, F. (1990) *Le Temps des Amphores en Gaule* Editions Errance

Laubenheimer, F. (1991) *Les amphores de Bibracte Le matériel des fouilles anciennes* Editions de la Maison des Sciences de l'Homme, Paris No. 29 Documents d'archéologie Française

Laubenheimer, F. (1993) 'Au dossier du vin italien en Gaule (IIe-Ier siècles av. J.-C.)' in Daubigney (ed.)

Laver, Philip G. (1926-27) 'The excavation of a tumulus at Lexden, Colchester' *Archaeologia*, Vol. 76

Lethbridge, T.C. (1953) 'Burial of an Iron Age warrior at Snailwell' *Proceedings of the Cambridgshire Antiquarian Society*, 47, p.25-37

Ling, R. (1995) 'The Decoration of Roman Triclinia' in Murray & Tecusan (eds.)

Macready, S. & Thompson, F.H. (1984) *Cross Channel Trade between Gaul and Britain in the pre-Roman Iron Age* Society of Antiquaries of London

Matthews, K.J. (1999) 'The Iron Age of North West England and Irish Sea Trade' in B. Bevan (ed.)

May, J. (1971) 'An Iron Age Spout from Kirmington, Lincolnshire' *Antiquaries Journal* 51

McGovern, P.E., Fleming, S.J. & Katz, S.H. (1996) *The Origins and Ancient History of Wine* Gordon and Breach Publishers

McPeake, J.C. & Moore, C.N. (1978) "A bronze skillet handle from Chester and other vessels from the British Isles" *Britannia* 9

Medleycott, M., Bedwin, O. & Godbold, S. (1995) 'South Weald Camp - a probable late Iron Age hill fort: excavations 1990' *Essex Archaeology and History*, 26

Metzler, J. (1984) 'Treverische Reitergräber von Goeblingen-Nospelt' in *Trier, Augustusstadt des Treverer* Catal. Expo., Rhein. Landesmus. Trier, v. Zabern, Mayence, 87-99

Metzler, J., Waringo, R., Bis, R. & Metzler-Zens, N. (1991) *Clemency et les tombes de l'aristocratie en Gaule Belgique* Dossiers d'Archeologie du Musée National d'Histoire et d'Art I

Miket, R. (1983) *The Roman Fort at South Shields: Excavation of the Defences 1977-1981*, Tyne & Wear County Council Museums

Miles, A. (1975) 'Salt-panning in Romano-British Kent' in de Brisay & Evans (eds.)

Mohen, J.-P., Duval, A. & Eluère, C. (1988) *Les Princes Celtes et la Méditerranée* Rencontres de l'École du Louvre: La Documentation Française

Moore, C.N. (1978) 'An enamelled skillet handle form Brough-on-Fosse and the distribution of similar vessels' *Britannia*, 9

Morris, E.L. (1994) 'Production and Distribution of Pottery and Salt in Iron Age Britain: a Review' *Proceedings of the Prehistoric Society*, 60

Murray, O. & Tecusan, M. (1995) *In Vino Veritas* British School at Rome

Murray, O. (1995) 'Histories of Pleasure' in Murray & Tecusan (eds.)

Nash, D. (1976) 'Reconstructing Poseidonios' Celtic Ethnography: some reconsiderations' *Britannia*, 7

Nash, D. (1984) 'The basis of contact between Britain and Gaul in late pre-Roman Iron Age' in Macready & Thompson (eds.)

107

Nash, D. (1985) 'Celtic territorial expansion and the Mediterranean World' in Champion & Megaw (eds.)

Nenquin, J. (1961) *Salt: A Study in Economic Prehistory* Brugge: De Tempel

Niblett, R. (1993) 'A Royal Burial at St. Albans' *Current Archaeology*, 132

Niblett, R. (1995) 'A Chieftain's burial from Verulamium' in Swaddling, Walker & Roberts (eds.)

Niblett, R. (1999) *The excavation of a ceremonial site at Folly Lane, Verulamium* Britannia Monograph Series No.14

Nilsson, M.P. (1957) *The Dionysiac Mysteries of the Hellenistic and Roman Age* Lund: C.W.K. Gleerup

Nurse, K. (1991) 'Unearthing the Unearthly' *Country Life*, No. 185 May 30th

Parfitt, K. (1995) *Iron Age Burials from Mill Hill, Deal* British Museum Press

Partridge, C. (1980) 'Excavations at Puckeridge and Braughing, 1975-79' *Hertfordshire Archaeology*, 7 p.28-132

Partridge, C. (1981) *Skeleton Green A Late Iron Age and Romano-British Site* Britannia Monograph Series No. 2 London

Pautreau, J.-P. (1999) *Antran: Un Ensemble Aristocratique du Premier Siècle* Musées de Poitiers

Peacock, D.P.S. (1971) 'Roman Amphorae in pre-Roman Britain' in Hill & Jesson (eds.)

Peacock, D.P.S. (1978) 'The Rhine and the problem of Gaulish wine in Roman Britain' in Taylor & Cleere (eds.)

Peacock, D.P.S. (1984) 'Amphorae in Iron Age Britain: A Reassessment' in Macready & Thompson (eds.)

Peacock, D.P.S. & Williams, D.F. (1986) *Amphorae and the Roman Economy: An Introductory Guide* London: Longman

Pearce, J. (1997) 'Death and time: the structure of a late Iron Age mortuary ritual' in Gwilt & Haselgrove (eds.)

Percival-Westell, W. (1931) 'A Romano-British cemetery at Baldock, Herts.' *Archaeological Journal*, 88

Percival-Westell, W. (1931-32) "Notes on a Romano-British cemetery in Hertfordshire" *Proceedings of the Society of Antiquaries of Scotland*, Vol. 65 p.105

Philpott, R. (1991) *Burial Practices in Roman Britain: A survey of grave treatment and furnishing AD 43-410*, British Archaeological Reports 219

Pitts, L.F. & St. Joseph, J.K. (1985) *Inchtuthill - The Roman Legionary Fortress. Excavations 1952-65* Britannia Monograph Series No. 6

Pliny (1952) *Natural History* (H. Rackham, trans.) Loeb Classical Library, London: William Heinemann Ltd.

Polybius (1889) *Histories* (E.S. Shuckburgh, trans.) London: MacMillan

Potter, T.W. & Trow, S.D. (1988) 'Puckeridge-Braughing, Herts: The Ermine Street Excavations, 1971-1972' *Hertfordshire Archaeology*, 10

Poux, M. (1997) 'Les amphores de Bâle-Gasfabrik: Approche taphonomique' *Annuaire de la Société Suisse de Préhistoire et d'Archéologie* 80, p.147-172

Poux, M. & Selles, H. (1998) 'Vin Italique en Pays Carnute A propos d'un lot d'amphores Dressel 1 découvert á Chartres, rue Sainte-Thérèse' *SFECAG, Actes du Congrès d'Istres*

Poux, M. (1999) 'Festins sacrés et ivresse collective en Gaule Celtique: traces littéraires, perspectives archéologiques' in *Rites et espace en pays celte et méditerranéen: étude comparée à partir du village d'Acy-Romance.* Actes du colloque de Rome (1997)

Py, M. (1993) Lattara 6

Reece, R. (1977) *Burial in the Roman World*, CBA Research Report

Reille, J.-L. & Abbas, G. (1992) 'Les inclusions minérales des amphores massaliètes et leur signification: le cas des formes archaïques et le problème de la localisation des sites de production' *Documents d'Archélogie Méridionale*, 15: 431-437

Renfrew, C. & Shennan, S. (1982) *Ranking, Resource and Exchange: Aspects of the Archaeology of Early European Society* Cambridge University Press

Richmond, I. (1968) *Hod Hill Volume II Excavations carried out between 1951 and 1958 for the Trustees of the British Museum* The Trustees of the British Museum: London

Rigby, V. (1995) 'Italic imports in late Iron Age Britain: a summary of the evidence from 'Chieftain burials''' in Swaddling, Walker & Roberts (eds.)

Robertson, A. (1970) "Roman Finds from non-Roman sites in Scotland" *Britannia* 1

Rodwell, K. & W. (1975) 'Kelvedon' *Current Archaeology*, Vol.48

Rodwell, W. (1976a) 'Coinage, oppida and the rise of Belgic power in south-east Britain' in Cunliffe & Rowley (eds.)

Rodwell, W. (1976b) 'A Dressel 1 amphora from the Thaxted area (and notes on amphorae from Sandon and Marks Tey)' *Essex Archaeology and History*, 8: 250-251

Rodwell, W. (1978) 'Rivenhall and the emergence of 1st century villas in North Essex' in *Studies in the Romano British Villa*, Todd, M. (ed.)

Rodwell, W. (1979) 'Iron Age and Roman salt-winning on the Essex coast' in Burnham & Johnson (eds.)

Rodwell, W. (1980) *Temples, Churches and Religion in Roman Britain* BAR 77 (2 volumes)

Rolley, C. (1988) 'Importations méditerranéennes et repères chronologiques' in Mohen, Duval & Eluère (eds.)

Rösler, W. (1995: 106-112) 'Wine and Truth in the Greek Symposion' in Murray & Tecusan (eds.)

Roymans, N. (1990) *Tribal Societies in Northern Gaul: An Anthropological Perspective* Amsterdam University Press

Scarre, C. & Healy, F. (1993) *Trade and Exchange in Prehistoric Europe* Oxbow 33

Scullard, H.H. (1981) *Festivals and Ceremonies of the Roman Republic* London: Thames & Hudson

Sealey, P.R. (1985) *Amphoras from the 1970 Excavations at Colchester Sheepen* British Archaeological Reports 142

Sealey, P.R. (1995) 'New light on the salt industry and Red Hills of prehistoric and Roman Essex' *Essex Archaeology and History*, 26 p.65-81

Sealey, P.R. (1997) *The Boudican Revolt against Rome* Shire Archaeology

Sealey, P.R. (forthcoming) *The Ardleigh Cauldron Pit*

Sealey, P.R. & Davies, G.M.R. (1984) 'Falernian Wine at Roman Colchester' *Britannia*, 15

Seltman, C. (1957) *Wine in the Ancient World* London: Routledge & Paul

Sharples, N.M. (1991) *Maiden Castle Excavations and Field Survey 1985-86* English Heritage

Sherwin, G.A. (1926) 'The Roman Villas on the Isle of Wight' *Proceedings of the Isle of Wight Natural History and Archaeologica Society* 1: Part 7

Sieveking, G. de G. (1971) *Prehistoric and Roman Studies* British Museum

Simmons, B.B. (1975) 'Salt Making Sites in the Silt Fens of Lincolnshire in the Iron Age and Roman Periods' in de Brisay & Evans (eds.)

Smith, Reginald A. (1911-12) 'On late Celtic antiquities discovered at Welwyn, Herts', *Archaeologia* 2nd series, Vol. XIII (Vol.63)

Stead, I.M. (1967) 'A La Téne burial at Welwyn Garden City' *Archaeologia*, Vol.101

Stead, I.M. (1971) "The reconstruction of Iron Age buckets from Aylesford and Baldock" in Sieveking, G. de G. (ed.)

Stead, I.M. & Rigby, V. (1989) *Verulamium: the King Harry Lane Site*, English Heritage

Strabo (1923) *Geography* Loeb Classical Library

Struck, M. (1993) *Römerzeitliche Gräber als Quellen zu Religion, Bevölkerungsstruktur und Sozialgeschichte* Internationale Fachkonferenz vom 18.-20. Februar 1991 im Institut für Vor- und Frühgeschichte der Johannes Gutenberg-Universität Mainz Mainz

Suetonius (1930) *Lives of Caesar* (G.M. Mooney, trans.) Dublin: Longmans, Green & Co.

Swaddling, J., Walker, S. & Roberts, P. (1995) *Italy in Europe: Economic Relations 700 BC - AD 50* British Museum Occasional Paper 97

Tacitus (1970) *Agricola* (M. Hutton, trans.) Loeb Classical Library, London & Cambridge, Mass.: Harvard University Press

Tacitus (1970) *Germania* (M. Hutton, trans.) Loeb Classical Library, London & Cambridge, Mass.: Harvard University Press

Taylor, J. du Plat & Cleere, H. (1978) *Roman Shipping and trade: Britain and the Rhine Provinces* CBA Research Report 24, London

Tchernia, A. (1983) 'Italian Wine in Gaul at the end of the Republic' in Garnsey, Hopkins & Whittaker (eds.)

Tchernia, A. (1986) *Le Vin de l'Italie Romaine* Ecole Française de Rome

Thoen, H. (1975) 'Iron Age and Roman Salt Making Sites on the Belgian Coast' in de Brisay & Evans (eds.)

Tierney, James T. (1964) 'The Celts and the Classical Authors' in Raftery, J. (ed.) *The Celts: The Thomas Davis Lectures* Dublin: Cork: Mercier Press

Todd, M. (1977) 'Germanic burials in the Roman Iron Age' in Reece, R. (ed.)

Tomalin, D.J. (forthcoming, A) 'The Wootton Haven Inter Tidal Survey'

Tomalin, D.J. & Loader, B. (forthcoming, B) 'The excavations of Combley Roman Villa, Arreton'

Tomalin, D.J. (1992) 'Ceramics of the Middle and Late Iron Age from Mount Joy Hill, Newport, Isle of Wight, and some cultural implications' *Proceedings of the Isle of Wight Natural History and Archaeological Society* 12: 125-133

Tomalin, D.J. (1979) 'Redcliff, Isle of Wight - Notes' *Proceedings of the Prehistoric Society* 45

Toynbee, J.M.C. (1971) *Death and Burial in the Roman World* London: John Hopkins University Press

Trott, K. (forthcoming) 'Implications regarding late Iron Age imports and the possible involvement of cross-Channel trade in relation to the Isle of Wight Iron Age community' *International Journal of Nautical Archaeology*

Trott, K. (in preparation, A) 'The Mersley and Knighton Farms Archaeological Survey'

Trott, K. (in preparation, B) 'Excavations at a coastal site at Grange Chine'

Trott, K. (in preparation, C) 'Excavations at a coastal site at Atherfield Point'

Trott, K. (in preparation, D) 'Excavations at St. Catherine's Point'

Trow, S.D. (1988) 'Braughing-Puckeridge in the late pre-Roman Iron Age' in Potter & Trow (eds.)

Trow, S.D. (1990) 'By the northern shores of Ocean. Some observations on acculturation process at the edge of the Roman world' in Blagg & Millett (eds.)

Tyers, P. (1996) *Roman Pottery in Britain* Batsford: London

Unwin, T. (1991) *Wine and the Vine* London & New York: Routledge

Veyne, P. (1987) *A History of Private Life From Pagan Rome to Byzantium* Cambridge, MA: Harvard University Press

Wait, G.A. (1985) *Ritual and Religion in Iron Age Britain* BAR No.149 Vols.I and II

Watson, W. (1949) 'Belgic bronzes and pottery found at Felmersham-on-Ouse, Bedfordshire' *Antiquaries Journal*, 29, p.37-61

Webster, J. (1995) 'Sanctuaries and Sacred Places' in M.J. Green (ed.)

Webster, J. (1997) 'Text expectations: the archaeology of 'Celtic' ritual wells and shafts' in Gwilt & Haselgrove (eds.)

Wells, C. (1995) 'Celts and Germans in the Rhineland' in M.J. Green (ed.)

Wells, P.S. (1980) *Culture Contact and Culture Change*

Werner, J. (1954) 'Die Bronzekanne von Kelheim' *Bayer. Vorgeschbl.*, 20 (re-edited in *Spätes Keltentum zwischen Rom und Germanien*, Munich (1978), p.68-108)

Wheeler, M. (1930) *London in Roman Times* London Museum Catalogues No. 3

Whimster, R. (1981) *Burial Practices in Iron Age Britain: A Discussion and Gazeteer of the Evidence c. 700BC- AD42*, Parts I and II BAR

Whitehead, B. (1996) 'Report on an archaeological excavation at Corralls Coal Yard, Newport' *Southern Archaeological Services*, 70

Williams, D. (1977) 'A consideration of the sub-fossil remains of *Vitis vinifera* L. as evidence for viticulture in Roman Britain' *Britannia*, 8

Williams, D. & Peacock, D. (1994) 'Roman Amphorae in Iron Age Wessex' in Fitzpatrick & Morris (eds.)

Williams, D. (1988) 'The amphorae' in Potter & Trow (eds.)

Woolf, G. (1993) 'The Social Significance of Trade in Late Iron Age Europe' in Scarre & Healy (eds.)

www.ingramcontent.com/pod-product-compliance
Lightning Source LLC
Chambersburg PA
CBHW061006030426
42334CB00033B/3375